DIALECTIC OF ENLIGHTENMENT

Cultural Memory

in

the

Present

Mieke Bal and Hent de Vries, Editors

DIALECTIC OF ENLIGHTENMENT

Philosophical Fragments

MAX HORKHEIMER *and*

THEODOR W. ADORNO

Edited by Gunzelin Schmid Noerr

Translated by Edmund Jephcott

STANFORD UNIVERSITY PRESS

STANFORD, CALIFORNIA

2002

Dialectic of Enlightenment: Philosophical Fragments is translated from Volume 5
of Max Horkheimer, *Gesammelte Schriften: Dialektik der Aufklärung und
Schriften 1940–1950*, edited by Gunzelin Schmid Noerr, ©1987 by S. Fischer
Verlag GmbH, Frankfurt am Main.

Asterisks in the text and display material mark editorial notes created for the
German edition. They include variant readings and other textual concerns.
They are keyed in the reference matter section via the number of the page on
which the asterisk appears and the preceding word. Numbered notes are those
created by Horkheimer and Adorno themselves.

Horkheimer, Max, 1895–1973
  [Philosophische Fragmente. English]
  Dialectic of enlightenment : philosophical fragments / Max Horkheimer and
Theodor W. Adorno ; edited by Gunzelin Schmid Noerr ; translated by
Edmund Jephcott.
     p. cm. — (Cultural memory in the present)
  Includes bibliographical references.
  ISBN 0-8047-3632-4 (alk. paper) — ISBN 0-8047-3633-2 (pbk: alk. paper)
  1. Philosophy. I. Adorno, Theodor W., 1903–1969. II. Schmid Noerr,
Gunzelin. III. Title. IV. Series.
  B3279.H8473 P513   2002
  193—dc21   2002000073

Printed in the United States of America

Original Printing 2002
Last figure below indicates year of this printing:
11   10   09   08   07   06   05   04   03   02

Typeset at Stanford University Press in 11/13.5 Adobe Garamond

For Friedrich Pollock*

Contents

Preface to the New Edition (1969)

Dialectic of Enlightenment was published in 1947 by Querido in Amsterdam. The book, which found readers only gradually, has been out of print for some time. We have been induced to reissue it after more than twenty years not only by requests from many sides but by the notion that not a few of the ideas in it are timely now and have largely determined our later theoretical writings. No one who was not involved in the writing could easily understand to what extent we both feel responsible for every sentence. We dictated long stretches together; the *Dialectic* derives its vital energy from the tension between the two intellectual temperaments which came together in writing it.

We do not stand by everything we said in the book in its original form. That would be incompatible with a theory which attributes a temporal core to truth instead of contrasting truth as something invariable to the movement of history. The book was written at a time when the end of the National Socialist terror was in sight. In not a few places, however, the formulation is no longer adequate to the reality of today. All the same, even at that time we did not underestimate the implications of the transition to the administered world.

In a period of political division into immense blocs driven by an objective tendency to collide, horror has been prolonged. The conflicts in the third world and the renewed growth of totalitarianism are not mere historical interludes any more than, according to the *Dialectic*, fascism was at that time. Critical thought, which does not call a halt before progress itself, requires us to take up the cause of the remnants of freedom, of tendencies toward real humanity, even though they seem powerless in face of the great historical trend.

The development toward total integration identified in the book has been interrupted but not terminated; it threatens to be consummated by means of dictators and wars. Our prognosis regarding the associated lapse from enlightenment into positivism, into the myth of that which is the case, and finally of the identity of intelligence and hostility to mind, has been overwhelmingly confirmed. Our concept of history does not believe itself elevated above history, but it does not merely chase after information in the positivist manner. As a critique of philosophy it does not seek to abandon philosophy itself.

From America, where the book was written, we returned to Germany with the conviction that, theoretically and practically, we would be able to achieve more there than elsewhere. Together with Friedrich Pollock, to whom the book is dedicated on his seventy-fifth birthday as it was then on his fiftieth, we built up the Institut für Sozialforschung once again, with the idea of taking further the concepts formulated in *Dialectic*. In continuing to develop our theory, and in the common experiences connected with it, Gretel Adorno has given us the most valuable assistance, as she did with the first version.

We have made changes far more sparingly than is usual with re-editions of books dating back several decades. We did not want to retouch what we had written, not even the obviously inadequate passages. To bring the text fully up to date with the current situation would have amounted to nothing less than writing a new book. That what matters today is to preserve and disseminate freedom, rather than to accelerate, however indirectly, the advance toward the administered world, we have also argued in our later writings. We have confined ourselves here to correcting misprints and suchlike matters. This restraint has made the book a piece of documentation; we hope that it is also more.

Max Horkheimer   Theodor W. Adorno

Frankfurt am Main, April 1969

Preface to the Italian Edition* (1962/1966)

The German text of *Dialectic of Enlightenment* is a fragment. Begun as early as 1942, during the Second World War, it was supposed to form the introduction to the theory of society and history we had sketched during the period of National Socialist rule. It is self-evident that, with regard to terminology and the scope of the questions investigated, the book is shaped by the social conditions in which it was written.

In keeping with its theme, our book demonstrates tendencies which turn cultural progress into its opposite. We attempted to do this on the basis of social phenomena of the 1930s and 1940s in America. However, to construct a systematic theory which would do justice to the present economic and political circumstances is a task which, for objective and subjective reasons, we are unable to perform today. We are therefore happy that the fragment is appearing in a series devoted predominantly to philosophical questions.

M.H. and T.W.A.

Frankfurt am Main, March 1966

Preface (1944 and 1947)

When* we began this work, the first samples of which we dedicate to Friedrich Pollock, we hoped to be able to present the whole book on his fiftieth birthday. But the further we proceeded with the task the more we became aware of the mismatch between it and our own capabilities. What we had set out to do was nothing less than to explain why humanity, instead of entering a truly human state, is sinking into a new kind of * barbarism. We underestimated the difficulty of dealing with the subject because we still placed too much trust in contemporary consciousness. While we had noted for many years that, in the operations of modern science, the major discoveries are paid for with an increasing* decline of theoretical education, we nevertheless believed that we could follow those operations to the extent of limiting our work primarily to a critique or a continuation of specialist theories. Our work was to adhere, at least thematically, to the traditional disciplines: sociology, psychology, and epistemology.

The fragments we have collected here show, however, that we had to abandon that trust. While attentive cultivation and investigation of the scientific heritage—especially when positivist new brooms have swept it away as useless lumber—does represent one moment of knowledge, in the present collapse of bourgeois civilization not only the operations but the purpose of science have become dubious. The tireless self-destruction of enlightenment hypocritically celebrated by implacable fascists and implemented by pliable experts in humanity* compels thought to forbid itself its last remaining innocence regarding the habits and tendencies of the *Zeitgeist*. If public life has reached a state in which thought is being turned inescapably into a commodity and language into celebration of the commodity, the attempt to trace the sources of this degradation must refuse obedience to the current linguistic and intellectual demands before it is rendered entirely futile by the consequence of those demands for world history.

If the only obstacles were those arising from the oblivious instrumentalization of science, thought about social questions could at least attach itself to tendencies opposed to official science. Those tendencies, too, however, are caught up in the general process of production. They have changed no less than the ideology they attacked. They suffer the fate which has always been reserved for triumphant thought. If it voluntarily leaves behind its critical element to become a mere means in the service of an existing order, it involuntarily tends to transform the positive cause it has espoused into something negative and destructive. The eighteenth-century philosophy which, defying the funeral pyres for books and people, put the fear of death into infamy, joined forces with it under Bonaparte. Finally, the apologetic school of Comte usurped the succession to the uncompromising *encyclopédistes*, extending the hand of friendship* to all those whom the latter had opposed. Such metamorphoses of critique into affirmation do not leave theoretical content untouched; its truth evaporates. Today, however, motorized history is rushing ahead of such intellectual developments, and the official spokesmen, who have other concerns, are liquidating the theory to which they owe their place in the sun* before it has time to prostitute itself completely.*

In reflecting on its own guilt, therefore, thought finds itself deprived not only of the affirmative reference to science and everyday phenomena but also of the conceptual language of opposition. No terms are available which do not tend toward complicity with the prevailing intellectual trends, and what threadbare language cannot achieve on its own is precisely made good by the social machinery. The censors voluntarily maintained by the film factories to avoid greater costs have their counterparts in all other departments. The process to which a literary text is subjected, if not in the automatic foresight of its producer then through the battery of readers, publishers, adapters, and ghost writers inside and outside the editorial office, outdoes any censor in its thoroughness. To render their function entirely superfluous appears, despite all the benevolent reforms, to be the ambition of the educational system. In the belief that without strict limitation to the observation of facts and the calculation of probabilities the cognitive mind would be overreceptive to charlatanism and

superstition, that system is preparing arid ground for the greedy acceptance of charlatanism and superstition. Just as prohibition has always
ensured the admission of the poisonous product, the blocking of the theoretical imagination has paved the way for political delusion. Even when
people have not already succumbed to such delusion, they are deprived by
the mechanisms of censorship, both the external ones and those implanted within them, of the means of resisting it.

The aporia which faced us in our work thus proved to be the first
matter we had to investigate: the self-destruction of enlightenment. We
have no doubt—and herein lies our *petitio principii*—that freedom in
society is inseparable from enlightenment thinking. We believe we have
perceived with equal clarity, however, that the very concept of that thinking, no less than the concrete historical forms, the institutions of society
with which it is intertwined, already contains the germ of the regression*
which is taking place everywhere today. If enlightenment does not assim-
ilate reflection on this regressive moment, it seals its own fate. By leaving
consideration of the destructive side of progress to its enemies, thought in
its headlong* rush into pragmatism is forfeiting its sublating character,
and therefore its relation to truth. In the mysterious willingness of the
technologically educated masses to fall under the spell of any despotism,
in its self-destructive affinity to nationalist paranoia, in all this uncomprehended senselessness the weakness of contemporary theoretical understanding is evident.

We believe that in these fragments we have contributed to such
understanding by showing that the cause of enlightenment's relapse into
mythology is to be sought not so much in the nationalist, pagan, or other
modern mythologies concocted specifically to cause such a relapse as in
the fear of truth which petrifies enlightenment itself. Both these terms,
enlightenment and truth, are to be understood as pertaining not merely to
intellectual history but also to current reality. Just as enlightenment expresses the real movement of bourgeois society as a whole from the perspective of the idea embodied in its personalities and institutions, truth
refers not merely to rational* consciousness but equally to the form it takes
in reality. The loyal son of modern civilization's fear of departing from the
facts, which even in their perception are turned into clichés by the prevailing usages in science, business, and politics, is exactly the same as the
fear of social deviation. Those usages also define the concept of clarity in

language and thought to which art, literature, and philosophy must conform today. By tabooing any thought which sets out negatively from the
facts and from the prevailing modes of thought as obscure, convoluted,
and preferably foreign, that concept holds mind captive in ever deeper
blindness. It is in the nature of the calamitous situation existing today that
even the most honorable reformer who recommends renewal in threadbare
language reinforces the existing order he seeks to break by taking over its
worn-out categorial apparatus and the pernicious power-philosophy lying
behind it. False clarity is only another name for myth. Myth was always
obscure and luminous at once. It has always been distinguished by its
familiarity and its exemption from the work of concepts.

The enslavement to nature of people today cannot be separated from
social progress. The increase in economic productivity which creates the
conditions for a more just world also affords the technical apparatus and
the social groups controlling it a disproportionate advantage over the rest
of the population. The individual is entirely nullified in face of the economic powers. These powers are taking society's domination over nature
to unimagined heights. While individuals as such are vanishing before the
apparatus they serve, they are provided for by that apparatus and better
than ever before. In the unjust state of society the powerlessness and pliability of the masses increase* with the quantity of goods allocated to them.
The materially considerable and socially paltry rise in the standard of living of the lower classes is reflected in the hypocritical propagation of intellect. Intellect's true concern is a negation of reification. It must perish
when it is solidified into a cultural asset and handed out for consumption
purposes. The flood of precise information and brand-new amusements
make people smarter and more stupid at once.

What is at issue here is not culture as a value, as understood by crit-
ics of civilization such as Huxley, Jaspers, and Ortega y Gasset, but the
necessity for enlightenment to reflect on itself if humanity is not to be
totally betrayed. What is at stake is not conservation of the past but the
fulfillment of past hopes. Today, however,* the past is being continued as
destruction of the past. If, up to the nineteenth century, respectable education was a privilege paid for by the increased sufferings* of the uneducated, in the twentieth the hygienic factory is bought with the melting
down of all cultural entities in the gigantic crucible.* That might not even
be so high a price as those defenders of culture believe if the bargain sale

of culture did not contribute to converting economic achievements into their opposite.

Under the given circumstances the gifts of fortune themselves become elements of misfortune. If, in the absence of the social subject, the volume of goods took the form of so-called overproduction in domestic economic crises in the preceding period, today, thanks to the enthronement of powerful groups as that social subject, it is producing the international threat of fascism: progress is reverting to regression. That the hygienic factory and everything pertaining to it, Volkswagen* and the sports palace, are obtusely liquidating metaphysics does not matter in itself, but that these things are themselves becoming metaphysics, an ideological curtain,* within the social whole, behind which real doom is gathering, does matter. That is the basic premise of our fragments.

The first essay, the theoretical basis of those which follow, seeks to gain greater understanding of the intertwinement of rationality and social reality, as well as of the intertwinement, inseparable from the former, of nature and the mastery of nature. The critique of enlightenment given in this section is intended to prepare a positive concept of enlightenment which liberates it from its entanglement in blind domination.

The critical part of the first essay can be broadly summed up in two theses: Myth is already enlightenment, and enlightenment reverts to mythology. These theses are worked out in relation to specific subjects in the two excurses. The first traces the dialectic of myth and enlightenment in the *Odyssey*, as one of the earliest representative documents of bourgeois Western civilization. It focuses primarily on the concepts of sacrifice and renunciation, through which both the difference between and the unity of mythical nature and enlightened mastery of nature become apparent. The second excursus is concerned with Kant, Sade, and Nietzsche, whose works represent the implacable consummation of enlightenment. This section shows how the subjugation of everything natural to the sovereign subject culminates in the domination of what is blindly objective and natural. This tendency levels all the antitheses of bourgeois thought, especially that between moral rigor and absolute amorality.

The section "The Culture Industry" shows the regression of enlightenment to ideology which is graphically expressed in film and radio. Here, enlightenment consists primarily in the calculation of effects and in the technology of production and dissemination; the specific content of the ideology is exhausted in the idolization of the existing order and of the power by which the technology is controlled. In the discussion of this contradiction the culture industry is taken more seriously than it might itself wish to be. But because its appeal to its own commercial character, its confession of its diminished truth, has long since become an excuse with which it evades responsibility for its lies, our analysis is directed at the claim objectively contained in its products to be aesthetic formations and thus representations of truth. It demonstrates* the dire state of society by the invalidity of that claim. Still more than the others, the section on the culture industry is fragmentary.*

The discussion, in the form of theses, of "Elements of Anti-Semitism" deals with the reversion of enlightened civilization to barbarism in reality. The not merely theoretical but practical tendency toward self-destruction has been inherent in rationality from the first, not only in the present phase when it is emerging nakedly. For this reason a philosophical prehistory of anti-Semitism is sketched. Its "irrationalism" derives from the nature of the dominant reason and of the world corresponding to its image. The "elements" are directly related to empirical research by the Institute of Social Research,* the foundation set up and kept alive by Felix Weil, without which not only our studies but the good part of the theoretical work of German emigrants carried forward despite Hitler would not have been possible. We wrote the first three theses jointly with Leo Löwenthal, with whom we have collaborated on many scholarly questions since the first years in Frankfurt.

In the last section we publish notes and sketches which, in part, form part of the ideas in the preceding sections, without having found a place in them, and in part deal provisionally with problems of future work. Most of them relate to a dialectical anthropology.*

Los Angeles, California, May 1944

The book contains no essential changes to the text completed during the war. Only the last thesis of "Elements of Anti-Semitism" was added subsequently.

Max Horkheimer   Theodor W. Adorno

June 1947

The Concept* of Enlightenment

Enlightenment, understood in the widest sense as the advance of thought, has always aimed at liberating human beings from fear and installing them as masters. Yet the wholly enlightened earth is radiant with triumphant calamity. Enlightenment's program was the disenchantment of the world.* It wanted to dispel myths, to overthrow fantasy with knowledge. Bacon, "the father of experimental philosophy,"[1] brought these motifs together. He despised the exponents of tradition, who substituted belief for knowledge and were as unwilling to doubt as they were reckless in supplying answers. All this, he said, stood in the way of "the happy match between the mind of man and the nature of things," with the result that humanity was unable to use its knowledge for the betterment of its condition. Such inventions as had been made—Bacon cites printing, artillery, and the compass—had been arrived at more by chance than by systematic enquiry into nature. Knowledge obtained through such enquiry would not only be exempt from the influence of wealth and power but would establish man as the master of nature:

Therefore, no doubt, the sovereignty of man lieth hid in knowledge; wherein many things are reserved, which kings with their treasure cannot buy, nor with their force command; their spials and intelligencers can give no news of them, their seamen and discoverers cannot sail where they grow: now we govern nature in opinions, but we are thrall unto her in necessity: but if we would be led by her in invention, we should command her by action.[2]

Although not a mathematician, Bacon well understood the scientific temper which was to come after him. The "happy match" between human understanding and the nature of things that he envisaged is a patriarchal one: the mind, conquering superstition, is to rule over disenchanted nature. Knowledge, which is power, knows no limits, either in its enslavement* of creation or in its deference to worldly masters. Just as it serves all the purposes of the bourgeois economy both in factories and on the battlefield, it is at the disposal of entrepreneurs regardless of their origins. Kings control technology no more directly than do merchants: it is as democratic as the economic system* with which it evolved. Technology is the essence of this knowledge. It aims to produce neither concepts nor images, nor the joy of understanding, but method, exploitation of the labor of others,* capital. The "many things" which, according to Bacon, knowledge still held in store are themselves mere instruments: the radio as a sublimated printing press, the dive bomber as a more effective form of artillery, remote control as a more reliable compass. What human beings seek to learn from nature is how to use it to dominate wholly both it and human beings. Nothing else counts. Ruthless toward itself, the Enlightenment has eradicated the last remnant of its own self-awareness. Only thought which does violence to itself is hard enough to shatter myths. Faced by the present triumph of the factual mentality, Bacon's nominalist credo would have smacked of metaphysics and would have been convicted of the same vanity for which he criticized scholasticism. Power and knowledge are synonymous.[3] For Bacon as for Luther, "knowledge that tendeth but to satisfaction, is but as a courtesan, which is for pleasure, and not for fruit or generation." Its concern is not "satisfaction, which men call truth," but "operation," the effective procedure. The "true end, scope or office of knowledge" does not consist in "any plausible, delectable, reverend or admired discourse, or any satisfactory arguments, but in effecting and working, and in discovery of particulars not revealed before, for the better endowment and help of man's life."[4] There shall be neither mystery nor any desire to reveal mystery.

The disenchantment of the world means the extirpation of animism. Xenophanes mocked the multiplicity of gods because they resembled their creators, men, in all their idiosyncrasies and faults, and the latest logic denounces the words of language, which bear the stamp of impressions, as counterfeit coin that would be better replaced by neutral counters. The world becomes chaos, and synthesis salvation. No difference is said to exist between the totemic animal, the dreams of the spirit-seer,* and the absolute Idea. On their way toward modern science human beings have discarded meaning. The concept is replaced by the formula, the cause by rules and probability. Causality was only the last philosophical concept on which scientific criticism tested its strength, because it alone of the old ideas still stood in the way of such criticism, the latest secular form of the creative principle. To define substance and quality, activity and suffering, being and existence in terms appropriate to the time has been a concern of philosophy since Bacon; but science could manage without such categories. They were left behind as *idola theatri* of the old metaphysics and even in their time were monuments to entities and powers from prehistory. In that distant time life and death had been interpreted and interwoven in myths. The categories by which Western philosophy defined its timeless order of nature marked out the positions which had once been occupied by Ocnus and Persephone, Ariadne and Nereus. The moment of transition is recorded in the pre-Socratic cosmologies. The moist, the undivided, the air and fire which they take to be the primal stuff of nature are early rationalizations precipitated from the mythical vision. Just as the images of generation from water and earth, that had come to the Greeks from the Nile, were converted by these cosmologies into Hylozoic principles and elements, the whole ambiguous profusion of mythical demons was intellectualized to become the pure form of ontological entities. Even the patriarchal gods of Olympus were finally assimilated by the philosophical *logos* as the Platonic Forms. But the Enlightenment discerned the old powers in the Platonic and Aristotelian heritage of metaphysics and suppressed the universal categories' claims to truth as superstition. In the authority of universal concepts the Enlightenment detected a fear of the demons through whose effigies human beings had tried to influence nature in magic rituals. From now on matter was finally to be controlled without the illusion of immanent powers or hidden properties. For enlightenment, anything which does not conform to the standard of calculability and utility must be viewed with suspicion. Once the movement is able to develop unhampered by external oppression, there is no holding it back. Its own ideas of human rights then fare no better than the older universals. Any intellectual resistance it encounters merely increases its strength.[5] The reason is that enlightenment also recognizes itself in the old myths. No matter which myths are invoked against it, by being used as arguments they are made to acknowledge the very principle of corrosive rationality of which enlightenment stands accused. Enlightenment is totalitarian.

Enlightenment has always regarded anthropomorphism, the projection of subjective properties onto nature, as the basis of myth.[6] The supernatural, spirits and demons, are taken to be reflections of human beings who allow themselves to be frightened by natural phenomena. According to enlightened thinking, the multiplicity of mythical figures can be reduced to a single common denominator, the subject. Oedipus's answer to the riddle of the Sphinx—"That being is man"—is repeated indiscriminately as enlightenment's stereotyped message, whether in response to a piece of objective meaning, a schematic order, a fear of evil powers, or a hope of salvation. For the Enlightenment, only what can be encompassed by unity has the status of an existent or an event; its ideal is the system from which everything and anything follows. Its rationalist and empiricist versions do not differ on that point. Although the various schools may have interpreted its axioms differently, the structure of unitary science has always been the same. Despite the pluralism of the different fields of research, Bacon's postulate of *una scientia universalis*[7] is as hostile to anything which cannot be connected as Leibniz's *mathesis universalis* is to discontinuity. The multiplicity of forms is reduced to position and arrangement, history to fact, things to matter. For Bacon, too, there was a clear logical connection, through degrees of generality, linking the highest principles to propositions based on observation. De Maistre mocks him for harboring this "idolized ladder."[8] Formal logic was the high school of unification. It offered Enlightenment thinkers a schema for making the world calculable. The mythologizing equation of Forms with numbers in Plato's last writings expresses the longing of all demythologizing: number became enlightenment's canon. The same equations govern bourgeois justice and commodity exchange. "Is not the rule, '*Si inaequalibus aequalia addas, omnia erunt inaequalia*,' [If you add like to unlike you will always end up with unlike] an axiom of justice as well as of mathematics? And is there not a true coincidence between commutative and distributive justice, and arithmetical and geometrical proportion?"[9] Bourgeois society is ruled by equivalence. It makes dissimilar things comparable by reducing them to abstract quantities. For the Enlightenment, anything which cannot be resolved into numbers, and ultimately into one, is illusion; modern positivism consigns it to poetry. Unity remains the watchword from Parmenides to Russell. All gods and qualities must be destroyed.

But the myths which fell victim to the Enlightenment were themselves its products. The scientific calculation of events annuls the account of them which thought had once given in myth. Myth sought to report, to name, to tell of origins—but therefore also to narrate, record, explain. This tendency was reinforced by the recording and collecting of myths. From a record, they soon became a teaching. Each ritual contains a representation of how things happen and of the specific process which is to be influenced by magic. In the earliest popular epics this theoretical element of ritual became autonomous. The myths which the tragic dramatists drew on were already marked by the discipline and power which Bacon celebrated as the goal. The local spirits and demons had been replaced by heaven and its hierarchy, the incantatory practices of the magician by the carefully graduated sacrifice and the labor of enslaved men mediated by command. The Olympian deities are no longer directly identical with elements, but signify them. In Homer Zeus controls the daytime sky, Apollo guides the sun; Helios and Eos are already passing over into allegory. The gods detach themselves from substances to become their quintessence. From now on, being is split between *logos*—which, with the advance of philosophy, contracts to a monad, a mere reference point—and the mass of things and creatures in the external world. The single distinction between man's own existence and reality swallows up all others. Without regard for differences, the world is made subject to man. In this the Jewish story of creation and the Olympian religion are at one: ". . . and let them have dominion over the fish of the sea, and over the fowl of the air, and over the cattle, and over all the earth, and over every creeping thing that creepeth upon the earth."[10] "O Zeus, Father Zeus, yours is the dominion of the heavens; you oversee the works of men, both the wicked and the just, and the unruly animals, you who uphold righteousness."[11] "It is so ordained that one atones at once, another later; but even should one escape the doom threatened by the gods, it will surely come to pass one day, and innocents shall expiate his deed, whether his children or a later generation."[12] Only those who subject themselves utterly pass muster with the gods. The awakening of the subject is bought with the recognition of power as the principle of all relationships. In face of the unity of such reason the distinction between God and man is reduced to an irrelevance, as reason has steadfastly indicated since the earliest critique of Homer. In their mastery of nature, the creative God and the ordering mind are alike. Man's likeness to God consists in sovereignty over existence, in the lordly gaze, in the command.

Myth becomes enlightenment and nature mere objectivity. Human beings purchase the increase in their power with estrangement from that over which it is exerted. Enlightenment stands in the same relationship to things as the dictator to human beings. He knows them to the extent that he can manipulate them. The man of science knows things to the extent that he can make them. Their "in-itself" becomes "for him." In their transformation the essence of things is revealed as always the same, a substrate of domination. This identity constitutes the unity of nature. Neither it nor the unity of the subject was presupposed by magical incantation. The rites of the shaman were directed at the wind, the rain, the snake outside or the demon inside the sick person, not at materials or specimens. The spirit which practiced magic was not single or identical; it changed with the cult masks which represented the multiplicity of spirits. Magic is bloody untruth, but in it domination is not yet disclaimed by transforming itself into a pure truth underlying the world which it enslaves. The magician imitates demons; to frighten or placate them he makes intimidating or appeasing gestures. Although his task was impersonation he did not claim to be made in the image of the invisible power, as does civilized man, whose modest hunting ground then shrinks to the unified cosmos, in which nothing exists but prey. Only when made in such an image does man attain the identity of the self which cannot be lost in identification with the other but takes possession of itself once and for all as an impenetrable mask. It is the identity of mind and its correlative, the unity of nature, which subdues the abundance of qualities. Nature, stripped of qualities, becomes the chaotic stuff of mere classification, and the all-powerful self becomes a mere having, an abstract identity. Magic implies specific representation. What is done to the spear, the hair, the name of the enemy, is also to befall his person; the sacrificial animal is slain in place of the god. The substitution which takes place in sacrifice marks a step toward discursive logic. Even though the hind which was offered up for the daughter, the lamb for the firstborn, necessarily still had qualities of its own, it already represented the genus. It manifested the arbitrariness of the specimen. But the sanctity of the *hic et nunc*, the uniqueness of the chosen victim which coincides with its representative status, distinguishes it radically, makes it non-exchangeable even in the exchange. Science puts an end to this. In it there is no specific representation: something which is a sacrificial animal cannot be a god. Representation gives way to universal fungibility. An atom is smashed not as a representative but as a specimen of matter, and the rabbit suffering the torment of the laboratory is seen not as a representative but, mistakenly, as a mere exemplar. Because in functional science the differences are so fluid that everything is submerged in one and the same matter, the scientific object is petrified, whereas the rigid ritual of former times appears supple in its substitution of one thing for another. The world of magic still retained differences whose traces have vanished even in linguistic forms.[13] The manifold affinities between existing things are supplanted by the single relationship between the subject who confers meaning and the meaningless object, between rational significance and its accidental bearer. At the magical stage dream and image were not regarded as mere signs of things but were linked to them by resemblance or name. The relationship was not one of intention but of kinship. Magic like science is concerned with ends, but it pursues them through mimesis, not through an increasing distance from the object. It certainly is not founded on the "omnipotence of thought," which the primitive is supposed to impute to himself like the neurotic;[14] there can be no "over-valuation of psychical acts" in relation to reality where thought and reality are not radically distinguished. The "unshakable confidence in the possibility of controlling the world"[15] which Freud anachronistically attributes to magic applies only to the more realistic form of world domination achieved by the greater astuteness of science. The autonomy of thought in relation to objects, as manifested in the reality-adequacy of the Ego, was a prerequisite for the replacement of the localized practices of the medicine man by all-embracing industrial technology.*

As a totality set out in language and laying claim to a truth which suppressed the older mythical faith of popular religion, the solar, patriarchal myth was itself an enlightenment, fully comparable on that level to the philosophical one. But now it paid the price. Mythology itself set in motion the endless process of enlightenment by which, with ineluctable necessity, every definite theoretical view is subjected to the annihilating criticism that it is only a belief, until even the concepts of mind, truth, and, indeed, enlightenment itself have been reduced to animistic magic.

The principle of the fated necessity which caused the downfall of the mythical hero, and finally evolved as the logical conclusion from the oracular utterance, not only predominates, refined to the cogency of formal logic, in every rationalistic system of Western philosophy but also presides over the succession of systems which begins with the hierarchy of the gods and, in a permanent twilight of the idols, hands down a single identical content: wrath against those of insufficient righteousness.* Just as myths already entail enlightenment, with every step enlightenment entangles itself more deeply in mythology. Receiving all its subject matter from myths, in order to destroy them, it falls as judge under the spell of myth. It seeks to escape the trial of fate and retribution by itself exacting retribution on that trial. In myths, everything that happens must atone for the fact of having happened. It is no different in enlightenment: no sooner has a fact been established than it is rendered insignificant. The doctrine that action equals reaction continued to maintain the power of repetition over existence long after humankind had shed the illusion that, by repetition, it could identify itself with repeated existence and so escape its power. But the more the illusion of magic vanishes, the more implacably repetition, in the guise of regularity, imprisons human beings in the cycle now objectified in the laws of nature, to which they believe they owe their security as free subjects. The principle of immanence, the explanation of every event as repetition, which enlightenment upholds against mythical imagination, is that of myth itself. The arid wisdom which acknowledges nothing new under the sun, because all the pieces in the meaningless game have been played out, all the great thoughts have been thought, all possible discoveries can be construed in advance, and human beings are defined by self-preservation through adaptation—this barren wisdom merely reproduces the fantastic doctrine it rejects: the sanction of fate which, through retribution, incessantly reinstates what always was. Whatever might be different is made the same. That is the verdict which critically sets the boundaries to possible experience. The identity of everything with everything is bought at the cost that nothing can at the same time be identical to itself. Enlightenment dissolves away the injustice of the old inequality of unmediated mastery, but at the same time perpetuates it in universal mediation, by relating every existing thing to every other. It brings about the situation for which Kierkegaard praised his Protestant ethic and which, in the legend-cycle of Hercules, constitutes one of the primal images of mythical violence: it amputates the incommensurable. Not merely are qualities dissolved in thought, but human beings are forced into real conformity. The blessing that the market does not ask about birth is paid for in the exchange society by the fact that the possibilities conferred by birth are molded to fit the production of goods that can be bought on the market. Each human being has been endowed with a self of his or her own, different from all others, so that it could all the more surely be made the same. But because that self never quite fitted the mold, enlightenment throughout the liberalistic period has always sympathized with social coercion. The unity of the manipulated collective consists in the negation of each individual and in the scorn poured on the type of society which could make people into individuals. The horde, a term which doubtless* is to be found in the Hitler Youth organization, is not a relapse into the old barbarism but the triumph of repressive *égalité*, the degeneration of the equality of rights into the wrong inflicted by equals. The fake myth of fascism reveals itself as the genuine myth of prehistory, in that the genuine myth beheld retribution while the false one wreaks it blindly on its victims. Any attempt to break the compulsion of nature by breaking nature only succumbs more deeply to that compulsion. That has been the trajectory of European civilization. Abstraction, the instrument of enlightenment, stands in the same relationship to its objects as fate, whose concept it eradicates: as liquidation. Under the leveling rule of abstraction, which makes everything in nature repeatable, and of industry, for which abstraction prepared the way, the liberated finally themselves become the "herd" (*Trupp*), which Hegel[16] identified as the outcome of enlightenment.

The distance of subject from object, the presupposition of abstraction, is founded on the distance from things which the ruler attains by means of the ruled. The songs of Homer and the hymns of the *Rig Veda* date from the time of territorial dominion and its strongholds, when a warlike race of overlords imposed itself on the defeated indigenous population.[17] The supreme god among gods came into being with this civil world in which the king, as leader of the arms-bearing nobility, tied the subjugated people* to the land while doctors, soothsayers, artisans, and traders took care of circulation. With the end of nomadism the social order is established on the basis of fixed property. Power and labor diverge. A property owner like Odysseus "controls from a distance a numerous, finely graded personnel of ox herds, shepherds, swineherds, and servants. In the evening, having looked out from his castle to see the countryside lit up by a thousand fires, he can go to his rest in peace. He knows that his loyal servants are watching to keep away wild animals and to drive away thieves from the enclosures which they are there to protect."[18] The generality of the ideas developed by discursive logic, power in the sphere of the concept, is built on the foundation of power in reality. The superseding of the old diffuse notions of the magical heritage by conceptual unity expresses a condition of life defined by the freeborn citizen and articulated by command. The self which learned about order and subordination through the subjugation of the world soon equated truth in general with classifying thought, without whose fixed distinctions it cannot exist. Along with mimetic magic it tabooed the knowledge which really apprehends the object. Its hatred is directed at the image of the vanquished primeval world and its imaginary happiness. The dark, chthonic gods of the original inhabitants are banished to the hell into which the earth is transformed under the religions of Indra and Zeus, with their worship of sun and light.

But heaven and hell were linked. The name Zeus was applied both to a god of the underworld and to a god of light in cults which did not exclude each other,[19] and the Olympian gods maintained all kinds of commerce with the chthonic deities. In the same way, the good and evil powers, the holy and the unholy, were not unambiguously distinguished. They were bound together like genesis and decline, life and death, summer and winter. The murky, undivided entity worshipped as the principle of *mana* at the earliest known stages of humanity lived on in the bright world of the Greek religion. Primal and undifferentiated, it is everything unknown and alien; it is that which transcends the bounds of experience, the part of things which is more than their immediately perceived existence. What the primitive experiences as supernatural is not a spiritual substance in contradistinction to the material world but the complex concatenation of nature in contrast to its individual link.* The cry of terror called forth by the unfamiliar becomes its name. It fixes the transcendence of the unknown in relation to the known, permanently linking horror to holiness. The doubling of nature into appearance and essence, effect and force, made possible by myth no less than by science, springs from human fear, the expression of which becomes its explanation. This does not mean that the soul is transposed into nature, as psychologism would have us believe; *mana*, the moving spirit, is not a projection but the echo of the real preponderance of nature in the weak psyches of primitive people. The split between animate and inanimate, the assigning of demons and deities to certain specific places, arises from this preanimism. Even the division of subject and object is prefigured in it. If the tree is addressed no longer as simply a tree but as evidence of something else, a location of *mana*, language expresses the contradiction that it is at the same time itself and something other than itself, identical and not identical.[20] Through the deity speech is transformed from tautology into language. The concept, usually defined as the unity of the features of what it subsumes, was rather, from the first, a product of dialectical thinking, in which each thing is what it is only by becoming what it is not. This was the primal form of the objectifying definition, in which concept and thing became separate, the same definition which was already far advanced in the Homeric epic and trips over its own excesses in modern positive science. But this dialectic remains powerless as long as it emerges from the cry of terror, which is the doubling, the mere tautology of terror itself. The gods cannot take away fear from human beings, the petrified cries of whom they bear as their names. Humans believe themselves free of fear when there is no longer anything unknown. This has determined the path of demythologization, of enlightenment, which equates the living with the nonliving as myth had equated the nonliving with the living. Enlightenment is mythical fear radicalized. The pure immanence of positivism, its ultimate product, is nothing other than a form of universal taboo. Nothing is allowed to remain outside, since the mere idea of the "outside" is the real source of fear. If the revenge of primitive people for a murder committed on a member of their family could sometimes be assuaged by admitting the murderer into that family,[21] both the murder and its remedy mean the absorption of alien blood into one's own, the establishment of immanence. The mythical dualism does not lead outside the circle of existence. The world controlled by *mana*, and even the worlds of Indian and Greek myth, are issueless and eternally the same. All birth is paid for with death, all fortune with misfortune. While men and gods may attempt in their short span to assess their fates by a measure other than blind destiny, existence triumphs over them in the end. Even their justice, wrested from calamity, bears its features; it corresponds to the way in which human beings, primitives no less than Greeks and barbarians, looked upon their world from within a society of oppression and poverty. Hence, for both mythical and enlightened justice, guilt and atonement, happiness and misfortune, are seen as the two sides of an equation. Justice gives way to law. The shaman wards off a danger with its likeness. Equivalence is his instrument; and equivalence regulates punishment and reward within civilization. The imagery of myths, too, can be traced back without exception to natural conditions. Just as the constellation Gemini, like all the other symbols of duality, refers to the inescapable cycle of nature; just as this cycle itself has its primeval sign in the symbol of the egg from which those later symbols are sprung, the Scales (Libra) held by Zeus, which symbolize the justice of the entire patriarchal world, point back to mere nature. The step from chaos to civilization, in which natural conditions exert their power no longer directly but through the consciousness of human beings, changed nothing in the principle of equivalence. Indeed, human beings atoned for this very step by worshipping that to which previously, like all other creatures, they had been merely subjected. Earlier, fetishes had been subject to the law of equivalence. Now equivalence itself becomes a fetish. The blindfold over the eyes of Justitia means not only that justice brooks no interference but that it does not originate in freedom.

The teachings of the priests were symbolic in the sense that in them sign and image coincided. As the hieroglyphs attest, the word originally also had a pictorial function. This function was transferred to myths. They, like magic rites, refer to the repetitive cycle of nature. Nature as self-repetition is the core of the symbolic: an entity or a process which is conceived as eternal because it is reenacted again and again in the guise of the symbol. Inexhaustibility, endless renewal, and the permanence of what they signify are not only attributes of all symbols but their true content. Contrary to the Jewish *Genesis*, the representations of creation in which the world emerges from the primal mother, the cow or the egg, are symbolic. The scorn of the ancients for their all-too-human gods left their core untouched. The essence of the gods is not exhausted by individuality. They still had about them a quality of *mana*; they embodied nature as a universal power. With their preanimistic traits they intrude into the enlightenment. Beneath the modest veil of the Olympian *chronique scandaleuse* the doctrine of the commingling and colliding of elements had evolved; establishing itself at once as science, it turned the myths into figments of fantasy. With the clean separation between science and poetry the division of labor which science had helped to establish was extended to language. For science the word is first of all a sign; it is then distributed among the various arts as sound, image, or word proper, but its unity can never be restored by the addition of these arts, by synaesthesia or total art.* As sign, language must resign itself to being calculation and, to know nature, must renounce the claim to resemble it. As image it must resign itself to being a likeness and, to be entirely nature, must renounce the claim to know it. With advancing enlightenment, only authentic works of art have been able to avoid the mere imitation of what already is. The prevailing antithesis between art and science, which rends the two apart as areas of culture in order to make them jointly manageable as areas of culture, finally causes them, through their internal tendencies as exact opposites, to converge. Science, in its neopositivist interpretation, becomes aestheticism, a system of isolated signs devoid of any intention transcending the system; it becomes the game which mathematicians have long since proudly declared their activity to be. Meanwhile, art as integral replication has pledged itself to positivist science, even in its specific techniques. It becomes, indeed, the world over again, an ideological doubling, a compliant reproduction. The separation of sign and image is inescapable. But if, with heedless complacency, it is hypostatized over again, then each of the isolated principles tends toward the destruction of truth.

Philosophy has perceived the chasm opened by this separation as the relationship between intuition and concept and repeatedly but vainly has attempted to close it; indeed, philosophy is defined by that attempt. Usually, however, it has sided with the tendency to which it owes its name. Plato banished poetry with the same severity with which positivism dismissed the doctrine of Forms. Homer, Plato argued, had procured neither public nor private reforms through his much-vaunted art, had neither won a war nor made an invention. We did not know, he said, of any numerous followers who had honored or loved him. Art had to demonstrate its usefulness.[22] The making of images was proscribed by Plato as it was by the Jews. Both reason and religion outlaw the principle of magic. Even in its resigned detachment from existence, as art, it remains dishonorable; those who practice it become vagrants, latter-day nomads, who find no domicile among the settled. Nature is no longer to be influenced by likeness but mastered through work. Art has in common with magic the postulation of a special, self-contained sphere removed from the context of profane exis-

tence. Within it special laws prevail. Just as the sorcerer begins the ceremony by marking out from all its surroundings the place in which the
sacred forces are to come into play, each work of art is closed off from reality by its own circumference. The very renunciation of external effects by
which art is distinguished from magical sympathy binds art only more
deeply to the heritage of magic. This renunciation places the pure image
in opposition to corporeal existence, the elements of which the image sub-
lates within itself. It is in the nature of the work of art, of aesthetic illusion, to be what was experienced as a new and terrible event in the magic
of primitives: the appearance of the whole in the particular. The work of
art constantly reenacts the duplication by which the thing appeared as
something spiritual, a manifestation of *mana*. That constitutes its aura. As
an expression of totality art claims the dignity of the absolute. This has
occasionally led philosophy to rank it higher than conceptual knowledge.
According to Schelling, art begins where knowledge leaves humans in the
lurch. For him art is "the model of science, and wherever art is, there science must go."[23] According to his theory the separation of image and sign
"is entirely abolished by each single representation of art."[24] The bourgeois
world was rarely amenable to such confidence in art. Where it restricted
knowledge, it generally did so to make room for faith, not art. It was
through faith that the militant religiosity of the modern age, of Tor-
quemada, Luther, and Mohammed, sought to reconcile spirit and existence. But faith is a privative concept: it is abolished as faith if it does not
continuously assert either its opposition to knowledge or its agreement
with it. In being dependent on the limits set to knowledge, it is itself limited. The attempt made by faith under Protestantism to locate the principle of truth, which transcends faith and without which faith cannot exist,
directly in the word itself, as in primeval times, and to restore the symbolic
power of the word, was paid for by obedience to the word, but not in its
sacred form. Because faith is unavoidably tied to knowledge as its friend
or its foe, faith perpetuates the split in the struggle to overcome knowledge: its fanaticism is the mark of its untruth, the objective admission that
anyone who *only* believes for that reason no longer believes. Bad conscience is second nature to it. The secret awareness of this necessary, inherent flaw, the immanent contradiction that lies in making a profession of
reconciliation, is the reason why honesty in believers has always been a
sensitive and dangerous affair. The horrors of fire and sword, of counter-

Reformation and Reformation, were perpetrated not as an exaggeration but as a realization of the principle of faith. Faith repeatedly shows itself of the same stamp as the world history it would like to command; indeed, in the modern period it has become that history's preferred means, its special ruse. Not only is the Enlightenment of the eighteenth century inexorable, as Hegel confirmed; so, too, as none knew better than he, is the movement of thought itself. The lowest insight, like the highest, contains the knowledge of its distance from the truth, which makes the apologist a liar. The paradox of faith degenerates finally into fraud, the myth of the twentieth century* and faith's irrationality into rational organization in the hands of the utterly enlightened as they steer society toward barbarism.

When language first entered history its masters were already priests and sorcerers. Anyone who affronted the symbols fell prey in the name of the unearthly powers to the earthly ones, represented by these appointed organs of society. What preceded that stage is shrouded in darkness. Wherever it is found in ethnology, the terror from which *mana* was born was already sanctioned, at least by the tribal elders. Unidentical, fluid *mana* was solidified, violently materialized by men. Soon the sorcerers had populated every place with its emanations and coordinated the multiplicity of sacred realms with that of sacred rites. With the spirit-world and its peculiarities they extended their esoteric knowledge and their power. The sacred essence was transferred to the sorcerers who managed it. In the first stages of nomadism the members of the tribe still played an independent part in influencing the course of nature. The men tracked prey while the women performed tasks which did not require rigid commands. How much violence preceded the habituation to even so simple an order cannot be known. In that order the world was already divided into zones of power and of the profane. The course of natural events as an emanation of *mana* had already been elevated to a norm demanding submission. But if the nomadic savage, despite his subjection, could still participate in the magic which defined the limits of that world, and could disguise himself as his quarry in order to stalk it, in later periods the intercourse with spirits and the subjection were assigned to different classes of humanity: power to one side, obedience to the other. The recurring, never-changing natural processes were drummed into the subjects, either by other tribes or by their own cliques, as the rhythm of work, to the beat of the club and the rod, which reechoed in every barbaric drum, in each monotonous ritual. The symbols take on the expression of the fetish. The repetition of nature which they signify always manifests itself in later times as the permanence of social compulsion, which the symbols represent. The dread objectified in the fixed image becomes a sign of the consolidated power of the privileged.* But general concepts continued to symbolize that power even when they had shed all pictorial traits. Even the deductive form of science mirrors hierarchy and compulsion. Just as the first categories represented the organized tribe and its power over the individual, the entire logical order, with its chains of inference and dependence, the superordination and coordination of concepts, is founded on the corresponding conditions in social reality, that is, on the division of labor.[25] Of course, this social character of intellectual forms is not, as Durkheim argues, an expression of social solidarity but evidence of the impenetrable unity of society and power. Power confers increased cohesion and strength on the social whole in which it is established. The division of labor, through which power manifests itself socially, serves the self-preservation of the dominated whole. But this necessarily turns the whole, as a whole, and the operation of its immanent reason, into a means of enforcing the particular interest. Power confronts the individual as the universal, as the reason which informs reality. The power of all the members of society, to whom as individuals no other way is open, is constantly summated, through the division of labor imposed on them, in the realization of the whole, whose rationality is thereby multiplied over again. What is done to all by the few always takes the form of the subduing of individuals by the many: the oppression of society always bears the features of oppression by a collective. It is this unity of collectivity and power, and not the immediate social universal, solidarity, which is precipitated in intellectual forms. Through their claim to universal validity, the philosophical concepts with which Plato and Aristotle represented the world elevated the conditions which those concepts justified to the status of true reality. They originated, as Vico put it,[26] in the marketplace of Athens; they reflected with the same fidelity the laws of physics, the equality of freeborn citizens, and the inferiority of women, children, and slaves. Language itself endowed what it expressed, the conditions of domination, with the universality it had acquired as the means of intercourse in civil society. The metaphysical emphasis, the sanction by ideas and norms, was no more than a hypostatization of the rigidity and exclusivity which concepts have necessarily taken on wherever language has consolidated the community of the rulers for the enforcement of commands. As a means of reinforcing the social power of language, ideas became more superfluous the more that power increased, and the language of science put an end to them altogether. Conscious justification lacked the suggestive power which springs from dread of the fetish. The unity of collectivity and power now revealed itself in the generality which faulty content necessarily takes on in language, whether metaphysical or scientific. The metaphysical apologia at least betrayed the injustice of the established order through the incongruence of concept and reality. The impartiality of scientific language deprived what was powerless of the strength to make itself heard and merely provided the existing order with a neutral sign for itself. Such neutrality is more metaphysical than metaphysics. Enlightenment finally devoured not only symbols but also their successors, universal concepts, and left nothing of metaphysics behind except the abstract fear of the collective from which it had sprung. Concepts in face of enlightenment are like those living on unearned income in face of industrial trusts:* none can feel secure. If logical positivism still allowed some latitude for probability, ethnological positivism already equates probability with essence. "Our vague ideas of chance and quintessence are pale relics of that far richer notion,"[27] that is, of the magical substance.

Enlightenment as a nominalist tendency stops short before the *nomen*, the non-extensive, restricted concept, the proper name. Although[28] it cannot be established with certainty whether proper names were originally generic names, as some maintain, the former have not yet shared the fate of the latter. The substantial ego repudiated by Hume and Mach is not the same thing as the name. In the Jewish religion, in which the idea of the patriarchy is heightened to the point of annihilating myth, the link between name and essence is still acknowledged in the prohibition on uttering the name of God. The disenchanted world of Judaism propitiates magic by negating it in the idea of God. The Jewish religion brooks no word which might bring solace to the despair of all mortality. It places all hope in the prohibition on invoking falsity as God, the finite as the infinite, the lie as truth. The pledge of salvation lies in the rejection of any faith which claims to depict it, knowledge in the denunciation of illusion. Negation, however, is not abstract. The indiscriminate denial of anything positive, the stereotyped formula of nothingness as used by Buddhism, ignores the ban on calling the absolute by its name no less than its opposite, pantheism, or the latter's caricature, bourgeois skepticism. Explanations of the world as nothingness or as the entire cosmos are mythologies, and the guaranteed paths to redemption sublimated magical practices. The self-satisfaction of knowing in advance, and the transfiguration of negativity as redemption, are untrue forms of the resistance to deception. The right of the image is rescued in the faithful observance of its prohibition. Such observance, "determinate negation,"[29] is not exempted from the enticements of intuition by the sovereignty of the abstract concept, as is skepticism, for which falsehood and truth are equally void. Unlike rigorism, determinate negation does not simply reject imperfect representations of the absolute, idols, by confronting them with the idea they are unable to match. Rather, dialectic discloses each image as script. It teaches us to read from its features the admission of falseness which cancels its power and hands it over to truth. Language thereby becomes more than a mere system of signs. With the concept of determinate negation Hegel gave prominence to an element which distinguishes enlightenment from the positivist decay to which he consigned it. However, by finally postulating the known result of the whole process of negation, totality in the system and in history, as the absolute, he violated the prohibition and himself succumbed to mythology.

That fate befell not only his philosophy, as the apotheosis of advancing thought, but enlightenment itself, in the form of the sober matter-of-factness by which it purported to distinguish itself from Hegel and from metaphysics in general. For enlightenment is totalitarian as only a system can be. Its untruth does not lie in the analytical method, the reduction to elements, the decomposition through reflection, as its Romantic enemies had maintained from the first, but in its assumption that the trial is prejudged. When in mathematics the unknown becomes the unknown quantity in an equation, it is made into something long familiar before any value* has been assigned. Nature, before and after quantum theory, is what can be registered mathematically; even what cannot be assimilated, the insoluble and irrational, is fenced in by mathematical theorems. In the preemptive identification of the thoroughly mathematized world with truth, enlightenment believes itself safe from the return of the mythical. It equates thought with mathematics. The latter is thereby cut loose, as it were, turned into an absolute authority. "An infinite world, in this case a world of idealities, is conceived as one in which objects are not accessible individually to our cognition in an imperfect and accidental way but are attained by a rational, systematically unified method which finally apprehends each object—in an infinite progression—fully as its own in-itself. . . . In Galileo's mathematization of nature, *nature itself* is idealized on the model of the new mathematics. In modern terms, it becomes a mathematical manifold."[30] Thought is reified as an autonomous, automatic process, aping the machine it has itself produced, so that it can finally be replaced by the machine. Enlightenment[31] pushed aside the classical demand to "think thinking"—Fichte's philosophy is its radical fulfillment—because it distracted philosophers from the command to control praxis, which Fichte himself had wanted to enforce. Mathematical procedure became a kind of ritual of thought. Despite its axiomatic self-limitation, it installed itself as necessary and objective: mathematics made thought into a thing—a tool, to use its own term. Through this mimesis, however, in which thought makes the world resemble itself, the actual has become so much the only concern that even the denial of God falls under the same judgment as metaphysics. For positivism, which has assumed the judicial office of enlightened reason, to speculate about intelligible worlds is no longer merely forbidden but senseless prattle. Positivism—fortunately for it—does not need to be atheistic, since objectified thought cannot even pose the question of the existence of God. The positivist sensor turns a blind eye to official worship, as a special, knowledge-free zone of social activity, just as willingly as to art—but never to denial, even when it has a claim to be knowledge. For the scientific temper, any deviation of thought from the business of manipulating the actual, any stepping outside the jurisdiction of existence, is no less senseless and self-destructive than it would be for the magician to step outside the magic circle drawn for his incantation; and in both cases violation of the taboo carries a heavy price for the offender. The mastery of nature draws the circle in which the critique of pure reason holds thought spellbound. Kant combined the doctrine of thought's restlessly toilsome progress toward infinity with insistence on its insufficiency and eternal limitation. The wisdom he imparted is oracular: There is no being in the world that knowledge cannot penetrate, but what can be penetrated by knowledge is not being. Philosophical judgment, according to Kant, aims at the new yet recognizes nothing new, since it always merely repeats what reason has placed into objects beforehand. However, this thought, protected within the departments of science from the dreams of a spirit-seer,* has to pay the price: world domination over nature turns against the thinking subject itself; nothing is left of it except that ever-unchanging "I think," which must accompany all my conceptions. Both subject and object are nullified. The abstract self, which alone confers the legal right to record and systematize, is confronted by nothing but abstract material, which has no other property than to be the substrate of that right. The equation of mind and world is finally resolved, but only in the sense that both sides cancel out. The reduction of thought to a mathematical apparatus condemns the world to be its own measure. What appears as the triumph of subjectivity, the subjection of all existing things to logical formalism, is bought with the obedient subordination of reason to what is immediately at hand. To grasp existing things as such, not merely to note their abstract spatial-temporal relationships, by which they can then be seized, but, on the contrary, to think of them as surface, as mediated conceptual moments which are only fulfilled by revealing their social, historical, and human meaning—this whole aspiration of knowledge is abandoned. Knowledge does not consist in mere perception, classification, and calculation but precisely in the determining negation of whatever is directly at hand. Instead of such negation, mathematical formalism, whose medium, number, is the most abstract form of the immediate, arrests thought at mere immediacy. The actual is validated, knowledge confines itself to repeating it, thought makes itself mere tautology. The more completely the machinery of thought subjugates existence, the more blindly it is satisfied with reproducing it. Enlightenment thereby regresses to the mythology it has never been able to escape. For mythology had reflected in its forms the essence of the existing order—cyclical motion, fate, domination of the world as truth—and had renounced hope. In the terseness of the mythical image, as in the clarity of the scientific formula, the eternity of the actual is confirmed and mere existence is pronounced as the meaning it obstructs. The world as a gigantic analytical judgment, the only surviving dream of science, is of the same kind as the cosmic myth which linked the alternation of spring and autumn to the abduction of Persephone. The uniqueness of the mythical event, which was intended to legitimize the factual one, is a deception. Originally, the rape of the goddess was directly equated with the dying of nature. It was repeated each autumn, and even the repetition was not a succession of separate events, but the same one each time. With the consolidation of temporal consciousness the process was fixed as a unique event in the past, and ritual assuagement of the terror of death in each new cycle of seasons was sought in the recourse to the distant past. But such separation is powerless. The postulation of the single past event endows the cycle with a quality of inevitability, and the terror radiating from the ancient event spreads over the whole process as its mere repetition. The subsumption of the actual, whether under mythical prehistory or under mathematical formalism, the symbolic relating of the present to the mythical event in the rite or to the abstract category in science, makes the new appear as something predetermined which therefore is really the old. It is not existence that is without hope, but knowledge which appropriates and perpetuates existence as a schema in the pictorial or mathematical symbol.

In the enlightened world, mythology has permeated the sphere of the profane. Existence, thoroughly cleansed of demons and their conceptual descendants, takes on, in its gleaming naturalness, the numinous character which former ages attributed to demons. Justified in the guise of brutal facts as something eternally immune to intervention, the social injustice from which those facts arise is as sacrosanct today as the medicine man once was under the protection of his gods. Not only is domination paid for with the estrangement of human beings from the dominated objects, but the relationships of human beings, including the relationship of individuals to themselves, have themselves been bewitched by the objectification of mind. Individuals shrink to the nodal points of conventional reactions and the modes of operation objectively expected of them. Animism had endowed things with souls; industrialism makes souls into things.* On its own account, even in advance of total planning, the economic apparatus endows commodities with the values which decide the behavior of people. Since, with the ending of free exchange, commodities have forfeited all economic qualities except their fetish character, this character has spread like a cataract across the life of society in all its aspects. The countless agencies of mass production and its culture* impress standardized behavior on the individual as the only natural, decent, and rational one. Individuals define themselves now only as things, statistical elements, successes or failures. Their criterion is self-preservation, successful or unsuccessful adaptation to the objectivity of their function and the schemata assigned to it. Everything which is different, from the idea to criminality, is exposed to the force of the collective, which keeps watch from the classroom to the trade union. Yet even the threatening collective is merely a part of the deceptive surface, beneath which are concealed the powers which manipulate the collective as an agent of violence. Its brutality, which keeps the individual up to the mark, no more represents the true quality of people than value* represents that of commodities. The demonically distorted form which things and human beings have taken on in the clear light of unprejudiced knowledge points back to domination, to the principle which already imparted the qualities of *mana* to spirits and deities and trapped the human gaze in the fakery of sorcerers and medicine men. The fatalism by which incomprehensible death was sanctioned in primeval times has now passed over into utterly comprehensible life. The noonday panic fear in which nature suddenly appeared to humans as an all-encompassing power has found its counterpart in the panic which is ready to break out at any moment today: human beings expect the world, which is without issue, to be set ablaze by a universal power which they themselves are and over which they are powerless.

Enlightenment's mythic terror springs from a horror of myth. It detects myth not only in semantically unclarified concepts and words, as linguistic criticism imagines, but in any human utterance which has no place in the functional context of self-preservation. Spinoza's proposition: "the endeavor of preserving oneself is the first and only basis of virtue,"[32] contains the true maxim of all Western civilization, in which the religious and philosophical differences of the bourgeoisie are laid to rest. The self which, after the methodical extirpation of all natural traces as mythological, was no longer supposed to be either a body or blood or a soul or even a natural ego but was sublimated into a transcendental or logical subject, formed the reference point of reason, the legislating authority of action. In the judgment of enlightenment as of Protestantism, those who entrust themselves directly to life, without any rational reference to self-preservation, revert to the realm of prehistory. Impulse as such, according to this view, is as mythical as superstition, and worship of any God not postulated by the self, as aberrant as drunkenness. For both—worship and self-immersion in immediate natural existence—progress holds the same fate in store. It has anathematized the self-forgetfulness both of thought and of pleasure. In the bourgeois economy the social work of each individual is mediated by the principle of the self; for some this labor is supposed to yield increased capital, for others the strength for extra work. But the more heavily the process of self-preservation is based on the bourgeois division of labor, the more it enforces the self-alienation of individuals, who must mold themselves to the technical apparatus body and soul. Enlightened thinking has an answer for this, too: finally, the transcendental subject of knowledge, as the last reminder of subjectivity, is itself seemingly abolished and replaced by the operations of the automatic mechanisms of order, which therefore run all the more smoothly. Subjectivity has volatilized itself into the logic of supposedly optional rules, to gain more absolute control. Positivism, which finally did not shrink from laying hands on the idlest fancy of all, thought itself, eliminated the last intervening agency between individual action and the social norm. The technical process, to which the subject has been reified after the eradication of that process from consciousness, is as free from the ambiguous meanings of mythical thought as from meaning altogether, since reason itself has become merely an aid to the all-encompassing economic apparatus.* Reason serves as a universal tool for the fabrication of all other tools, rigidly purpose-directed and as calamitous as the precisely calculated operations of material production, the results of which for human beings escape all calculation. Reason's old ambition to be purely an instrument of purposes has finally been fulfilled. The exclusivity of logical laws stems from this obdurate adherence to function and ultimately from the compulsive character of self-preservation. The latter is constantly magnified into the choice between survival and doom, a choice which is reflected even in the principle that, of two contradictory propositions, only one can be true and the other false. The formalism of this principle and the entire logic established around it stem from the opacity and entanglement of interests in a society in which the maintenance of forms and the preservation of individuals only fortuitously coincide. The expulsion of thought from logic ratifies in the lecture hall the reification of human beings in factory and office. In this way the taboo encroaches on the power imposing it, enlightenment on mind, which it itself is. But nature as true self-preservation is thereby unleashed, in the individual as in the collective fate of crisis and war, by the process which promised to extirpate it. If unitary knowledge* is the only norm which theory has left, praxis must be handed over to the unfettered operations of world history. The self, entirely encompassed by civilization, is dissolved in an element composed of the very inhumanity which civilization has sought from the first to escape. The oldest fear, that of losing one's own name, is being fulfilled. For civilization, purely natural existence, both animal and vegetative, was the absolute danger. Mimetic, mythical, and metaphysical forms of behavior were successively regarded as stages of world history which had been left behind, and the idea of reverting to them held the terror that the self would be changed back into the mere nature from which it had extricated itself with unspeakable exertions and which for that reason filled it with unspeakable dread. Over the millennia the living memory of prehistory, of its nomadic period and even more of the truly prepatriarchal stages, has been expunged from human consciousness with the most terrible punishments. The enlightened spirit replaced fire and the wheel by the stigma it attached to all irrationality, which led to perdition. Its hedonism was moderate, extremes being no less repugnant to enlightenment than to Aristotle. The bourgeois ideal of naturalness is based not on amorphous nature but on the virtue of the middle way. For this ideal, promiscuity and asceticism, superfluity and hunger, although opposites, are directly identical as powers of disintegration. By subordinating life in its entirety to the requirements of its preservation, the controlling minority guarantees, with its own security, the continuation of the whole. From Homer to modernity the ruling spirit has sought to steer between the Scylla of relapse into simple reproduction and the Charybdis of unfettered fulfillment; from the first it has mistrusted any guiding star other than the lesser evil. The German neopagans and administrators of war fever want to reinstate pleasure.* But since, under the work-pressure of the millennium now ending, pleasure has learned to hate itself, in its totalitarian emancipation it remains mean and mutilated through self-contempt.* It is still in the grip of the self-preservation inculcated in it by the reason which has now been deposed. At the turning points of Western civilization, whenever new peoples and classes have more heavily repressed myth, from the beginnings of the Olympian religion to the Renaissance, the Reformation, and bourgeois atheism, the fear of unsubdued, threatening nature—a fear resulting from nature's very materialization and objectification—has been belittled as animist superstition, and the control of internal and external nature has been made the absolute purpose of life. Now that self-preservation has been finally automated, reason is dismissed by those who, as controllers of production, have taken over its inheritance and fear it in the disinherited. The essence of enlightenment is the choice between alternatives, and the inescapability of this choice is that of power. Human beings have always had to choose between their subjugation to nature and its subjugation to the self. With the spread of the bourgeois commodity economy the dark horizon of myth is illuminated by the sun of calculating reason, beneath whose icy rays the seeds of the new barbarism are germinating. Under the compulsion of power, human labor has always led away from myth and, under power, has always fallen back under its spell.

The intertwinement of myth, power, and labor is preserved in one of the tales of Homer. Book XII of the *Odyssey* tells how Odysseus sailed past the Sirens. Their allurement is that of losing oneself in the past. But the hero exposed to it has come of age in suffering. In the multitude of mortal dangers which he has had to endure, the unity of his own life, the identity of the person, have been hardened. The realms of time have been separated for him like water, earth, and air. The tide of what has been has receded from the rock of the present, and the future lies veiled in cloud on the horizon. What Odysseus has left behind him has passed into the world of shades: so close is the self to the primeval myth from whose embrace it has wrested itself that its own lived past becomes a mythical prehistory. It seeks to combat this by a fixed order of time. The tripartite division is intended to liberate the present moment from the power of the past by banishing the latter beyond the absolute boundary of the irrecoverable and placing it, as usable knowledge, in the service of the present. The urge to rescue the past as something living, instead of using it as the material of progress, has been satisfied only in art, in which even history, as a representation of past life, is included. As long as art does not insist on being treated as knowledge, and thus exclude itself from praxis, it is tolerated by social praxis in the same way as pleasure. But the Sirens' song has not yet been deprived of power as art. They have knowledge "of all that has ever happened on this fruitful earth"[33] and especially of what has befallen Odysseus himself: "For we know all that the Argives and the Trojans suffered on the broad plain of Troy by the will of the gods."[34] By directly invoking the recent past, and with the irresistible promise of pleasure which their song contains, the Sirens threaten the patriarchal order, which gives each person back their life only in exchange for their full measure of time. When only unfailing presence of mind wrests survival from nature, anyone who follows the Sirens' phantasmagoria is lost. If the Sirens know everything that has happened, they demand the future as its price, and their promise of a happy homecoming is the deception by which the past entraps a humanity filled with longing. Odysseus has been warned by Circe, the divinity of regression to animal form, whom he has withstood and who therefore gives him the strength to withstand other powers of dissolution. But the lure of the Sirens remains overpowering. No one who hears their song can escape. Humanity had to inflict terrible injuries on itself before the self—the identical, purpose-directed, masculine character of human beings—was created, and something of this process is repeated in every childhood. The effort to hold itself together attends the ego at all its stages, and the temptation to be rid of the ego has always gone hand-in-hand with the blind determination to preserve it. Narcotic intoxication, in which the euphoric suspension of the self is expiated by deathlike sleep, is one of the oldest social transactions mediating between self-preservation and self-annihilation, an attempt by the self to survive itself. The fear of losing the self, and suspending with it the boundary between oneself and other life, the aversion to death and destruction, is twinned with a promise of joy which has threatened civilization at every moment. The way of civilization has been that of obedience and work, over which fulfillment shines everlastingly as mere illusion, as beauty deprived of power. Odysseus's idea, equally inimical to his death and to his happiness, shows awareness of this. He knows only two possibilities of escape. One he prescribes to his comrades. He plugs their ears with wax and orders them to row with all their might. Anyone who wishes to survive must not listen to the temptation of the irrecoverable, and is unable to listen only if he is unable to hear. Society has always made sure that this was the case. Workers must look ahead with alert concentration and ignore anything which lies to one side. The urge toward distraction must be grimly sublimated in redoubled exertions. Thus the workers are made practical. The other possibility Odysseus chooses for himself, the landowner, who has others to work for him. He listens, but does so while bound helplessly to the mast, and the stronger the allurement grows the more tightly he has himself bound, just as later the bourgeois denied themselves happiness the closer it drew to them with the increase in their own power. What he hears has no consequences for him; he can signal to his men to untie him only by movements of his head, but it is too late. His comrades, who themselves cannot hear, know only of the danger of the song, not of its beauty, and leave him tied to the mast to save both him and themselves. They reproduce the life of the oppressor as a part of their own, while he cannot step outside his social role. The bonds by which he has irrevocably fettered himself to praxis at the same time keep the Sirens at a distance from praxis: their lure is neutralized as a mere object of contemplation, as art. The fettered man listens to a concert, as immobilized as audiences later, and his enthusiastic call for liberation goes unheard as applause. In this way the enjoyment of art and manual work diverge as the primeval world is left behind. The epic already contains the correct theory. Between the cultural heritage and enforced work there is a precise correlation, and both are founded on the inescapable compulsion toward the social control of nature.

Measures like those taken on Odysseus's ship in face of the Sirens are a prescient allegory of the dialectic of enlightenment. Just as the capacity to be represented is the measure of power, the mightiest person being the one who can be represented in the most functions, so it is also the vehicle of both progress and regression. Under the given conditions, exclusion from work means mutilation, not only for the unemployed but also for people at the opposite social pole. Those at the top experience the existence with which they no longer need to concern themselves as a mere substrate, and are wholly ossified as the self which issues commands. Primitive man experienced the natural thing only as the fugitive object of desire, "but the lord, who has interposed the bondsman between it and himself, takes to himself only the dependent aspect of the thing and has the pure enjoyment of it. The aspect of its independence he leaves to the bondsman, who works on it."[35] Odysseus is represented in the sphere of work. Just as he cannot give way to the lure of self-abandonment, as owner he also forfeits participation in work and finally even control over it, while his companions, despite their closeness to things, cannot enjoy their work because it is performed under compulsion, in despair, with their senses forcibly stopped. The servant is subjugated in body and soul, the master regresses. No system of domination has so far been able to escape this price, and the circularity of history in its progress is explained in part by this debilitation, which is the concomitant of power. Humanity, whose skills and knowledge become differentiated with the division of labor, is thereby forced back to more primitive anthropological stages, since, with the technical facilitation of existence, the continuance of domination demands the fixation of instincts by greater repression. Fantasy withers. The calamity is not that individuals have fallen behind society or its material production. Where the development of the machine has become that of the machinery of control, so that technical and social tendencies, always intertwined, converge in the total encompassing of human beings, those who have lagged behind represent not only untruth. Adaptation to the power of progress furthers the progress of power, constantly renewing the degenerations which prove successful progress, not failed progress, to be its own antithesis. The curse of irresistible progress is irresistible regression.

This regression is not confined to the experience of the sensuous world, an experience tied to physical proximity, but also affects the autocratic intellect, which detaches itself from sensuous experience in order to subjugate it. The standardization of the intellectual function through which the mastery of the senses is accomplished, the acquiescence of thought to the production of unanimity, implies an impoverishment of thought no less than of experience; the separation of the two realms leaves both damaged. A consequence of the restriction of thought to organization and administration, rehearsed by the those in charge from artful Odysseus to artless chairmen of the board, is the stupidity which afflicts the great as soon as they have to perform tasks other than the manipulation of the small. Mind becomes in reality the instrument of power and self-mastery for which bourgeois philosophy has always mistaken it. The deafness which has continued to afflict the submissive proletarians since the myth is matched by the immobility of those in command. The over-ripeness of society lives on the immaturity of the ruled. The more complex and sensitive the social, economic, and scientific mechanism, to the operation of which the system of production has long since attuned the body, the more impoverished are the experiences of which the body is capable. The elimination of qualities, their conversion into functions, is transferred by rationalized modes of work to the human capacity for experience, which tends to revert to that of amphibians. The regression of the masses today lies in their inability to hear with their own ears what has not already been heard, to touch with their hands what has not previously been grasped; it is the new form of blindness which supersedes that of vanquished myth. Through the mediation of the total society, which encompasses all relationships and impulses, human beings are being turned back into precisely what the developmental law of society, the principle of the self, had opposed: mere examples of the species, identical to one another through isolation within the compulsively controlled collectivity. The rowers, unable to speak to one another, are all harnessed to the same rhythms, like modern workers in factories, cinemas, and the collective. It is the concrete conditions of work in society* which enforce conformism—not the conscious influences which additionally render the oppressed stupid and deflect them from the truth. The powerlessness of the workers is not merely a ruse of the rulers but the logical consequence of industrial society, into which the efforts to escape it have finally transformed the ancient concept of fate.

This logical necessity, however, is not conclusive. It remains tied to domination, as both its reflection and its tool. Its truth, therefore, is no less questionable than its evidence is inescapable. Thought, however, has always been equal to the task of concretely demonstrating its own equivocal nature. It is the servant which the master cannot control at will. Domination, in becoming reified as law and organization, first when humans formed settlements and later in the commodity economy, has had to limit itself. The instrument is becoming autonomous: independently of the will of the rulers,* the mediating agency of mind moderates the immediacy of economic injustice.* The instruments of power—language, weapons, and finally machines—which are intended to hold everyone in their grasp, must in their turn be grasped by everyone. In this way, the moment of rationality in domination also asserts itself as something different from it. The thing-like quality of the means, which makes the means universally available, its "objective validity" for everyone, itself implies a criticism of the domination from which thought has arisen as its means. On the way from mythology to logistics, thought has lost the element of reflection on itself, and machinery mutilates people today, even if it also feeds them. In the form of machines, however, alienated reason is moving toward a society which reconciles thought, in its solidification as an apparatus both material and intellectual, with a liberated living element, and relates it to society itself as its true subject. The particularist origin and the universal perspective of thought have always been inseparable. Today, with the transformation of the world into industry, the perspective of the universal, the social realization of thought, is so fully open to view that thought is repudiated by the rulers themselves as mere ideology. It is a telltale manifestation of the bad conscience of the cliques in whom economic necessity is finally embodied* that its revelations, from the "intuitions" of the *Führer* to the "dynamic worldview," no longer acknowledge their own atrocities as necessary consequences of logical regularities, in resolute contrast to earlier bourgeois apologetics. The mythological lies about "mission" and "fate"* which they use instead do not even express a complete untruth: it is no longer the objective laws of the market which govern the actions of industrialists and drive humanity toward catastrophe. Rather, the conscious decisions of the company chairmen* execute capitalism's old law of value, and thus its fate, as resultants no less compulsive than the blindest price mechanisms. The rulers themselves do not believe in objective necessity, even if they sometimes call their machinations by that name. They posture as engineers of world history. Only their subjects accept the existing development, which renders them a degree more powerless with each prescribed increase in their standard of living, as inviolably necessary. Now that the livelihood of those still* needed to operate the machines can be provided with a minimal part of the working time which the masters of society have at their disposal, the superfluous remainder, the overwhelming mass of the population, are trained as additional guards of the system, so that they can be used today and tomorrow as material for its grand designs. They are kept alive as an army of unemployed. Their reduction to mere objects of administration, which preforms every department of modern life right down to language and perception, conjures up an illusion of objective necessity before which they believe themselves powerless. Poverty* as the antithesis between power and impotence is growing beyond measure, together with the capacity permanently to abolish poverty. From the commanding heights of the economy* to the latest professional rackets,* the tangled mass of cliques and institutions which ensures the indefinite continuation of the status quo is impenetrable to each individual. Even for a union boss, to say nothing of a manager, a proletarian is no more than a superfluous specimen, should he catch his notice at all, while the union boss in turn must live in terror of his own liquidation.

The absurdity of a state of affairs in which the power of the system over human beings increases with every step they take away from the power of nature denounces the reason of the reasonable* society as obsolete. That reason's necessity is illusion, no less than the freedom of the industrialists, which reveals its ultimately compulsive nature in their inescapable struggles and pacts. This* illusion, in which utterly enlightened humanity is losing itself, cannot be dispelled by a thinking which, as an instrument of power, has to choose between command and obedience. Although unable to escape the entanglement in which it was trapped in prehistory, that thinking* is nevertheless capable of recognizing the logic of either/or, of consequence and antinomy, by means of which it emancipated itself radically from nature, as that same nature, unreconciled and self-estranged. Precisely by virtue of its irresistible logic, thought, in whose compulsive mechanism nature is reflected and perpetuated, also reflects itself as a nature oblivious of itself, as a mechanism of compulsion. Of course, mental representation is only an instrument. In thought, human beings distance themselves from nature in order to arrange it in such a way that it can be mastered. Like the material tool which, as a thing, is held fast as that thing in different situations and thereby separates the world, as something chaotic, multiple, and disparate, from that which is known, single, and identical, so the concept is the idea-tool which fits into things at the very point from which one can take hold of them. Thought thus becomes illusory whenever it seeks to deny its function of separating, distancing, and objectifying. All mystical union remains a deception, the impotently inward trace of the forfeited revolution. But while enlightenment is right in opposing any hypostatization of utopia and in dispassionately denouncing power as division, the split between subject and object, which it will not allow to be bridged, becomes the index of the untruth both of itself and of truth.* The proscribing of superstition has always signified not only the progress of domination but its exposure. Enlightenment is more than enlightenment, it is nature made audible in its estrangement. In mind's self-recognition as nature divided from itself, nature, as in prehistory, is calling to itself, but no longer directly by its supposed name, which, in the guise of *mana*, means omnipotence, but as something blind and mutilated. In the mastery of nature, without which mind does not exist, enslavement to nature persists. By modestly confessing itself to be power and thus being taken back into nature, mind rids itself of the very claim to mastery which had enslaved it to nature. Although humanity may be unable to interrupt its flight away from necessity and into progress and civilization without forfeiting knowledge itself, at least it no longer mistakes the ramparts it has constructed against necessity, the institutions and practices of domination which have always rebounded against society from the subjugation of nature, for guarantors of the coming freedom. Each advance of civilization has renewed not only mastery but also the prospect of its alleviation. However, while real history is woven from real suffering, which certainly does not diminish in proportion to the increase in the means of abolishing it, the fulfillment of that prospect depends on the concept. For not only does the concept, as science, distance human beings from nature, but, as the self-reflection of thought—which, in the form of science, remains fettered to the blind economic tendency—it enables the distance which perpetuates injustice to be measured. Through this remembrance of nature within the subject, a remembrance which contains the unrecognized truth of all culture, enlightenment is opposed in principle to power, and even in the time of Vanini the call to hold back enlightenment was uttered less from fear of exact science than from hatred of licentious thought, which had escaped the spell of nature by confessing itself to be nature's own dread of itself. The priests have always avenged *mana* on any exponent of enlightenment who propitiated *mana* by showing fear before the frightening entity which bore that name, and in their hubris the augurs of enlightenment were at one with the priests. Enlightenment in its bourgeois form had given itself up to its positivist moment long before Turgot and d'Alembert. It was never immune to confusing freedom with the business of self-preservation. The suspension of the concept, whether done in the name of progress or of culture, which had both long since formed a secret alliance against truth, gave free rein to the lie. In a world which merely verified recorded evidence and preserved thought, debased to the achievement of great minds, as a kind of superannuated headline, the lie was no longer distinguishable from a truth neutralized as cultural heritage.

But to recognize power even within thought itself as unreconciled nature would be to relax the necessity which even socialism, in a concession to reactionary common sense, prematurely confirmed as eternal.* In declaring necessity the sole basis of the future and banishing mind, in the best idealist fashion, to the far pinnacle of the superstructure, socialism clung all too desperately to the heritage of bourgeois philosophy. The relationship of necessity to the realm of freedom was therefore treated as merely quantitative, mechanical, while nature, posited as wholly alien, as in the earliest mythology, became totalitarian, absorbing socialism along with freedom. By sacrificing thought, which in its reified form as mathematics, machinery, organization, avenges itself on a humanity forgetful of it, enlightenment forfeited its own realization. By subjecting everything particular to its discipline, it left the uncomprehended whole free to rebound as mastery over things against the life and consciousness of human beings. But a true praxis capable of overturning the status quo depends on theory's refusal to yield to the oblivion in which society allows thought to ossify. It is not the material preconditions of fulfillment, unfettered technology* as such, which make fulfillment uncertain. That is the argument of sociologists who are trying to devise yet another antidote, even a collectivist one, in order control that antidote.[36] The fault lies in a social context which induces blindness. The mythical scientific respect of peoples for the given reality, which they themselves constantly create, finally becomes itself a positive fact, a fortress before which even the revolutionary imagination feels shamed as utopianism, and degenerates to a compliant trust in the objective tendency of history. As the instrument of this adaptation, as a mere assemblage of means, enlightenment is as destructive as its Romantic enemies claim. It will only fulfill itself if it forswears its last complicity with them and dares to abolish the false absolute, the principle of blind power. The spirit of such unyielding theory would be able to turn back from its goal even the spirit of pitiless progress. Its herald, Bacon, dreamed of the many things "which kings with their treasure cannot buy, nor with their force command, [of which] their spials and intelligencers can give no news."* Just as he wished, those things have been given to the bourgeois, the enlightened heirs of the kings. In multiplying violence through the mediation of the market, the bourgeois economy has also multiplied its things and its forces to the point where not merely kings or even the bourgeoisie are sufficient to administrate them: all human beings are needed. From the power of things they finally learn to forgo power. Enlightenment consummates and abolishes itself when the closest practical objectives reveal themselves to be the most distant goal already attained, and the lands of which "their spials and intelligencers can give no news"—that is, nature misunderstood by masterful science—are remembered as those of origin. Today, when Bacon's utopia, in which "we should command nature in action," has been fulfilled on a telluric scale, the essence of the compulsion which he ascribed to unmastered nature is becoming apparent. It was power itself. Knowledge, in which, for Bacon, "the sovereignty of man" unquestionably lay hidden, can now devote itself to dissolving that power. But in face of this possibility enlightenment, in the service of the present, is turning itself into an outright deception of the masses.

Excursus I: Odysseus or Myth and Enlightenment

Just as the story of the Sirens illustrates the intertwinement of myth and rational labor, the *Odyssey* as a whole bears witness to the dialectic of enlightenment. In its oldest stratum, especially, the epic shows clear links to myth: the adventures are drawn from popular tradition. But as the Homeric spirit takes over and "organizes" the myths, it comes into contradiction with them. The familiar equation of epic and myth, which in any case has been undermined by recent classical philology, proves wholly misleading when subjected to philosophical critique. The two concepts diverge. They mark two phases of an historical process, which are still visible at the joints where editors have stitched the epic together. The Homeric discourse creates a universality of language, if it does not already presuppose it; it disintegrates the hierarchical order of society through the exoteric form of its depiction, even and especially when it glorifies that order. The celebration of the wrath of Achilles and the wanderings of Odysseus is already a nostalgic stylization of what can no longer be celebrated; and the hero of the adventures turns out to be the prototype of the bourgeois individual, whose concept originates in the unwavering self-assertion of which the protagonist driven to wander the earth is the primeval model. Finally, the epic, which in terms of the philosophy of history is the counterpart of the novel, exhibits features reminiscent of that genre, and the venerable cosmos of the Homeric world, a world charged with meaning, reveals itself as an achievement of classifying reason, which destroys myth by virtue of the same rational order which is used to reflect it.

Understanding of the element of bourgeois enlightenment in Homer has been advanced by the German late-Romantic interpretation of antiquity based on the early writings of Nietzsche. Like few others since Hegel, Nietzsche recognized the dialectic of enlightenment. He formulated the ambivalent relationship of enlightenment to power. Enlightenment must be "drummed into the people, so that the priests all turn into priests with a bad conscience—and likewise with the state. That is the task of enlightenment: to show up the pompous behavior of princes and statesmen as a deliberate lie."[1] However, enlightenment had always been a means employed by the "great artists of government (Confucius in China, the Roman Empire, Napoleon, the Papacy, when it was concerned with power and not just with the world) . . . The self-deception of the masses in this respect—for instance, in all democracies—is highly advantageous: making people small and governable is hailed as 'progress'!"[2] As this twofold character of enlightenment emerged more clearly as a basic motif of history, its concept, that of advancing thought, was traced back to the beginning of recorded history. However, whereas Nietzsche's attitude to enlightenment, and thus to Homer, remained ambivalent; whereas he perceived in enlightenment both the universal movement of sovereign mind, whose supreme exponent he believed himself to be, and a "nihilistic," life-denying power, only the second moment was taken over by his pre-fascist followers and perverted into ideology. This ideology became a blind eulogy of blind life, which imposes a praxis by which everything living is suppressed. This is seen in the cultural fascists' attitude to Homer. In the Homeric depiction of feudal conditions they detect a democratic element, brand the work a product of seafarers and traders, and condemn the Ionian epic for its of overly rational discourse and its communication of the commonplace. Nevertheless, the evil eye of these sympathizers with all seemingly immediate power, who reject mediation and "liberalism" of any degree, discerns an element of truth. Connections with reason, liberality, and middle-class qualities do indeed extend incomparably further back than is assumed by historians who date the concept of the burgher from the end of medieval feudalism. In identifying the burgher where earlier bourgeois humanism had imagined some pristine dawn of culture, which was taken to legitimize that humanism, the neo-Romantic reaction equates world history with enlightenment. The fashionable ideology, whose most urgent concern is to liquidate enlightenment, thus pays it involuntary homage. It is forced to acknowledge enlightened thinking even in the remotest past. For the bad conscience of present-day devotees of the archaic it is especially the earliest traces of enlightenment which threaten to unleash the process they seek to hold back, but which they themselves obliviously promote.

But a recognition of Homer's antimythological, enlightened character, his opposition to chthonic mythology, remains untrue because limited. Rudolf Borchardt,* for example, the most prominent and therefore the most impotent of the esoteric apologists of German heavy industry, prematurely breaks off his analysis in the service of repressive ideology. He fails to perceive that the primal powers he extols themselves represent a stage of enlightenment. By indiscriminately denouncing the epic as a form of novel he overlooks what epic and myth actually have in common: power and exploitation. The ignoble qualities he condemns in the epic, mediation and circulation, are only a further development of the dubious nobility he idolizes in myth: naked force. The alleged authenticity of the archaic, with its principle of blood and sacrifice, is already tainted by the devious bad conscience of power characteristic of the "national regeneration" today, which uses primeval times for self-advertising. The original myth itself contains the moment of mendacity which triumphs in the fraudulent myth of fascism and which the latter imputes to enlightenment. But no work bears more eloquent witness to the intertwinement of enlightenment and myth than that of Homer, the basic text of European civilization. In Homer, epic and myth, form and subject matter do not simply diverge; they conduct an argument. The aesthetic dualism of the work gives evidence of the historical-philosophical tendency. "The Apollonian Homer is merely a continuation of the general human artistic process to which we owe individuation."[3]

Myths are precipitated in the different strata of Homer's subject matter; but at the same time the reporting of them, the unity imposed on the diffuse legends, traces the path of the subject's flight from the mythical powers. This is already true, in a profound sense, of the *Iliad*. The anger of the mythical son of a goddess against the rational* warrior king and organizer; the hero's undisciplined inactivity; finally, the enlistment of the victorious, doomed hero in a cause which is national, Hellenic, and no

longer tribal, an allegiance mediated by mythic loyalty to his dead comrade—all these reflect the intertwinement of history and prehistory. The
same development is still more vividly present in the *Odyssey*, since it is
closer in form to the picaresque novel. The contrast between the single surviving ego and the multiplicity of fate reflects the antithesis between
enlightenment and myth. The hero's peregrinations from Troy to Ithaca
trace the path of the self through myths, a self infinitely weak in comparison to the force of nature and still in the process of formation as self-consciousness. The primeval world is secularized as the space he measures out;
the old demons populate only the distant margins and islands of the civilized Mediterranean, retreating into the forms of rock and cave from
which they had originally sprung in the face of primal dread. The adventures bestow names on each of these places, and the names give rise to a
rational overview of space. The shipwrecked, tremulous navigator anticipates the work of the compass. His powerlessness, leaving no part of the
sea unknown, aims to undermine the ruling powers. But, in the eyes of
the man who has thus come of age, the plain untruth of the myths, the
fact that sea and earth are not actually populated by demons but are a
magic delusion propagated by traditional popular religion, becomes something merely "aberrant" in contrast to his unambiguous purpose of self-
preservation, of returning to his homeland and fixed property. All the adventures Odysseus survives are dangerous temptations deflecting the self
from the path of its logic. Again and again he gives way to them, experi-
menting like a novice incapable of learning—sometimes, indeed, out of
foolish curiosity, like a mime insatiably trying out roles. "But where danger threatens / That which saves from it also grows":[4] the knowledge which
makes up his identity and enables him to survive has its substance in the
experience of diversity, distraction, disintegration; the knowing survivor is
also the man who exposes himself most daringly to the threat of death,
thus gaining the hardness and the strength to live. That is the secret underlying the conflict between epic and myth: the self does not exist simply in
rigid antithesis to adventure but takes on its solidity only through this
antithesis, and its unity through the very multiplicity which myth in its
oneness denies.[5] Odysseus, like the heroes of all true novels after him,
throws himself away, so to speak, in order to win himself; he achieves his
estrangement from nature by abandoning himself to nature, trying his
strength against it in all his adventures; ironically, it is implacable nature

that he now commands, which triumphs on his return home as the implacable judge, avenging the heritage of the very powers he has escaped.
At the Homeric stage, the identity of the self is so much a function of the
nonidentical, of dissociated, unarticulated myths, that it must derive itself
from them. The element which shapes and organizes individuality inter-
nally, time, is still so weak that the unity of the adventures remains an outward one, their sequence being formed by the spatial changes of scene, the
succession of sites of local divinities on which the hero is flung by the
storm. Whenever, at later historical stages, the self has again experienced
such weakness, or narration has presupposed it in the reader, the manner
of depicting life has slipped back into the form of successive adventures.
Laboriously and revocably, in the image of the journey, historical time has
detached itself from space, the irrevocable schema of all mythical time.

The faculty by which the self survives adventures, throwing itself
away in order to preserve itself, is cunning. The seafarer Odysseus outwits
the natural deities as the civilized traveler was later to swindle savages,
offering them colored beads for ivory. It is true that Odysseus is only occasionally seen bartering, when gifts of hospitality are given and received. In
Homer the gift which accompanies hospitality falls midway between
exchange and sacrifice. Like a sacrificial act it is intended to compensate
for wrongfully spilled blood, whether of the stranger or of settlers defeated by pirates, and represents an oath of truce. At the same time, however,
the gift to the host anticipates the principle of equivalence: the host
receives really or symbolically the equivalent value of the service he has
performed, while the guest takes away provisions which, in principle, are
intended to enable him to reach home. Even though the host receives no
direct compensation for this, he can expect the same treatment to be given
to him or his kinsmen one day: as a sacrifice to elemental deities the hospitality gift is at the same time a rudimentary insurance against them. The
extensive but perilous nautical activities of the early Greeks were the pragmatic reason for the custom. Even Poseidon, Odysseus's elemental foe,
thinks in terms of equivalence, constantly complaining that the gifts
received by Odysseus at the stations of his journey are worth more than his
full share of the spoils of Troy would have been had he been allowed to
carry it home without hindrance from Poseidon. And in Homer this kind
of rationalization can be traced back to the sacrificial acts themselves.
Hecatombs of a certain size are intended to secure the goodwill of partic-

ular deities. If exchange represents the secularization of sacrifice, the sacrifice itself, like the magic schema of rational exchange, appears as a human contrivance intended to control the gods, who are overthrown precisely by the system created to honor them.[6]

The moment of fraud in sacrifice is the prototype of Odyssean cunning, just as many of Odysseus's ruses are wrapped up, as it were, in an offering to natural deities.[7] The deities are duped not only by the hero but also by the solar gods. Odysseus's Olympian friends take advantage of Poseidon's sojourn among the Ethiopians, the backwoodsmen who still worship him and offer him bloody sacrifices, in order to escort Odysseus in safety. Even the sacrifice which Poseidon is glad to accept involves deception: the amorphous sea-god's confinement to a certain locality, the sacred precinct, also restricts his power, and in exchange for sating himself on Ethiopian oxen he is denied the opportunity to cool his temper on Odysseus. All sacrificial acts, deliberately planned by humans, deceive the god for whom they are performed: by imposing on him the primacy of human purposes they dissolve away his power, and the fraud against him passes over seamlessly into that perpetrated by unbelieving priests against believing congregations. Cunning originates in the cult. Odysseus himself acts as both victim and priest. By calculating the risk he incurs as victim, he is able to negate the power to which the risk exposes him. By such bargaining he retrieves the life he has staked. However, deception, cunning, and rationality do not form a simple antithesis to the archaism of sacrifice. Only the moment of fraud in sacrifice, perhaps the innermost reason for the illusory character of myth, is raised to self-consciousness through Odysseus. The awareness that the symbolic communication with the deity through sacrifice was not real must have been age-old. The representative character of sacrifice, glorified by fashionable irrationalists, cannot be separated from the deification of the sacrificial victim, from the fraudulent priestly rationalization of murder through the apotheosis of the chosen victim. Something of this fraud, which elevates the perishable person as bearer of the divine substance, has always been detectable in the ego, which owes its existence to the sacrifice of the present moment to the future. Its substance is as illusory as the immortality of the slaughtered victim. Not without reason was Odysseus regarded by many as a deity.*

For as long as individuals are sacrificed, for as long as the sacrifice contains the antithesis between collective and individual, deception is objectively implicit in it. If the belief in the representative character of sacrifice springs from recollection of the nonoriginal quality of the self, from its emergence through the history of domination, at the same time, in relation to the fully developed self, this belief becomes untruth: the self is precisely the human being to whom the magic power of representation is no longer attributed. The formation of the self severs the fluctuating connection with nature which the sacrifice of the self is supposed to establish. Each sacrifice is a restoration of the past, and is given the lie by the historical reality in which it is performed. The venerable belief in sacrifice is probably itself a behavior pattern drilled into the subjugated, by which they reenact against themselves the wrong done to them in order to be able to bear it. Sacrifice as representative restoration does not reinstate immediate communication, which had been merely interrupted, as present-day mythologies claim; rather, the institution of sacrifice is itself the mark of an historical catastrophe, an act of violence done equally to human beings and to nature. Cunning is nothing other than the subjective continuation of the objective untruth of sacrifice, which it supersedes. That untruth may not have been always only untruth. At one stage[8] of prehistory sacrifices may have possessed a kind of bloody rationality, which even then, however, could hardly have been separated from the thirst for privilege. The theory of sacrifice prevalent today relates it to the idea of a collective body, the tribe, into which the spilled blood of the tribe's sacrificed member is supposed to flow back. While totemism was an ideology even in its own time, it nevertheless marks a real state in which the dominant reason required sacrificial victims. It is a state of archaic shortage, in which human sacrifice can hardly be distinguished from cannibalism. At some times the numerically increased collective can keep itself alive only by consuming human flesh; perhaps, in some ethnic and social groups, pleasure was linked in some way to cannibalism, a link to which only the aversion to human flesh now bears witness. Customs from later times, such as the *ver sacrum*, whereby a whole age-group of young men was forced into exile with accompanying rites at times of hunger, bear clear traces of such barbaric, idealized rationality. Long before the emergence of mythical popular religions, that rationality must have revealed itself as illusory; as systematic hunting provided the tribe with enough animals to make devouring its own members superfluous, it must have been the medicine men who deluded the shrewd hunters and trappers into believing that people

still needed to be consumed.[9] The magic, collective interpretation of sacrifice, which entirely denies the rationality of sacrifice, is its rationalization; but the straightforward assumption of enlightened thinking that
what today is ideology may once have been truth is too uncritical:[10] the
newest ideologies are a mere reprise of the oldest, which long antedate
those hitherto known, in the same way as the development of the class
society refutes the previously sanctioned ideologies. The frequently cited
irrationality of sacrifice is no more than an expression of the fact that the
praxis of sacrifice outlasted its rational necessity, which was replaced by
particular interests. This split between the rational and the irrational
aspects of sacrifice gave cunning a point at which to take hold.
Demythologization always takes the form of the irresistible revelation of
the futility and the superfluity of sacrifices.

If the principle of sacrifice was proved transient by its irrationality,
at the same time it survives through its rationality. This rationality has
transformed itself, not disappeared. The self wrests itself from dissolution
in blind nature, whose claims are constantly reasserted by sacrifice. But it
still remains trapped in the context of the natural, one living thing seeking to overcome another. Bargaining one's way out of sacrifice by means
of self-preserving rationality is a form of exchange no less than was sacrifice itself. The identical, enduring self which springs from the conquest of
sacrifice is itself the product of a hard, petrified sacrificial ritual in which
the human being, by opposing its consciousness to its natural context, celebrates itself. That much is true of the famous story in Nordic mythology
according to which Odin was hung from a tree as a sacrifice to himself,
and of Klages's thesis that every sacrifice is a sacrifice of the god to the god,
as is still apparent in Christology, the monotheistic disguise of myth.[11] The
difference is that the stratum of mythology in which the self manifests
itself as a sacrifice to itself expresses not so much the original conception
of popular religions as the absorption of myth into civilization. In class
society, the self's hostility to sacrifice included a sacrifice of the self, since
it was paid for by a denial of nature in the human being for the sake of
mastery over extrahuman nature and over other human beings. This very
denial, the core of all civilizing rationality, is the germ cell of proliferating
mythical irrationality: with the denial of nature in human beings, not only
the *telos* of the external mastery of nature but also the *telos* of one's own
life becomes confused and opaque. At the moment when human beings

cut themselves off from the consciousness of themselves as nature, all the purposes for which they keep themselves alive—social progress, the heightening of material and intellectual forces, indeed, consciousness itself—become void, and the enthronement of the means as the end, which in late capitalism is taking on the character of overt madness, is already detectable in the earliest history of subjectivity. The human being's mastery of itself, on which the self is founded, practically always involves the annihilation of the subject in whose service that mastery is maintained, because the substance which is mastered, suppressed, and disintegrated by self-preservation is nothing other than the living entity, of which the achievements of self-preservation can only be defined as functions—in other words, self-preservation destroys the very thing which is to be preserved. The antireason of totalitarian capitalism, whose technique of satisfying needs, in their objectified form determined by domination, makes the satisfaction of needs impossible and tends toward the extermination of humanity—this antireason appears prototypically in the hero who escapes the sacrifice by sacrificing himself. The history of civilization is the history of the introversion of sacrifice—in other words, the history of renunciation. All who renounce give away more of their life than is given back to them, more than the life they preserve. This process unfolds within the framework of wrong society. In that society everyone is one too many, and is cheated. But society's predicament* is that the person who escaped the universal, unequal, and unjust exchange, who did not renounce but immediately seized the undiminished whole, would thereby lose everything, even the meager residue of oneself granted by self-preservation. All the superfluous sacrifices are needed: against sacrifice. Even Odysseus is a sacrificial victim, the self which incessantly suppresses its impulses,[12] and thus he lets slip his own life, that he saves only to recall it as a path of error. Nevertheless, he is sacrificed, also, for the abolition of sacrifice. His lordly renunciation, as a struggle with myth, is representative of a society which no longer needs renunciation and domination—which masters itself not in order to do violence to itself and others but for the sake of reconciliation.

The transformation of the sacrificial victim into subjectivity is done under the aegis of the same cunning which always had its share in sacrifice. In the untruth of guile the deception inherent in sacrifice becomes an element of character; it becomes the mutilation of the cheat [*Ver-*

schlagener], whose shifty look still cowers from the blows [*Schläge*] self-preservation has brought down on him. This look expresses the relation of mind to physical strength. The bearer of mind, the one who issues commands—as Odysseus almost always appears—is in all cases physically weaker than the primeval powers with which he has to wrestle for his life, despite all the reports of his heroic deeds. The occasions when naked bodily strength is celebrated, the fistfight with the beggar Irus instigated by the Suitors and the drawing of the great bow, are sporting in nature. Self-preservation and physical strength have diverged: Odysseus's athletic accomplishments are those of the gentleman who, free of practical cares, can train himself in lordly self-mastery. Precisely the strength which is detached from self-preservation benefits self-preservation: in the struggle with the feeble, gluttonous, undisciplined vagabond or with those who have basked in idleness, Odysseus inflicts on the stay-at-homes symbolically what organized landowning has long since done to them in reality, and legitimizes himself as a nobleman. But when he encounters primeval powers which are neither domesticated nor weakened by indolence, he faces a harder test. He can never engage the exotically persisting mythical powers in physical combat. He has to accept as a given reality the sacrificial ceremony in which he is repeatedly caught up: he is unable to break it. Instead, he makes sacrifice the formal precondition of his own rational decision. This decision is always carried out within the terms of the primeval judgment on which the sacrificial situation is based. That the old sacrifice has meanwhile become irrational presents itself to the cleverness of the weaker party as the stupidity of ritual. The ritual remains accepted, its letter is strictly observed. But its now senseless judgment refutes itself, since its terms constantly leave scope for evasion. The superiority of nature in the competitive struggle is repeatedly confirmed by the very mind which has mastered nature. All bourgeois enlightenment is agreed in its demand for sobriety, respect for facts, a correct appraisal of relative strength. Wishful thinking is banned. The reason, however, is that all power in class society is beset by the gnawing consciousness of its powerlessness in face of physical nature and its social successor, the many. Only deliberate adaptation to it brings nature under the power of the physically weaker. The reason that represses mimesis is not merely its opposite. It is itself mimesis: of death. The subjective mind which disintegrates the spiritualization of nature masters spiritless nature only by imitating its rigidity, disintegrating itself as animistic. Imitation enters the service of power when even the human being becomes an anthropomorphism for human beings. The pattern of Odysseus's guile is mastery of nature by such adaptation. In the assessment of power relationships that admits defeat in advance and makes survival virtually dependent on death, the principle of bourgeois disillusionment, the external schema for the internalization of sacrifice, is already latent. The nimble-witted man survives only at the cost of his own dream, which he forfeits by disintegrating his own magic along with that of the powers outside him. He can never have the whole, he must always be able to wait, to be patient, to renounce; he may not eat the lotus or the cattle of Hyperion, and when he steers through the narrows he must include in his calculation the loss of the companions snatched from the ship by Scylla. He wriggles through—that is his survival, and all the renown he gains in his own and others' eyes merely confirms that the honor of heroism is won only by the humbling of the urge to attain entire, universal, undivided happiness.

The formula for Odysseus's cunning is that the detached, instrumental mind, by submissively embracing nature, renders to nature what is hers and thereby cheats her. The mythical monsters under whose power he falls represent, as it were, petrified contracts and legal claims dating from primeval times. In the developed patriarchal era the earlier popular religion manifests itself in these scattered relics: beneath the Olympian heaven they have become figures of abstract fate, of a necessity remote from sensuous experience. The fact that it would be impossible to choose any route other than that between Scylla and Charybdis may be interpreted rationalistically as the mythical representation of the preponderant power of sea currents over the little ships of ancient times. But translated into the objectifying language of myth, it means that the natural relationship between strength and powerlessness has already taken on the character of a legal relationship. Scylla and Charybdis have a claim on whatever comes between their teeth, just as Circe has a right to metamorphose those who are not immune, or Polyphemus a right to the bodies of his guests. Every mythical figure is compelled to do the same thing over and over again. Each of them is constituted by repetition: its failure would mean their end. They all bear features of the fate which, in the myths of punishment in the underworld, is meted out by Olympian judgment to Tantalus, Sisyphus, and the Danaids. They are figures of compulsion: the horrors they commit are the curse which has fallen on them. Mythical inevitability is defined by the equivalence between the curse, the abominable act which expiates it, and the guilt arising from that act, which reproduces the curse. All law in history up to now bears the trace of this pattern. In myth each moment of the cycle pays off the preceding moment and thereby helps to establish the continuity of guilt as law. Against this Odysseus fights. The self represents rational universality against the inevitability of fate. But as it finds the universal and the inevitable already inextricably entwined, its rationality necessarily takes a restrictive form, that of an exception. It has to extricate itself from the legal terms encompassing and threatening it, terms which, in a sense, are inscribed in every mythical figure. Odysseus satisfies the legal statutes, but in such a way that by conceding their power he deprives them of it. It is impossible to hear the Sirens and not succumb to them: they cannot be defied. Defiance and beguilement are one and the same, and whoever defies them is lost to the very myth he challenges. Cunning, however, is defiance made rational. Odysseus does not try to steer a different course to the one past the Sirens' island. Nor does he try to insist on the superiority of his knowledge and listen freely to the temptresses, believing his freedom protection enough. He cowers, the ship takes its preordained, fateful course, and he realizes that however he may consciously distance himself from nature, as a listener [*Hörender*] he remains under its spell. He complies with the contract of his bondage [*Hörigkeit*] and, bound to the mast, struggles to throw himself into the arms of the seductresses. But he has found a loophole in the agreement, through which he eludes it while fulfilling its terms. The primeval contract did not specify whether the mariner sailing past should be bound or unbound while listening to the song. The use of bonds belongs to a later era, in which prisoners were not killed straightaway. Technically enlightened, Odysseus acknowledges the archaic supremacy of the song by having himself bound. By yielding to the song of pleasure he thwarts both it and death. The bound listener is drawn to the Sirens like any other. But he has taken the precaution not to succumb to them even while he succumbs. Despite the power of his desire, which reflects the power of the demigoddesses themselves, he cannot go to them, just as his companions at the oars, their ears stopped with wax, are deaf not only to the demigoddesses but to the desperate cries of their commander. The Sirens have a life of their own, but in this bourgeois prehistory it has already been neutralized as the yearning of those who pass it by. The epic does not say what happens to the singers once the ship has passed. But in a tragedy this would have been their last hour, as it was for the Sphinx when Oedipus solved the riddle, fulfilling her command and thereby causing her downfall. For the law of the mythical figures, being that of the stronger, depends on the impossibility of fulfilling their statutes. If they are fulfilled, then the myths are finished, down to their most distant descendants. Since the happily hapless meeting of Odysseus with the Sirens all songs have ailed; the whole of western music suffers from the absurdity of song in civilization, yet the motive force of all art-music is song.

With the dissolution of the contract through its literal fulfilment a change occurs in the historical situation of language: it begins to pass over into designation. Mythical fate had been one with the spoken word. Within the sphere of ideas in which mythical figures executed the unalterable edicts of fate, the distinction between word and object was unknown. The word was thought to have direct power over the thing, expression merged with intention. Cunning, however, consists in exploiting the difference. One clings to the word in order to change the thing. In this way consciousness arises out of intention: in his extremity Odysseus becomes aware of dualism, as he discovers that an identical word can mean different things. Since the name *Udeis* can mean either "hero" or "nobody," the hero is able to break the spell of the name. Unchangeable words remain formulae for the implacable continuities of nature. In magic their fixity was intended to challenge that of fate, which it reflected. The opposition between the word and what it imitated was already implicit in this challenge. At the Homeric stage that opposition became decisive. Odysseus discovered in words what in fully developed bourgeois society is called *formalism*: their perennial ability to designate is bought at the cost of distancing themselves from any particular content which fulfills them, so that they refer from a distance to all possible contents, both to nobody and to Odysseus himself. From the formalism of mythical names and statutes, which, indifferent like nature, seek to rule over human beings and history, emerges nominalism, the prototype of bourgeois thinking. Self-preserving guile lives on the argument between word and thing. Odysseus's two contradictory actions in his meeting with Polyphemus, his obedience to his name and his repudiation of it, are really the same thing. He declares allegiance to himself by disowning himself as Nobody; he saves his life by making himself disappear. This adaptation to death through language contains the schema of modern mathematics.

Cunning as a means of exchange, in which everything is done correctly, the contract is fulfilled yet the other party is cheated, points back to a form of economic activity which is found, if not in mythical prehistory, at least in early antiquity: the ancient practice of "occasional exchange" between self-sufficient households. "Surpluses are occasionally exchanged, but provisions are predominantly produced by the consumers themselves."[13] The behavior of the adventurer Odysseus recalls that of the parties to the occasional exchange. Even in the pathetic guise of the beggar the feudal lord bears features of the oriental merchant[14] who returns home with untold wealth because he has once, against tradition, stepped outside the confines of the domestic economy and "put to sea." The adventurous element in his undertaking is, in economic terms, nothing other than the irrational aspect his reason takes on in face of the prevailing traditional economic forms. This irrationality of reason has been precipitated in cunning, as the adaptation of bourgeois reason to any unreason which confronts it as a stronger power. The lone voyager armed with cunning is already *homo oeconomicus,* whom all reasonable people will one day resemble: for this reason the *Odyssey* is already a Robinsonade. Both these prototypical shipwrecked sailors make their weakness—that of the individual who breaks away from the collective—their social strength. Abandoned to the vagaries of the waves, helplessly cut off, they are forced by their isolation into a ruthless pursuit of their atomistic interest. They embody the principle of the capitalist economy* even before they make use of any worker;* but the salvaged goods they bring with them to the new venture idealize the truth that the entrepreneur* has always entered the competition armed with more than the industry of his hands. Their powerlessness in face of nature already functions as an ideology for their social predominance. Odysseus's defenselessness against the foaming sea sounds like a legitimation of the enrichment of the voyager at the expense of indigenous inhabitants. Bourgeois economics later enshrined this principle in the concept of risk: the possibility of foundering is seen as a moral justification for profit.* From the standpoint of the developed exchange society and its individuals, the adventures of Odysseus are no more than a depiction of the risks which line the path to success. Odysseus lives according to the ancient principle which originally constituted bourgeois society. One had to choose between cheating and going under. Fraud was the stigma of reason, which betrayed its particular interest. The universal socialization for which the globetrotter Odysseus and the solo manufacturer Robinson Crusoe provide a preliminary sketch was attended from the first by the absolute loneliness which at the end of the bourgeois era is becoming overt. Radical socialization means radical alienation. Both Odysseus and Crusoe deal in totality: the former measures it out; the latter fabricates it. They can do so only in total isolation from all other human beings, who appear to both men only in estranged forms, as enemies or allies, but always as instruments, things.

One of the first adventures in the *nostos** proper does, admittedly, originate much further back, far beyond even the barbaric age of demonic masks and gods of magic. It is the story of the Lotus-eaters. Whoever tastes their food is as much in thrall as those who listen to the Sirens' song or are touched by the wand of Circe. But no harm is done to those who succumb: "Now it never entered the heads of these natives to kill my friends."[15] They are threatened only by forgetfulness and loss of will. The curse condemns them to nothing worse than a primal state exempt from labor and struggle in the "fertile land":[16] "As soon as each had eaten the honeyed fruit of the plant, all thoughts of reporting to us or escaping were banished from his mind. All they now wished for was to stay where they were with the Lotus-eaters, to browse on the lotus, and to forget that they had a home to return to."[17] Self-preserving reason cannot permit such an idyll—reminiscent of the bliss induced by narcotics, by which subordinate classes have been made capable of enduring the unendurable in ossified social orders—among its own people. And indeed, it is only an illusion of bliss, a dull aimless vegetating, as impoverished as the life of animals. At best, it would be an absence of the awareness of unhappiness. But happiness contains truth within itself. It is in essence a result. It unfolds from suffering removed. The enduring Odysseus is therefore right not to endure life among the Lotus-eaters. Against them he asserts their own cause, the realization of utopia through historical work, whereas simply abiding within an image of bliss deprives them of their strength. But in being exerted by rationality, by Odysseus, this right is inevitably drawn into the realm of wrong. His immediate action is one which reasserts domination. Self-preserving reason can no more tolerate this bliss "near the rim of the world"[18] than the more dangerous form it takes in later stages. The indolent defectors are fetched back to the galleys: "I had to use force to bring them back to the ships, and they wept on the way, but once on board I dragged them under the benches and left them in irons."[19] Lotus is an oriental food. Its thin-cut slices still play a part in Chinese and Indian cooking. Perhaps the temptation ascribed to it is no other than that of regression to the stage of gathering the fruits of the earth[20] and the sea, older than agriculture, cattle-rearing, or even hunting—older, in short, than any production. It is hardly an accident that the epic connects the idea of the life of idleness with the eating of flowers, whereas no such use is associated with them today. The eating of flowers, as is still customary during dessert in the East and is known to European children from baking with rosewater and from candied violets, bears the promise of a state in which the reproduction of life is independent of conscious self-preservation, the bliss of satiety uncoupled from the utility of planned nutrition. The memory of the remote and ancient joy which flashes up before the sense of smell is still inseparable from the extreme proximity of ingestion. It points back to earliest prehistory. No matter how copious the torments endured by the people of that time, they cannot conceive of a happiness not nourished by the image of that primal age: "So we left that country and sailed on sick at heart."[21]

The next figure on whose shore Odysseus is cast up [*verschlagen*]—being cast up and being cunning [*verschlagen*] are equivalents in Homer—is the Cyclops Polyphemus, who wears his single wheel-sized eye as a trace of the same primal world: the singleness of the eye suggests the nose and mouth, more primitive than the symmetry of eyes and ears[22] without which, and the combining of their dual perceptions, no identification, depth, or objectivity is possible. But, compared to the Lotus-eaters, he represents a later, truly barbaric age, one of hunters and shepherds. For Homer, the definition of barbarism coincides with that of a state in which no systematic agriculture, and therefore no systematic, time-managing organization of work and society, has yet been achieved. He calls the Cyclopes "fierce, uncivilized people"[23] because—and his words seem to contain a secret confession of the guilt of civilization itself—they "never lift a hand to plant or plough but put their trust in Providence. All the crops they require spring up unsown and untilled, wheat and barley and the vines whose generous clusters give them wine when ripened for them by the timely rains."[24] Abundance needs no law, and civilization's accusation of anarchy sounds almost like a denunciation of abundance: "The Cyclopes have no assemblies for the making of laws, nor any settled customs, but live in hollow caverns in the mountain heights, where each man is lawgiver to his children and his wives, and nobody cares a jot for his neighbors."[25] This is already a patriarchal society based on kinship and the suppression of the physically weaker, but it is not yet organized on the model of fixed property and its hierarchy; it is the lack of contact between the cave dwellers which is the true reason for the absence of objective laws and which calls forth Homer's accusation of their mutual disregard and their state of savagery. In a later passage, however, the narrator's pragmatic fidelity to his story contradicts his civilized judgment: despite their disregard for one another, the tribe gather round the blinded Polyphemus's cave when they hear his anguished cry, and only Odysseus's trick with his name prevents the simpletons from coming to his aid.[26] Stupidity and lawlessness share a common definition: when Homer calls the Cyclops a "lawless-minded monster"[27] he does not mean simply that the Cyclops does not respect the laws of morality but that his thinking itself is lawless, unsystematic, rhapsodic—as when he is unable to perform the straightforward mental task of working out how his uninvited guests are able to leave his cave, by clinging underneath the sheep instead of riding on them; or to decipher the sophistic double meaning in Odysseus's false name. Polyphemus, although he trusts in the power of the Immortals, is a cannibal; accordingly, he refuses to show reverence for the gods despite his trust in them: "Stranger, you must be a fool, or must have come from very far afield"—in later times fools and strangers were less scrupulously distinguished, and ignorance of custom, like all foreignness, was branded straight away as folly—"to preach to me of fear or reverence for the gods. We Cyclopes care not a jot for Zeus with his aegis, nor for the rest of the blessed gods, since we are much stronger than they."[28] "We are stronger," Odysseus mockingly reports; but what the giant really meant was: "We are older." The power of the solar system is acknowledged, but much as a feudal lord might acknowledge that of bourgeois wealth, while tacitly regarding himself as more noble and failing to perceive that the wrong done to him is of the same kind as the wrong he himself represents. The nearby sea-god Poseidon, Polyphemus's father and Odysseus's enemy, is older than the universal Zeus in his remote heaven, and the feud between the elemental popular religion and the logocentric religion of laws is fought out, so to speak, on the backs of the subjects. However, the lawless Polyphemus is not simply the villain he appears to be according to the taboos of civilization and as the giant Goliath appears in the fables of enlightened childhood. In the meager domain in which his self-preservation has taken on orderly habits, he is not without redeeming traits. When he puts the young sheep and goats to their mothers' udders, this practical action shows a concern for creaturely life itself, and the famous speech of the blinded Polyphemus in which he calls the leading ram his friend, asking whether it is the last to leave the cave because it is grieving for its master's eye, has a power and poignancy equaled only at the highest point of the *Odyssey*, when the homecoming Odysseus is recognized by the old dog Argus—despite the appalling brutality with which the speech ends. The giant's behavior has not yet been objectified as character. When Odysseus begs for hospitality he does not reply simply with an expression of savage hatred but only by refusing to respect a law which does not yet apply to him. He says merely that "it would not occur to him"[29] to spare Odysseus and his companions, and it is open to question whether his next question, about the whereabouts of Odysseus's ship, is as devious as Odysseus reports it to be. Boastful and beguiled, the drunken Polyphemus promises Odysseus gifts of hospitality,[30] and it is only the notion of Odysseus as Nobody that gives him the malicious idea of showing his hospitality by eating the leader last—perhaps because he has called himself Nobody and thus may be considered nonexistent in terms of the Cyclops's feeble wit.[31] The physical crudity of the overpowerful creature is the source of his gullible trust. In this way the observance of the mythical law, always an injustice to the judged, also becomes an injustice to the natural power which imposes that law. Polyphemus and the other monsters that Odysseus outwits are models for the stupidly litigious devils of the Christian era, right down to Shylock and Mephistopheles. The giant's stupidity, the basis of his barbaric brutality as long as his cause prospers, represents something better once it is overthrown by one who should know better. Odysseus insinuates himself into Polyphemus's trust and thus subverts the captor's right to human flesh, according to the artful schema whereby the statute is breached in the observance: "Here, Cyclops, have some wine to wash down that meal of human flesh, and find out for yourself what kind of vintage was stored away in our ship's hold,"[32] the bearer of culture recommends.

However, the adaptation of reason to its opposite, a state of consciousness in which no firm identity has yet crystallized—represented by the bungling giant—culminates in the stratagem of the name. This is a widespread motif in folklore. In the Greek version it is a play on words; in a single word the name—Odysseus—and the intention—nobody—diverge. To modern ears *Odysseus* and *Udeis* still sound similar, and it is conceivable that in one of the dialects in which the story of the return to Ithaca was handed down, the name of the island's king did indeed sound the same as "nobody." The calculation that, once the deed was done, Polyphemus would answer "Nobody" when the tribe asked who was to blame, thus allowing the perpetrator to escape pursuit, is a thin rationalistic screen. In reality, Odysseus, the subject, denies his own identity, which makes him a subject, and preserves his life by mimicking the amorphous realm. He calls himself nobody because Polyphemus is not a self, and confusion of the name with the thing prevents the duped barbarian from escaping the trap: his cry for retribution remains magically tied to the name of the one on whom he wants to avenge himself, and this name condemns the cry to impotence. For by inserting his own intention into the name, Odysseus has withdrawn it from the magical sphere. But his self-assertion, as in the entire epic, as in all civilization, is self-repudiation. Thereby the self is drawn back into the same compulsive circle of natural connections from which it sought through adaptation to escape. The man who, for the sake of his own self, calls himself Nobody and manipulates resemblance to the natural state as a means of controlling nature, gives way to hubris. The artful Odysseus cannot do otherwise: as he flees, while still within the sphere controlled by the rock-hurling giant, he not only mocks Polyphemus but reveals to him his true name and origin, as if the primeval world still had such power over Odysseus, who always escaped only by the skin of his teeth, that he would fear to become Nobody again if he did not reestablish his own identity by means of the magical word which rational identity had just superseded. His friends try to restrain him from the folly of proclaiming his cleverness but do not succeed, and he narrowly escapes the hurled rocks, while the mention of his name probably brings down on him the hatred of Poseidon—who is hardly presented as omniscient. The cunning by which the clever man assumes the form of stupidity reverts to stupidity as soon as he discards that form. That is the dialectic of eloquence. From antiquity to fascism, Homer has been criticised for garrulousness—both in the hero and in the narrator. But the

Ionian has proved himself prophetically superior to Spartans old and new in his depiction of the doom which the fluency of the sly fox, the middleman, brings down on the latter. The speech which gets the better of physical strength is unable to curb itself. Its spate accompanies the stream of consciousness, thought itself, like a parody: thought's unwavering autonomy takes on a moment of manic folly when it enters reality as speech, as if thought and reality were synonymous, whereas the former has power over the latter only through distance. Such distance, however, is also suffering. For this reason the astute hero is always tempted to ignore the proverbial wisdom that silence is golden. He is driven objectively by the fear that, if he does not constantly uphold the fragile advantage the word has over violence, this advantage will be withdrawn by violence. For the word knows itself to be weaker than the nature it has duped. By talking too much he gives away the principle of violence and injustice underlying discourse and provokes in the feared adversary the very action he fears. The mythical compulsion acting on language in prehistory is perpetuated in the calamity which enlightened language brings on itself. "Udeis," who compulsively proclaims himself to be Odysseus, already bears features of the Jew who, in fear of death, continues to boast of a superiority which itself stems from the fear of death; revenge on the middleman stands not only at the end of bourgeois society but at its beginning, as the negative utopia toward which coercive violence tends in all its forms.

Unlike the stories of the escape from myth as an escape from barbaric cannibalism, the magical tale of Circe points back once more to the stage of actual magic. Magic disintegrates the self which falls back into its power and thus into the form of an earlier biological species. The power which causes the self's dissolution is, again, that of oblivion. With the fixed order of time, it gains control of the fixed will of the subject, which is based on that order. Circe seduces Odysseus's men into abandoning themselves to instinct, with which the animal form assumed by the victims has always been associated, while Circe has become the prototype of the courtesan, probably on the strength of the words of Hermes, which take her erotic initiatives for granted: "She will shrink from you in terror and invite you to her bed. Nor must you hesitate to accept the goddess' favors."[33] Circe's signature is ambiguity, and in the story she appears by turns as corrupter and helper; ambiguity is expressed even in her lineage: she is the daughter of Helios and the granddaughter of Oceanus.[34] In her the elements of fire and water are not yet separated, and it is this indeterminacy—in contrast to the primacy of a particular aspect of nature, whether matriarchal or patriarchal—which constitutes the essence of promiscuity and of the courtesan, reappearing as a watery lunar reflection even in the gaze of a nineteenth-century prostitute.[35] The hetaera both bestows joy and destroys the autonomy of its recipient—that is her ambiguity. But she does not necessarily destroy the recipient himself: she holds fast to an older form of life.[36] Like the Lotus-eaters, Circe does not cause lethal harm to her guests, and even those she has turned into wild beasts are peaceable: "Prowling about the place were mountain wolves and lions, actually the drugged victims of Circe's magic, for they not only refrained from attacking my men but rose on their hind legs to caress them, with much wagging of their long tails, like dogs fawning on their master, as he comes from table, for the tasty bits they know he always brings."[37] The bewitched humans behave in a similar way to the wild animals which listen to the playing of Orpheus. The mythical command to which they have been subjected at the same time liberates the very nature which is suppressed in them. What is revoked by their relapse into myth is myth itself. The suppression of instinct which constitutes them as selves and separates them from beasts was the introverted form of the repression existing within the hopelessly closed cycle of nature, to which, according to an earlier theory, the name Circe alludes. But, as the idyll of the Lotus-eaters had done earlier, the violent magic which recalls them to an idealized prehistory not only makes them animals but brings about, in however delusive a form, a semblance of reconciliation. But because they were once men the civilizing epic cannot present their fate as anything other than a calamitous lapse, and in Homer's account there is hardly a trace of the pleasure which went with it. It is all the more emphatically expunged the more civilized the victims themselves are.[38] Odysseus's companions are not turned into sacred creatures of the wilderness, like earlier guests, but into squalid domestic animals, swine. The story of Circe may contain echoes of the chthonic cult of Demeter, for whom the pig was sacred.[39] But perhaps it is also the humanoid anatomy of the pig and its nakedness which explain this motif: as if the same taboo on mingling with the blood of similar species, which has survived among the Jews, already existed among the Ionians. Finally, one may think of the prohibition on cannibalism, since, as in Juvenal, the taste of human flesh has repeatedly been compared to that of pigs. At any rate, later civilizations have always liked to apply the name of pig or swine to anyone whose impulses tended toward other pleasures than those sanctioned by society for its purposes. Magic and countermagic in the metamorphoses of Odysseus's companions are linked to herbs and wine, as intoxication and waking are to the sense of smell, which is increasingly suppressed and repressed and is closest not only to sex but to the remembrance of prehistory.[40] In the image of the pig, however, the joy of scent is distorted into the unfree snuffling[41] of someone who has his nose to the ground and has renounced the upright posture. It is as if, in the ritual to which she subjects the men, the sorceress-courtesan were reenacting the one to which she herself is repeatedly subjected by patriarchal society. Like her, women are predisposed, under the pressure of civilization, to adopt its judgment on women and to denigrate sex. In the conflict between enlightenment and myth, the traces of which are preserved in the epic, the powerful seductress is at the same time weak, obsolete, and vulnerable and needs the enslaved beasts as her escort.[42] As a representative of nature, woman in bourgeois society has become an enigma of irresistibility[43] and powerlessness. Thus she reflects back the vain lie of power, which substitutes the mastery over nature for reconciliation with it.

Marriage is society's middle way in dealing with this question: woman remains powerless in that her power is mediated to her only through her husband. Something of this is reflected in the defeat of the courtesan-goddess of the *Odyssey*, while the fully evolved marriage with Penelope, more recent in literary terms, represents a later stage in the objective structure of patriarchal arrangements. With the arrival of Odysseus on Aeaea,* the double meaning of the relationship of man to woman, of yearning to command, already takes on the form of an exchange underpinned by contracts. Odysseus resists Circe's magic. And he therefore receives actually what her magic promises only deceptively to those who fail to resist. Odysseus sleeps with her. But beforehand he makes her swear a solemn oath by the blessed gods. The oath is intended to protect the male from the mutilation which avenges the ban on promiscuity and male domination—although that domination, as a permanent suppression of instinct, symbolically performs the self-mutilation of the man in any case. Because of his resistance to metamorphosis, Circe accuses Odysseus of having "a heart in [his] breast which nothing enchants."[44] But she is also willing to submit to the man who has resisted her, the master, the self: "I beg you now to put up your sword and come with me to my bed, so that in love and sleep we may learn to trust each other."[45] The price she places on the pleasure she bestows is the condition that pleasure should first have been spurned; the last hetaera emerges as the first female character. In the transition from legend to history she makes a decisive contribution to the bourgeois chill. Her behavior puts into effect the ban on love which later became all the more powerful the more love as ideology was obliged to dissimulate the hatred between the competing partners. In the world of exchange the one who gives more is in the wrong; but the one who loves is always the one who loves more. While the lover's sacrifice is glorified, the making of that sacrifice is jealously enforced. It is precisely in love itself that the lover is incriminated and punished. The inability to master himself and others demonstrated by his love is reason enough to deny him fulfillment. With society, loneliness reproduces itself on a wider scale. The mechanism operates even within the tenderest ramifications of feeling, until love itself, in order to have contact with another person at all, is forced to assume such coldness that it shatters at the moment of its realization. Circe's power, which subjugates men as her slaves, gives way to her enslavement to the man who, through renunciation, has refused to submit. The goddess Circe's influence over nature, ascribed to her by the poet, is reduced to priestly soothsaying and even to clever foresight with regard to coming nautical difficulties. This lives on in the caricature of feminine wisdom. In the end, the prophecies of the disempowered sorceress regarding the Sirens, Scylla, and Charybdis merely serve the purposes of male self-preservation.

How high a price was paid for the establishing of orderly arrangements for procreation is hinted at by the obscure passage on the behavior of Odysseus's friends when Circe had transformed them back into men as required by her contractual lord. First we read that "they not only became men again but looked younger and much handsomer and taller than before."[46] But those who are thus confirmed and strengthened in their manhood are not happy: "We were so moved that we all wept for happiness. It was a strange sound for those walls to echo."[47] The earliest wedding song, the accompaniment of the feast celebrating the rudimentary marriage which lasts only a year, may have sounded like this. The actual marriage to Penelope has more in common with it than might be supposed. Harlot and wife are complementary forms of female self-alienation in the patriarchal world: the wife betrays pleasure to the fixed order of life and property, while the harlot, as her secret accomplice, brings within the property relationship that which the wife's property rights do not include—pleasure—by selling it. Circe and Calypso, the courtesans, are introduced as diligent weavers, thus resembling both mythical powers of fate and bourgeois housewives,[48] while Penelope, like a harlot, mistrustfully scrutinizes the returning Odysseus to make sure he is not really just an old beggar or even a god trying his luck. The much-lauded recognition scene is a truly patrician encounter: "For a long while Penelope, overwhelmed by wonder, sat there without a word. But her eyes were busy, at one moment resting full on his face, and at the next falling on the ragged clothes that made him seem a stranger once again."[49] There is no spontaneous upsurge of feeling; she is determined to avoid a mistake, which she can hardly afford under the weight of the order bearing down on her. This annoys the young Telemachus, who has not yet fully adapted himself to his future position yet already feels man enough to admonish his mother. By reproaching her with obstinacy and hardness, he exactly repeats the accusation of Circe against Odysseus. If the hetaera makes the patriarchal world order her own, the monogamous wife is not satisfied even with this and cannot rest until she has made herself conform to the male character. In this way the spouses settle their differences. The test she sets Odysseus concerns the immovable position of the marriage bed which her husband, as a young man, had constructed around an olive tree, a symbol of the unity of sex and property. With touching artfulness she refers to this bed as if it could be moved from the spot, whereupon her husband, "flaring up" and "rounding on" his wife, proceeds to give a circumstantial account of his durable amateur handiwork: as a prototypical bourgeois he is smart enough to have a hobby. It consists in a resumption of the craft work from which, within the framework of differentiated property relations, he has long since been exempted. He enjoys this occupation, as his freedom to perform superfluous tasks confirms his power over those who have to do such work in order to live. By this the ingenious Penelope recognizes him, flattering him with praise of his exceptional intelligence. But her flattery, which is not without a touch of mockery, is followed, in an abrupt caesura, by words which seek the reason for the suffering of all spouses in the gods' envy of the happiness guaranteed only by marriage, the "confirmation of the concept of permanence":[50] "All our unhappiness is due to the gods, who couldn't bear to see us share the joys of youth and reach the threshold of old age together."[51] Marriage represents not only the account-balancing order of the living but also solidarity and steadfastness in face of death. In it reconciliation grows up around subjugation, just as in history up to now true humanity has flourished only in conjunction with the barbaric element which is veiled by "humane values." Even if the contract between the spouses sets aside the old hostility only with difficulty, nevertheless the couple aging in peace merges into the image of Philemon and Baucis, as the smoke from the sacrificial altar is transmuted into that rising beneficently from the hearth. Undoubtedly, marriage forms part of the primal rock of myth at the base of civilization. But its mythic solidity and permanence jut from myth, as the small island realm rises from the endless sea.

The farthest point reached on the odyssey proper is no such homely refuge. It is Hades. The images which appear to the adventurer in the first visit to the Underworld* are of matriarchal shades[52] who have been banished by the religion of light: his own mother, before whom Odysseus forces himself to maintain a purposive patriarchal hardness,[53] is followed by heroines from primeval times. The image of the mother, however, is powerless, blind, and speechless,[54] a phantom, like epic narrative at the moments when language gives way to images. Sacrificial blood is required as a pledge of living memory before the shades can speak, breaking free, however vainly and ephemerally, from mythic muteness. Only when subjectivity masters itself by recognizing the nullity of images does it begin to share the hope which images vainly promise. The Promised Land for Odysseus is not the archaic realm of images. Finally, all the images reveal their true essence as shades in the world of the dead, as illusion. Having recognized them as dead he dismisses them with the lordly gesture of self-preservation, banishing them from the sacrifice which he reserves for those who grant him knowledge which benefits his life. In such knowledge the power of myth, transposed into mental forms, survives only as imagination. The realm of the dead, where the disempowered myths gather, is farthest from his homeland, with which it can communicate only from the remotest distance. If one follows Kirchhoff in supposing that Odysseus's visit to the Underworld forms part of the oldest stratum of the epic, composed of actual legends,[55] then this oldest stratum also contains a tendency which—as in the tradition of the journeys to the Underworld of

Orpheus and Heracles—most decisively transcends myth. Indeed, the motif of forcing the gates of hell, of abolishing death, is the innermost cell of all antimythological thought. This antimythological element is contained in Teiresias's prophecy of the possible placation of Poseidon. Odysseus is to wander ever farther, carrying on his shoulder an oar, until he reaches a people "who know nothing of the sea and never use salt with their food."[56] When he meets another traveler who refers to the oar on his shoulder as a "winnowing fan," he will have reached the proper place to offer a sacrifice to Poseidon. The core of the prophecy is the mistaking of the oar for a winnowing fan. This must have struck the Ionian as compellingly comic. However, this comic effect, on which the reconciliation is made to depend, cannot have been directed at humans but at the wrathful Poseidon.[57] The misunderstanding is meant to amuse the fierce elemental god, in the hope that his anger might be dispersed in laughter. That would be analogous to the neighbor's advice in Grimm, explaining how a mother can rid herself of a changeling: "She should carry the changeling into the kitchen, set it on the hearth, light the fire and boil water in two eggshells. That would make the changeling laugh, and if he laughed then that would make an end of him."[58] If laughter up to now* has been a sign of violence, an outbreak of blind, obdurate nature, it nevertheless contains the opposite element, in that through laughter blind nature becomes aware of itself as such and thus abjures its destructive violence. This ambiguity of laughter is closely related to that of name; perhaps names are nothing but petrified laughter, as nicknames still are—the only ones in which the original act of name-giving still persists. Laughter is in league with the guilt of subjectivity, but in the suspension of law which it announces it also points beyond that complicity. It promises a passage to the homeland. It is a yearning for the homeland which sets in motion the adventures by which subjectivity, the prehistory of which is narrated in the *Odyssey*, escapes the primeval world. The fact that— despite the fascist lies to the contrary—the concept of homeland is opposed to myth constitutes the innermost paradox of epic. Precipitated in the epic is the memory of an historical age in which nomadism gave way to settlement, the precondition of any homeland. If the fixed order of property implicit in settlement is the source of human alienation, in which all homesickness and longing spring from a lost primal state, at the same time it is toward settlement and fixed property, on which alone the concept of homeland is based, that all longing and homesickness are directed. Novalis's definition according to which all philosophy is homesickness holds good only if this longing is not dissipated in the phantasm of a lost original state, but homeland, and nature itself, are pictured as something that have had first to be wrested from myth. Homeland is a state of having escaped. For this reason the criticism that the Homeric legends "withdraw from the earth" is a warranty of their truth. They "turn to men."[59] The transposition of myths into the novel, as in the adventure story, does not falsify myth so much as drag it into the sphere of time, exposing the abyss which separates it from homeland and reconciliation. The vengeance wreaked by civilization on the primeval world has been terrible, and in this vengeance, the most horrifying document of which in Homer is to be found in the account of the mutilation of the goatherd Melanthios, civilization itself resembles the primeval world. It is not in the content of the deeds reported that civilization transcends that world. It is in the self-reflection which causes violence to pause at the moment of narrating such deeds. Speech itself, language as opposed to mythical song, the possibility of holding fast the past atrocity through memory, is the law of Homeric escape. Not without reason is the fleeing hero repeatedly introduced as narrator. The cold detachment of narrative, which describes even the horrible as if for entertainment, for the first time reveals in all their clarity the horrors which in song are solemnly confused with fate. But when speech pauses, the caesura allows the events narrated to be transformed into something long past, and causes to flash up a semblance of freedom that civilization has been unable wholly to extinguish ever since. Book XXII of the *Odyssey* describes the punishment meted out by the son of the island's king to the faithless maidservants who have sunk into harlotry. With an unmoved composure comparable in its inhumanity only to the *impassibilité* of the greatest narrative writers of the nineteenth century, the fate of the hanged victims is described and expressionlessly compared to the death of birds in a trap; and, as of the numb pause surrounding the narration at this point, it can truly be said that the rest of all speech is silence. This is followed by a statement reporting that "For a little while their feet kicked out, but not for very long."[60] The exactitude of the description, which already exhibits the coldness of anatomy and vivisection,[61] keeps a record, as in a novel, of the twitching of the subjugated women, who, under the aegis of justice and law, are thrust down into the realm from which Odysseus the judge has escaped. As a citizen reflecting on the execution, Homer comforts himself and his listeners, who are really readers, with the certified observation that the kicking did not last long—a moment, and all was over.[62] But after the words "not for long" the inner flow of the narrative comes to rest. "Not for long?" the narrator asks by this device, giving the lie to his own composure. In being brought to a standstill, the report is prevented from forgetting the victims of the execution and lays bare the unspeakably endless torment of the single second in which the maids fought against death. No echo remains of the words "not for long" except Cicero's *Quo usque tandem* ["How much longer (will you try our patience)?"], which later rhetoricians unwittingly desecrated by claiming that patience for themselves. But in the report of the infamous deed, hope lies in the fact that it is long past. Over the raveled skein of prehistory, barbarism, and culture, Homer passes the soothing hand of remembrance, bringing the solace of "once upon a time." Only as the novel is the epic transmuted into fairy tale.

Excursus II: Juliette or Enlightenment and Morality

Enlightenment, in Kant's words, is "the human being's emergence from self-incurred minority. Minority is inability to make use of one's own understanding without direction from another."[1] "Understanding without direction from another" is understanding guided by reason. That amounts to saying that the mind combines its individual cognitions into a system in accordance with its own internal logic. "Reason has . . . as its sole object the understanding and its effective application."[2] It posits "a certain collective unity as the goal of the activities of the understanding,"[3] and this unity is the system. Reason's rules are instructions for a hierarchical ordering of concepts. For Kant, as for Leibniz and Descartes, rationality consists in "processes of ascending to the higher genera and of descending to the lower species [by which] we obtain the idea of systematic connection in its completeness."[4] The "systematization" of knowledge lies in "the connection of its parts in conformity with a single principle."[5] Thinking, as understood by the Enlightenment, is the process of establishing a unified, scientific order and of deriving factual knowledge from principles, whether these principles are interpreted as arbitrarily posited axioms, innate ideas, or the highest abstractions. The laws of logic establish the most universal relationships within the order and define them. Unity lies in self-consistency. The principle of contradiction is the system *in nuce*. Knowledge consists in subsumption under principles. It is one with judgment, by which perceptions are incorporated into the system. Any thinking not guided by the system is directionless or authoritarian. Reason contributes nothing but the idea of systematic unity, the formal elements of fixed conceptual relationships. Any substantial objective which might be put forward as a rational insight is, according to the Enlightenment in its strict sense, delusion, falsehood, "rationalization," no matter what pains individual philosophers may take to steer us away from this conclusion and toward a reliance on philanthropic feeling. Reason is "a faculty of deducing the particular from the universal."[6] According to Kant, the homogeneity of the general and the particular is guaranteed by the "schematism of pure understanding," by which he means the unconscious activity of the intellectual mechanism which structures perception in accordance with the understanding. The intelligibility which subjective judgment discovers in any matter is imprinted on that matter by the intellect as an objective quality before it enters the ego. Without such a schematism—in short, without the intellectual element in perception—no impression would conform to the corresponding concept, no category to the particular example; thought, not to speak of the system toward which everything is directed, would be devoid of unity. To establish this unity is the conscious task of science. If "all empirical laws [are] only special determinations of the pure laws of understanding,"[7] research must always ensure that the principles are properly linked to the factual judgments. "This harmony of nature with our cognitive faculty is presupposed *a priori* by the Judgment."[8] It is the "guiding thread"[9] of organized experience.

The system must be kept in harmony with nature; just as facts are predicted from the system, so they must confirm it. Facts, however, form part of praxis; they everywhere characterize the contact of the individual subject with nature as social object: experience is always real action and suffering. In physics, to be sure, the perception by which a theory can be proved is usually reduced to the electrical spark appearing in the experimental apparatus. Its nonappearance is generally of no practical consequence; it merely destroys the theory or, at most, the career of the research assistant responsible for setting up the experiment. However, laboratory conditions are the exception. A thinking which fails to maintain agreement between system and perception does not merely violate isolated visual impressions; it conflicts with real praxis. Not only does the expected event fail to occur but the unexpected happens: the bridge collapses, the crop fails, the medicine causes illness. The spark which most conclusively indicates a lack of systematic thinking, a violation of logic, is not a fleeting perception but sudden death. The system which enlightenment aims for is the form of knowledge which most ably deals with the facts, most effectively assists the subject in mastering nature. The system's principles are those of self-preservation. Immaturity amounts to the inability to survive. The bourgeois in the successive forms of the slave-owner, the free entrepreneur, and the administrator is the logical subject of enlightenment.

The difficulties within this concept of reason, arising from the fact that its subjects, the bearers of one and the same reason, are in real opposition to each other, are concealed in the Western Enlightenment behind the apparent clarity of its judgments. In the *Critique of Pure Reason,* however, those difficulties make themselves apparent in the unclear relationship of the transcendental to the empirical ego and in the other irreconcilable contradictions. Kant's concepts are ambiguous. Reason as the transcendental, supraindividual self contains the idea of a free coexistence in which human beings organize themselves to form the universal subject and resolve the conflict between pure and empirical reason in the conscious solidarity of the whole. The whole represents the idea of true universality, utopia. At the same time, however, reason is the agency of calculating thought, which arranges the world for the purposes of self-preservation and recognizes no function other than that of working on the object as mere sense material in order to make it the material of subjugation. The true nature of the schematism which externally coordinates the universal and the particular, the concept and the individual case, finally turns out, in current science, to be the interest of industrial society. Being is apprehended in terms of manipulation and administration. Everything—including the individual human being, not to mention the animal—becomes a repeatable, replaceable process, a mere example of the conceptual models of the system. Conflict between administrative, reifying science, between the public mind and the experience of the individual, is precluded by the prevailing circumstances. The senses are determined by the conceptual apparatus in advance of perception; the citizen sees the world as made *a priori* of the stuff from which he himself constructs it. Kant intuitively anticipated what Hollywood has consciously put into practice: images are precensored during production by the same standard of understanding which will later determine their reception by viewers.

The perception by which public judgment feels itself confirmed has been shaped by that judgment even before the perception takes place. Although the secret utopia harbored within the concept of reason may have glimpsed the repressed identical interest which lies beyond the diverse accidental interests of subjects, reason, operating under the pressure of purposes merely as systematic science, not only levels out the differences but standardizes the identical interest. It acknowledges no determination other than the classifications of the social operation. No one is different to the purpose for which he has been produced: a useful, successful, or failed member of professional and national groups. He is a single, random representative of his geographical, psychological, and sociological type. Logic is democratic: in this respect the great have no advantage over the most menial. The former are counted as prominent citizens while the latter are prospective objects of welfare relief. Science stands in the same relationship to nature and human beings in general as insurance theory stands to life and death in particular. Who dies is unimportant; what matters is the ratio of incidences of death to the liabilities of the company. It is the law of large numbers, not the particular case, which recurs in the formula. Nor is the concordance of general and particular concealed any longer within an intellect which always perceives the particular as a case of the general and the general only as the aspect of the particular by which it can be grasped and manipulated. Science itself has no awareness of itself; it is merely a tool. Enlightenment, however, is the philosophy which equates truth with the scientific system. Kant's attempt to justify this identity, which was still made with a philosophical intention, gave rise to concepts which have no meaning for science, since they are not simply instructions for performing manipulations according to certain rules. The notion of the self-understanding of science conflicts with the concept of science itself. Kant's work transcends experience as mere operation, and for that reason—and in accordance with its own principles—is rejected as dogmatic by enlightenment today. In confirming the scientific system as the embodiment of truth—the result arrived at by Kant—thought sets the seal on its own insignificance, because science is a technical operation, as far removed from reflection on its own objectives as is any other form of labor under the pressure of the system.

The moral teachings of the Enlightenment bear witness to the hopelessness of attempting to replace enfeebled religion by an intellectual

motive for enduring within society when material interest no longer suf-
fices. As solid citizens, philosophers ally themselves in practice with the
powers they condemn in theory. The theories are logical and hard while
the moral philosophies are propagandistic and sentimental, even when rig-
orous in tone, or else the moral philosophies are acts of violence performed
in the awareness that morality is nondeducible, like Kant's recourse to
treating moral forces as facts. His attempt to derive the duty of mutual
respect from a law of reason, although more cautious than any other such
undertaking in Western philosophy, has no support within the *Critique*. It
is the usual endeavor of bourgeois thought to ground the respect without
which civilization cannot exist on something other than material interest—an attempt more sublime and paradoxical than any that went before,
but just as ephemeral. The citizen who renounced a profit out of the
Kantian motive of respect for the mere form of the law would not be
enlightened but superstitious—a fool. The root of Kantian optimism,
according to which moral actions are reasonable even when base ones are
likely to prosper, is a horror of relapsing into barbarism. If—Kant writes
in response to Haller[10]—one of these great moral forces, reciprocal love
and respect, were to collapse, "then nothingness (immorality) with gaping
maw would drink the whole realm of (moral) beings like a drop of water."
But, according to Kant, from the standpoint of scientific reason moral
forces are neutral drives and forms of behavior, no less than immoral ones,
which they immediately become when no longer directed at that hidden
possibility but at reconciliation with power. Enlightenment expels difference from theory. It considers "human actions and desires exactly as if I
were dealing with lines, planes, and bodies."[11] The totalitarian order has
put this into effect in utter seriousness. Freed from supervision by one's
own class, which had obliged the nineteenth-century businessman to
maintain Kantian respect and reciprocal love, fascism,* which by its iron
discipline relieves its peoples of the burden of moral feelings, no longer
needs to observe any discipline. Contrary to the categorical imperative,
and all the more deeply in accord with pure reason, it treats human beings
as things, centers of modes of behavior. The rulers sought to shield the
bourgeois world from the flood of naked violence, which now has broken
over Europe, only for as long as economic concentration was insufficient-
ly advanced. Previously only the poor and savages had been exposed to the
untrammeled force of the capitalist elements. But the totalitarian order has

granted unlimited rights to calculating thought and puts its trust in science as such. Its canon is its own brutal efficiency.* From Kant's *Critique* to Nietzsche's *Genealogy of Morals*, the hand of philosophy had traced the writing on the wall; one individual put that writing into practice, in all its details. The work of the Marquis de Sade exhibits "understanding without direction from another"—that is to say, the bourgeois subject freed from all tutelage.

Self-preservation is the constitutive principle of science, the soul of the table of categories, even if, as in Kant, it has to be deduced idealistically. Even the ego, the synthetic unity of apperception, the agency which Kant calls the highest point, from which the whole of logic must be suspended,[12] is really both the product and the condition of material existence. Individuals, in having to fend for themselves, develop the ego as the agency of reflective foresight and overview; over successive generations it expands and contracts with the individual's prospects of economic autonomy and productive ownership. Finally it passes from the expropriated citizens to the totalitarian trust-masters, whose science has become the quintessence of the methods by which the subjugated mass society reproduces itself. Sade erected an early monument to their planning skills. The conspiracy of rulers against peoples, implemented by relentless organization, finds the Enlightenment spirit since Machiavelli and Hobbes no less compliant than the bourgeois republic. That spirit is hostile to authority only when authority lacks the strength to enforce obedience, and to violence only when violence is not an established fact. As long as one does not ask who is applying it, reason has no greater affinity with violence than with mediation; depending on the situation of individuals and groups, it presents either peace or war, tolerance or repression, as the given state of affairs. Because it unmasks substantial goals as asserting the power of nature over mind and as curtailing its own self-legislation, reason, as a purely formal entity, is at the service of every natural interest. Becoming simply an organ, thinking reverts to nature. For the rulers, however, human beings become mere material, as the whole of nature has become material for society. After the brief interlude of liberalism in which the bourgeois kept one another in check, power is revealing itself as archaic terror in a fascistically rationalized form.* "The religious chimeras," says the Prince of Francavilla at the court of King Ferdinand of Naples, "must be replaced by utmost terror. The people must be freed from the fear of a future Hell. Once that is destroyed they will abandon themselves to anything. But that chimerical fear must be replaced by penal laws of enormous severity, which apply, of course, only to the people, since they alone cause unrest in the state. Malcontents are born only to the lower classes. What do the rich care for the idea of a leash they will never feel themselves, if this empty semblance gives them the right to grind down those living under their yoke? You will find no one in that class who will not permit the darkest shadow of tyranny to fall on him, provided it really falls on others."[13] Reason is the organ of calculation, of planning; it is neutral with regard to ends; its element is coordination. More than a century before the emergence of sport, Sade demonstrated empirically what Kant grounded transcendentally: the affinity between knowledge and planning which has set its stamp of inescapable functionality on a bourgeois existence rationalized even in its breathing spaces. The precisely coordinated modern sporting squad, in which no member is in doubt over his role and a replacement is held ready for each, has its exact counterpart in the sexual teams of Juliette, in which no moment is unused, no body orifice neglected, no function left inactive. In sport, as in all branches of mass culture, a tense, purposive bustle prevails, although none but the wholly initiated observer could fathom the different combinations or the meaning of the game's changing fortunes, governed by arbitrarily chosen rules. The special architectonic structure of the Kantian system, like the gymnasts' pyramids in Sade's orgies and the formalized principles of early bourgeois freemasonry—cynically reflected in the strict regime of the libertine society of the *120 Days of Sodom*—prefigures the organization, devoid of any substantial goals, which was to encompass the whole of life. What seems to matter in such events, more than pleasure itself, is the busy pursuit of pleasure, its organization; just as in other demythologized epochs, imperial Rome, the Renaissance, and the Baroque, the schema of activity counted for more than its content. In the modern period enlightenment has released the ideas of harmony and perfection from their hypostatization in a religious Beyond and made them available as criteria for human endeavor within the form of the system. Once the utopia which inspired the hopes of the French Revolution had been absorbed, potently and impotently, into German music and philosophy, the established bourgeois order entirely functionalized reason. It became a purposiveness without purpose, which for that very reason could be harnessed to any end. It is planning considered as an end in itself. The totalitarian state manipulates nations. "Just so," replies the Prince in Sade to the speaker just quoted, "the government itself must control the population. It must possess the means to exterminate the people, should it fear them, or to increase their numbers, should it consider that necessary. And nothing should weigh in the balance of its justice except its own interests or passions, together only with the passions and interests of those who, as we have said, have been granted just enough power to multiply our own."[14] The Prince points the path which imperialism, reason in its most terrible form, has always followed. "Take away its god from the people you wish to subjugate and you will demoralize it. As long as it has no other god than yours, you will always be its master . . . Grant it in return the widest, most criminal license. Never punish it, except when it turns against you."[15]

As reason posits no substantial goals, all affects are equally remote to it. They are merely natural. The principle according to which reason is simply opposed to everything unreasonable underlies the true opposition between enlightenment and mythology. The latter recognizes spirit only as something immersed in nature, a natural power. For it, inward impulses, like outward forces, are living powers of divine or demonic origin. Enlightenment, by contrast, relocates context, meaning, and life entirely within a subjectivity which is actually constituted only by this relocation. For enlightenment, reason is the chemical agent which absorbs the real substance of things and volatilizes it into the mere autonomy of reason. In order to escape the superstitious fear of nature, enlightenment has presented effective objective entities and forms without exception as mere veils of chaotic matter and condemned matter's influence on the human agent as enslavement, until the subject, according to its own concept, had been turned into a single, unrestricted, empty authority. The whole force of nature became a mere undifferentiated resistance to the abstract power of the subject. The particular mythology which the Western Enlightenment, including Calvinism, had to do away with was the Catholic doctrine of the *ordo* and the pagan popular religion which continued to flourish beneath it. To liberate human beings from such beliefs was the objective of bourgeois philosophy. However, the liberation went further than its humane originators had intended. The market economy it unleashed was at once the prevailing form of reason and the power which ruined reason. The Romantic reactionaries only expressed what the bourgeois themselves had realized: that freedom in their world tended toward organized anarchy. The Catholic counterrevolution's critique of the Enlightenment proved no less valid than the Enlightenment's critique of Catholicism. The Enlightenment had pinned its colors to liberalism. If all affects are of equal value, then self-preservation, which dominates the form of the system in any case, seems to offer the most plausible maxims for action. It was to be given free rein in the free economy. The somber writers of the early bourgeois period, such as Machiavelli, Hobbes, and Mandeville, who spoke up for the egoism of the self, thereby recognized society as the destructive principle and denounced harmony before it was elevated to the official doctrine by the bearers of light, the classicists. The former writers exposed the totality of the bourgeois order as the horrifying entity which finally engulfed both, the general and the particular, society and the self. With the development of the economic system* in which the control of the economic apparatus by private groups creates a division between human beings, self-preservation, although treated by reason as identical, had become the reified drive of each individual citizen and proved to be a destructive natural force no longer distinguishable from self-destruction. The two principles combined in a murky fusion. Pure reason became unreason, a procedure as immune to errors as it was devoid of content. However, with the revolutionary avant-garde, the utopia which proclaimed the reconciliation between nature and the self emerged from its hiding place in German philosophy as something at once irrational and reasonable, as the idea of the community of free individuals*—and brought down on itself the full fury of reason. In society as it is, despite feeble moralistic attempts to propagate humanity as the most rational means, self-preservation remains unencumbered by a utopia denounced as myth. For those at the top, shrewd self-preservation means the fascist struggle for power, and for individuals it means adaptation to injustice at any price. Enlightened reason no more possesses the means of measuring one drive within itself against others than of ordering the universe into spheres. It rightly exposes the notion of hierarchy in nature as a reflection of medieval society, and later attempts to demonstrate a new order of values bear the unmistakable taint of mendacity. The irrationalism which is evident in such futile reconstructions is far from opposing industrial reason.* Whereas great philosophy, in Leibniz and Hegel, had recognized a claim to truth even in subjective and objective forms of expression—feelings, institutions, works of art—which do not amount to actual ideas, irrationalism, here as elsewhere showing its kinship to the last dregs of the Enlightenment, modern positivism, draws a strict line between feeling, in the form of religion and art, and anything deserving the name of knowledge. Although irrationalism restricts cold reason in favor of immediate life, it turns the latter into a principle merely hostile to thought. Under cover of this illusory enmity feeling, and finally all human expression, indeed culture itself, is stripped of any responsibility to thought and transformed into the neutralized element of the all-embracing rationality of an economic system* long since grown irrational. From the first, that reason has been unable to rely on its attractive power alone and has supplemented it with the cult of emotions. In appealing to this cult, it turns against its own medium, thought, which was always suspect to this self-estranged form of reason. The tender effusions of lovers in films already function as a blow against dispassionate theory, and that is taken further in the sentimental argument against any thought which attacks injustice. This elevation of feelings to an ideology does not abolish the contempt in which they are really held. The fact that, compared to the starry heights into which ideology transposes them, they appear all the more vulgar merely contributes to their ostracism.. The verdict on feelings was already implicit in the formalization of reason. Even self-preservation, as a natural drive like other impulses, has a bad conscience; only bustling efficiency and the institutions created to serve it—mediation, apparatus, organization, systematization as ends in themselves—enjoy the esteem, in practice as in theory, of being deemed reasonable; the emotions are incorporated into this spurious reason.

The Enlightenment of the modern age has been marked from the first by radicalism: This fact distinguishes it from all earlier stages of demythologization. As a rule, whenever a new religion and a new mentality have won a place in world history, bringing a new mode of social existence, the old gods have been cast into the dust together with the old classes, tribes, and peoples. But especially when a people, such as the Jews, has taken on a new form of social life as a result of its own fate, its venerable customs, sacred actions, and objects of worship have been magically transformed into abominable misdeeds and terrifying specters. The phobias and idiosyncrasies of today, the character traits which are most despised and derided, can be deciphered as marks of a huge advance in human development. From the disgust aroused by excrement and human flesh to the contempt for fanaticism, idleness, and poverty, both spiritual and material, a line connects behavioral forms which were once adequate and necessary to those which are abominated. This line is at once that of destruction and of civilization. Each step has been an advance, a stage of enlightenment. But whereas all the earlier changes, from preanimism to magic, from matriarchal to patriarchal culture, from the polytheism of the slave traders to the Catholic hierarchy, replaced the older mythologies with new albeit enlightened ones, the Great Mother with the God of Hosts, the totem with the veneration of the Lamb, in the glare of enlightened reason any devotion which believed itself objective, grounded in the matter at hand, was dispelled as mythological. All preexisting ties were tabooed by this verdict, not excluding those which were necessary to the existence of the bourgeois order itself. The instrument by means of which the bourgeoisie had come to power, the unfettering of forces, universal freedom, self-determination—in short, enlightenment—turned against the bourgeoisie as soon as that class, as a system of rule, was forced to suppress those it ruled. By virtue of its principle, enlightenment does not stop short at the minimum of belief without which the bourgeois world could not exist. It does not render to power the reliable services which had always been performed for it by the old ideologies. Its antiauthoritarian tendency, which communicates, if only subterraneously, with the utopia contained in the concept of reason, finally made it as inimical to the established bourgeoisie as to the aristocracy, with which, indeed, it lost no time in forming alliances. Ultimately, the antiauthoritarian principle necessarily becomes its own antithesis, the agency opposed to reason: its abolition of all absolute ties allows power to decree and manipulate any ties which suit its purposes. After civic virtue and charity, for which it never offered good reasons, philosophy proclaimed authority and hierarchy as virtues, when enlightenment had long since revealed them as lies. But against such perversion of itself enlightenment, too, had no arguments, since pristine truth has no advantage over distortion, or rationalization over reason, unless it can demonstrate a practical one as well. With the formalization of reason, theory itself, if it seeks to be more than a cipher for neutral procedures, becomes an incomprehensible concept, and thought is deemed meaningful only after the sacrifice of meaning. Once harnessed to the dominant mode of production, enlightenment, which strives to undermine any order which has become repressive, nullifies itself. This is expressed in the early attacks of the current form of enlightenment on the "all-crushing" Kant. Just as Kant's moral philosophy set limits to his enlightened critique in order to rescue the possibility of reason, unreflecting enlightened thinking has always sought, for its own survival, to cancel itself with skepticism, in order to make room for the existing order.

In contrast to such precautions, the work of Sade, like that of Nietzsche, is an intransigent critique of practical reason, beside which even that of Kant himself appears like a revocation of his own thought. It pushes the scientific principle to annihilating extremes. Kant, to be sure, had so purified the moral law within the self of any heteronymous belief that respect, despite his assurances, could be no more than a psychological fact of nature, as the starry sky above the self was a physical one. "A fact of reason," he called it,[16] while Leibniz termed it "a general instinct of society."[17] But facts count for nothing where they do not exist. Sade does not deny their occurrence. Justine, the virtuous sister, is a martyr to the moral law. Juliette, however, draws the conclusion the bourgeoisie sought to avoid: she demonizes Catholicism as the latest mythology, and with it civilization as a whole. The energies previously focused on the sacrament are now devoted, perversely, to sacrilege. This inversion is extended to community in general. In all this Juliette does not proceed fanatically, as Catholicism had done with the Incas, but merely attends to the business of sacrilege in the efficient, enlightened way that Catholics, too, still had in their blood from archaic times. The primeval forms of behavior which had been tabooed by civilization, and had grown destructive under the stigma of bestiality, had led an underground life. Juliette revives them in their outlawed, not their natural form. She compensates the value judgment against them—which, like all value judgments, was unfounded—by its opposite. Thus, when she reenacts the primitive reactions they are no longer primitive but bestial. In psychological terms Juliette, not unlike Merteuil in *Les Liaisons Dangereuses*,[18] embodies neither unsublimated nor regressive libido but intellectual pleasure in regression, *amor intellectualis diaboli*, the joy of defeating civilization with its own weapons. She loves systems and logic. She wields the instrument of rational thought with consummate skill. As far as self-mastery is concerned, her instructions sometimes stand in the same relation to Kant's as the special application does to the principle. "Virtue," writes the latter,[19] "in so far as it is grounded on inner freedom, also contains an affirmative imperative for men, namely to place all their capacities and inclinations under the power [of reason] and therefore under the authority over oneself, which imperative is added to the interdiction on allowing oneself to be commanded by one's feelings and inclinations [the duty of apathy]. For unless reason takes the reins of government into its hands, those feelings and inclinations will play the master over men." Juliette teaches as follows on the self-discipline of the criminal: "First, reflect on your plan for several days in advance. Consider all its consequences, paying attention to what can be useful to you . . . and what might possibly betray you. Weigh these things just as soberly as if you were sure to be discovered."[20] The murderer's face must show utmost calm. "Let your features show calm and indifference. Try to acquire the greatest possible callousness in this situation. . . . If you are unsure of being free of pangs of conscience—and you will gain such certainty only through the habit of crime—if you are unsure of this, I say, then you will labor in vain to master the play of your features."[21] To be free of the stab of conscience is as essential to formalistic reason as to be free of love or hate. Remorse posits the past—which, contrary to popular ideology, has always meant nothing to the bourgeoisie—as something which exists; it is a relapse, to prevent which, for bourgeois praxis, would be remorse's only justification. Spinoza, following the Stoics, states the matter as follows: "Repentance is not a virtue, or, in other words, it does not arise from reason, but he who repents of an action is twice as unhappy or as weak as before."[22] But he goes on at once, quite in the spirit of Francavilla: "If the mob is not in fear, it threatens in its turn,"[23] thus maintaining, as a good student of Machiavelli, that modesty and remorse, like fear and hope, are undoubtedly useful, however contrary to reason. "Apathy (considered as a strength) is a necessary presupposition of virtue," writes Kant,[24] distinguishing, not unlike Sade, between this "moral apathy" and insensibility in the sense of indifference to sensory stimulation. Enthusiasm is bad. Calm and resolution constitute the strength of virtue. "That is the state of health in moral life, whereas the affect, even when it is excited by the idea of the good, is a momentarily lustrous phenomenon which leaves behind lassitude."[25] Juliette's friend Clairwil makes exactly the same observation with regard to vice.[26] "My soul is hardened, and I am far from preferring sensibility to the happy indifference I now enjoy. Oh Juliette . . . perhaps you are deceiving yourself about the dangerous sensibility prized by so many fools." Apathy arises at the turning points in bourgeois history, as in the history of antiquity, when the *pauci beati* become aware of their powerlessness in face of the overwhelming historical tendency. It marks the retreat of the individual's spontaneity into the private sphere, which is thus established as the truly bourgeois form of existence. Stoicism—which is the bourgeois philosophy—makes it easier for the privileged to look what threatens them in the eye by dwelling on the suffering of others. It affirms the general by elevating private existence, as protection from it, to the status of a principle. The private sphere of the bourgeois* is an upper-class cultural asset which has come down in the world.

Juliette's *credo* is science. She abominates any veneration which cannot be shown to be rational: belief in God and his dead son, obedience to the Ten Commandments, preference of the good to the wicked, salvation to sin. She is attracted by those reactions which have been proscribed by the legends of civilization. She manipulates semantics and logical syntax like the most up-to-date positivist, but unlike that employee of the latest administration she does not direct her linguistic criticism primarily against thought and philosophy but, as a daughter of the militant Enlightenment, against religion. "A dead God!" she says of Christ. "Nothing is more comical than this nonsensical combination of words from the Catholic dictionary: God, which means eternal; death, which means not eternal. Idiotic Christians, what do you intend to do with your dead God?"[27] The conversion of what is condemned without scientific proof into something to be striven for, and of what is respected without proof into an object of revulsion, the transvaluation of values, the "courage to do the forbidden,"[28] though without the telltale histrionics of Nietzsche's "*Wohlan!*" [Onward!] and without his biological idealism, is her specific passion. "Are pretexts needed, to commit crimes?" asks Princess Borghese, Juliette's friend, quite in Nietzsche's spirit.[29] Nietzsche proclaims the quintessence of her doctrine.[30] "Let the weaklings and failures go to ruin: the *first* principle of our philanthropy. And we should help them on their way. What is more damaging than any vice? The pity of active people for the unsuccessful and the weak—Christianity."[31] The latter, "with its curious interest in overthrowing tyrants and making them submit to principles of brotherhood . . . plays the game of the weak. It represents the weak, and has to speak like them. . . . We may be sure that such fraternal bonds were not only proposed but put in place by the weak, when priestly power had chanced to fall into their hands."[32] This contribution to the genealogy of morals is made by Noirceuil, Juliette's mentor. Nietzsche maliciously celebrates the mighty and their cruelty when it is directed "outside their circle," that is, against everything alien to themselves. "Once abroad in the wilderness, they revel in the freedom from social constraint and compensate for their long confinement in the quietude of their own community. They revert to the innocence of wild animals: we can imagine them returning from an orgy of murder, arson, rape, and torture, jubilant and at peace with themselves as though they had committed a ·fraternity prank—convinced, moreover, that the poets for a long time to come will have something to sing about and praise. . . . This 'boldness' of noble races, so headstrong, absurd, incalculable, sudden, improbable, . . . their utter indifference to safety and comfort, their terrible pleasure in destruction, their taste for cruelty,"[33] this boldness, stridently proclaimed by Nietzsche, has also taken hold of Juliette. "Live dangerously" is her message, too: "Dare henceforth to do anything without fear."[34] There are the strong and the weak, there are classes, races, and nations which dominate and others which are subjected. "Where, I ask you," cries Verneuil, "is the mortal stupid enough in face of all the evidence to claim that all men are born equal, in law and in fact? It was left to a misanthropist like Rousseau to put forward such a paradox, since, being extremely weak, he wanted to pull down those to whose level he was unable to raise himself. What effrontery did it take, I ask you, for this pygmy four feet two inches tall to compare himself to the model of stature and strength whom nature had endowed with the strength and figure of a Hercules? Is that not the same as comparing a fly to an elephant? Strength, beauty, stature, eloquence: those are the virtues which were decisive when authority passed to the rulers at the dawn of society."[35] "To expect that strength will not manifest itself as strength," Nietzsche goes on,[36] "as the desire to overcome, to appropriate, to have enemies, obstacles, and triumphs, is every bit as absurd as to expect that weakness will manifest itself as strength."—"How do you really expect" says Verneuil,[37] "a man endowed by nature with the highest predisposition for crime, whether through his superior strength, the refinement of his senses or as a result of an education fitting to his class or his wealth—how, I ask, do you expect this individual to be judged by the same law as those whom everything constrains to act virtuously and moderately? Would the law be more just if it punished both in the same way?

Is it natural for someone whom everything invites to do evil to be treated like someone whom everything impels to behave with prudence?"

Once the objective order of nature has been dismissed as prejudice and myth, nature is no more than a mass of material. For Nietzsche there is no law "which we not only recognize but recognize over us."[38] To the extent that the understanding, which was formed against the standard of self-preservation, recognizes any law of life, it is that of the stronger. While reason, because of its formalism, is unable to yield any necessary model for humanity, it has the advantage of actuality, in contrast to mendacious ideology. It is the weak who are guilty, according to Nietzsche's doctrine, since they use cunning to circumvent the natural law. "It is the diseased who imperil mankind, and not the 'beasts of prey.' It is the predestined failures and victims who undermine the social structure, who poison our faith in life and our fellow men."[39] They have spread throughout the world the Christianity which Nietzsche hates and abominates no less than Sade. "It is not the reprisals of the weak against the strong which truly conform to nature. They exist in the mental realm, not the physical. To carry out such reprisals the weak man would need strength he has not been given. He would have to assume a character which is by no means his—in a certain way he would do violence to nature. What is truthful in the laws of this wise mother is that the strong are allowed to injure the weak, since, to act in this way, they must only use the gifts they have received. The strong individual does not, like the weak, disguise himself with a character other than his own. He merely expresses in action what he has received from nature. Everything which follows from that is therefore natural: his oppression, his violence, his cruelties, his tyrannies, his injustices . . . are pure, like the hand which has imprinted them on him. And if the strong person exercises all his rights to oppress and pillage the weak, he is only doing the most natural thing in the world. . . . We should never, therefore, have scruples over what we are able to take from the weak, since it is not we who are committing the crime. Rather, it is the defense or revenge of the weak which are characteristic of crime."[40] If a weak person defends himself, he does wrong, "the wrong of stepping outside his own character of weakness, which nature has impressed on him. She created him to be a slave, and poor. He refuses to submit; that is his wrong."[41] In such magisterial speeches Dorval, the leader of a respectable Paris gang, expounds for Juliette the secret creed of all ruling classes, a creed to which Nietzsche, proclaiming it to his own time, added the psychology of resentment. Like Juliette he admired "the beautiful terribleness of the deed,"[42] even though, as a German professor, he differed from Sade in rejecting criminality, because its egoism "is restricted to such base goals. If its goals are lofty humanity has a different standard, judging 'crime,' even when committed with the most terrible means, not to be such."[43] The enlightened Juliette is still free of such prejudice in favor of greatness, a prejudice which, indeed, is characteristic of the bourgeois world; for her the racketeer is not less admirable than the minister because his victims are fewer. For the German, however, beauty is a function of size, and amid the twilight of the idols he cannot shake off the idealistic habit of wanting to see the petty thief hanged while imperialist raids are transfigured into world-historical missions. By elevating the cult of strength to a world-historical doctrine, German fascism took it to its absurd conclusion. As a protest against civilization the master morality perversely upheld the oppressed: hatred of stunted instincts objectively exposes the true nature of the slave masters, which reveals itself only in their victims. But, in the guise of a great power and a state religion, the master morality places itself entirely in the service of the civilizing powers that be, of the solid majority, of resentment and everything it once opposed. The realization of Nietzsche's doctrines both refutes them and reveals their truth—a truth which, despite his yea-saying affirmation of life, was hostile to the spirit of reality.

If remorse was contrary to reason, pity was outright sin. Anyone who yields to it "perverts the general law; whence it follows that pity, far from being a virtue, becomes truly a vice as soon as it induces us to interfere with the inequality required by the laws of nature."[44] Sade and Nietzsche realized that once reason had been formalized pity was left behind as a kind of sensuous awareness of the identity of general and particular, as naturalized mediation. It then forms a highly compelling prejudice: "compassion . . . does not appertain to the use of reason . . . although it seems to bear in it a sort of piety," writes Spinoza,[45] and "he who is moved neither by reason nor pity to help others is rightly called inhuman."[46] *Commiseratio* is humanity in its immediate form, but at the same time "bad and useless,"[47] since it is the opposite of the manly competence which, from Roman *virtus* through the Medici to efficiency under the Fords, has always been the true bourgeois virtue. Womanish and childish, Clairwil calls pity, vaunting her own "stoicism," the "tranquility of the passions" which enables her "to accomplish and endure everything without agitation."[48] "Pity is anything but a virtue. It is a weakness, born of fear and misfortune, a weakness that must be overcome most of all if one is striving to conquer excessive nervous sensibility, which is irreconcilable with the maxims of philosophy."[49] Women are the source of "outbursts of unrestrained compassion."[50] Sade and Nietzsche knew that their doctrine of the sinfulness of pity was an old bourgeois heritage. The latter speaks of "strong times" and "aristocratic cultures," while the former refers to Aristotle[51] and the Peripatetics.[52] Pity could not withstand the scrutiny of philosophy. Nor did Kant make an exception. Pity was, he said, "a certain soft-heartedness" and lacked "the dignity of virtue."[53] He failed to notice, however, that the principle of "general benevolence toward the human race,"[54] by which, in contrast to Clairwil's rationalism, he sought to replace pity, falls under the same curse of irrationality as "this well-meaning passion" which can easily seduce a person into becoming "a tender-hearted idler." Enlightenment cannot be duped; for it the general has no advantage over the particular fact, or an all-embracing love over a limited one. Pity stands in disrepute. Like Sade, Nietzsche cites the *Ars poetica* in passing judgment. "According to Aristotle, the Greeks often suffered an excess of pity: hence its necessary discharge through tragedy. We can see how suspect this inclination appeared to them. It endangers the state, takes away the necessary hardness and discipline, makes heroes howl like women."[55] Zarathustra preaches: "I see as much weakness as goodness. As much weakness as justice and pity."[56] Pity has, in fact, a moment which conflicts with justice, although Nietzsche lumps the two together. It confirms the rule of inhumanity by the exception it makes. By limiting the abolition of injustice to fortuitous love of one's neighbor, pity accepts as unalterable the law of universal estrangement which it would like to alleviate. It is true that the person who shows pity upholds as an individual the claim of the general, that is, the claim to life, against the general in the form of nature and society, which deny it. But the unity with the general as something inward, practiced by such an individual, is shown to be deceptive by his own weakness. It is not the softness but the restrictive nature of pity which makes it questionable—it is always too little. Just as the Stoic indifference on which bourgeois coldness, the counterpart of pity, has modeled itself was more loyal, however wretchedly, to the universal it had rejected than the compassionate baseness which adapted itself to the world, so it was those who unmasked pity who, however negatively, espoused the Revolution. The narcissistic deformations of pity, like the effusions of philanthropists and the moral complacency of the social welfare worker, are still an internalized endorsement of the difference between rich and poor. Admittedly, by imprudently confessing the joys of hardness, philosophy has put itself at the disposal of those who least forgive it the admission. The fascist masters* of the world translated the vilification of pity into that of political respect and the appeal to martial law, in which they were at one with Schopenhauer, the metaphysician of pity. For him the establishment of a humane order was the presumptuous delusion of someone who could hope only for misfortune. The enemies of pity were unwilling to equate humanity with misfortune. For them, the existence of misfortune was a scandal. With their impotent delicacy, they could not bear to see humanity pitied. In desperation their powerlessness switched to the glorification of power, while disowning it in practice whenever it gave them leave.

Kindness and good deeds become a sin, domination and suppression virtue. "All good things have at one time been considered evil; every original sin has, at some point, turned into an original virtue."[57] In the new epoch Juliette applies this principle in earnest, for the first time consciously performing the transvaluation of all values. After the destruction of all ideologies she elevates as her own morality what Christianity, in its ideology if not always in its practice, held to be abominable. As a good philosopher she remains cool and reflective. All is done without illusions. To Clairwil's proposal for a sacrilegious act she responds: "Now that we do not believe in God, my dear, . . . the desecrations you desire are no more than useless childish games. . . . I may be still firmer in my disbelief than you; my atheism is unshakable. So do not imagine that I need the childish pranks you propose to confirm it. I shall take part because it amuses you, but only for entertainment"—the American murderess Annie Henry* would have said "just for fun"—"and never as something necessary, either to strengthen my way of thinking, or to convince others of it."[58] Though swayed by momentary kindness toward her accomplice, she still upholds her principles. Even injustice, hatred, and destruction become merely operations, now that the formalization of reason has stripped all goals of the character of necessity and objectivity, which is dismissed as illusion. Magic passes into mere activity, into the means—in short, into industry. The formalization of reason is merely the intellectual expression of mechanized production. The means is fetishized: it absorbs pleasure. Just as the goals with which the old system of rule had veiled itself are rendered illusory by enlightenment in theory, the possibility of abundance removes their justification in practice. Domination survives as an end in itself, in the form of economic power. Pleasure itself shows traces of the outdated, the irrelevant, like the metaphysics which forbade it. Juliette speaks of the motives of crime.[59] She herself is no less ambitious and avaricious than her friend Sbrigani, but she idolizes the forbidden. Sbrigani, a man devoted to the means and to duty, is more advanced. "To enrich ourselves—that is what matters. It would be the height of guilt if we failed to reach that goal. Only if one is truly on the way to becoming wealthy is one permitted to reap one's pleasures: until then one must forget them." For all her rational superiority, Juliette still clings to one superstition. While she recognizes the naivety of sacrilege, in the end it still gives her pleasure. But every pleasure betrays idolization: it is self-abandonment to an Other. Nature actually does not know pleasure: it does not go beyond the satisfaction of needs. All pleasure is social, in the unsublimated affects no less than in the sublimated. It springs from alienation. Even when enjoyment is ignorant of the prohibition it infringes, it owes its origin to civilization, to the fixed order from which it yearns to return to the very nature from which that order protects it. Only when dream absolves them of the compulsion of work, of the individual's attachment to a particular social function and finally to a self, leading back to a primal state free of domination and discipline, do human beings feel the magic of pleasure. It was the homesickness of those enmeshed in civilization, the "objective despair" of those who had to turn themselves into elements of the social order, which nourished the love of gods and demons; to them as transfigured nature this love turned in adoration. Thought arose in the course of liberation from terrible nature, which is finally subjugated utterly. Pleasure, so to speak, is nature's revenge. In it human beings divest themselves of thought, escape from civilization. In earlier societies such homecoming was provided by communal festivals. Primitive orgies are the collective origin of pleasure. "The interlude of universal confusion represented by the festival," writes Roger Caillois, "seems truly like the moment when the world's order is suspended. All excesses are permitted. Rules must be broken, everything must be turned upside down. In the mythic epoch the course of time was reversed: one was born aged, died as a child. . . . All the precepts protecting the good, natural, and social order are systematically violated."[60] One abandons oneself to the transfigured powers of origin; but from the standpoint of the suspended interdiction these actions appear as dissipated and insane.[61] Only with increasing civilization and enlightenment do the strengthened self and the secure system of power reduce the festival to farce. The rulers introduce pleasure as a rational measure, a tribute paid to imperfectly subdued nature; they seek at once to detoxify it and to preserve it in higher culture; to administer it to their subjects in controlled doses where it cannot be entirely withdrawn. Pleasure becomes an object of manipulation, until it finally perishes in the administrative arrangements. This development extends from the primitive feast to the holiday. "The more dominant the complex social organism becomes, the less it tolerates interruptions of the ordinary course of life. Today as yesterday, tomorrow as today, everything must follow the same course. The general overflowing is no longer possible. The period of turbulence has been individualized. Holidays have supplanted the feast."[62] In fascism they are supplemented by the collective fake intoxication, concocted from radio, headlines, and Benzedrine.* Sbrigani has a presentiment of this. He grants himself amusements "on the road to fortune," as vacations. Juliette, by contrast, still emulates the *ancien régime*. She deifies sin. Her libertinism is in thrall to Catholicism as the nun's ecstasy is to paganism.

Nietzsche is aware of the still mythical nature of pleasure. In its abandonment to nature pleasure renounces the possible, just as pity renounces the transformation of the whole. Both contain a moment of resignation. Nietzsche tracks down pleasure in all its hiding places, as narcissism in solitude, as masochistic enjoyment in the depressions of the self-tormentor. "Against all who merely enjoy!"[63] Juliette tries to rescue pleasure by rejecting love in its bourgeois form as devotion, which, as resistance to the bourgeoisie's own shrewdness, is characteristic of that class in its last century. In love, pleasure was linked to the deification of the person who bestowed it and was the truly human passion. It is being finally revoked as a value judgment conditioned by sexuality. In the enraptured adoration of the lover, as in the boundless admiration shown in return by the beloved, the actual servitude of the woman was endlessly transfigured. Again and again, the sexes were reconciled on the basis of their recognition of this servitude: the woman seemed freely to accept her defeat, the man to grant her victory. Under Christianity the hierarchy of the sexes, the yoke placed on the feminine character by the masculine order of property, was idealized as the union of hearts in marriage, and the memory of sexuality's better, prepatriarchal past appeased. Under big industry* love is annulled. The decline of middle-class property, the downfall of the free economic subject, affects the family: it is no longer the celebrated cell of society it once was, since it no longer forms the basis of the citizen's economic existence. For adolescents the family no longer marks out the horizon of their lives; the autonomy of the father is vanishing and with it resistance to his authority. Earlier, the girl's servitude in the paternal home inflamed in her the passion which seemed to lead to freedom but was fulfilled neither in marriage nor anywhere outside. As the prospect of a job opens for the girl, that of love is closed. The more universally the system of modern industry* requires everyone to enter its service, the more all those who do not form part of the ocean of "white trash,"* which is absorbing the unqualified employed and unemployed, are turned into petty experts, into employees who must fend for themselves. In the form of skilled work the autonomy of the entrepreneur, which is over, is spreading to all those admitted as producers, including the "working" woman, and is becoming their character. Their self-respect grows in proportion to their fungibility. Defiance of the family is no more an act of daring than the leisure-time relationship with the boyfriend is the gateway to heaven. People are taking on the rational, calculating attitude to their own sexuality long since proclaimed as ancient wisdom by Juliette's enlightened circle. Mind and body are being separated in reality, just as those indiscreet bourgeois libertines demanded: "It appears to me," Noirceuil states rationalistically,[64] "that love and pleasure are two very different things . . . because tender feelings correspond to relationships of caprice and decorum, but in no way spring from the beauty of a neck or the pretty curve of a hip. And these objects, which, in accordance with our taste, can keenly excite our physical affects, have, it seems to me, no rights over our mental affections. To complete my thought, Bélize is ugly, is forty years old, entirely lacks grace of person, is without regular features or any physical charm. But Bélize has intelligence, a precious character, a million things which attach my feelings and preferences. I shall never wish to sleep with Bélize, but I shall love her to the point of madness, whereas I shall lust after Araminthe but heartily detest her as soon as the fever of desire is past." Here, the inevitable consequence implicit in the Cartesian division of the human being into thinking and extensive substance is expressed with total clarity as the destruction of Romantic love. The latter is taken to be a mask, a rationalization of the physical drive, "a false and always dangerous metaphysics,"[65] as Count Belmor explains in his great speech on love. For all their libertinism, Juliette's friends conceive of sexuality, as against tenderness, of earthly as against heavenly love, not just as a degree too powerful but also as oversimplified. The beauty of a neck or the curve of a hip acts on sexuality not as unhistorical, merely natural facts but as images in which the whole of social experience is contained; this experience harbors an intention toward something different to nature, a love not restricted to sexuality. But even the most incorporeal tenderness is transformed sexuality; the hand stroking the hair, the kiss on the brow, which express the rapture of spiritual love, are in pacified form the beating and biting which accompany the sexual act among Australian aborigines. The distinction is abstract. Metaphysics, Belmor teaches, falsifies the factual situation, it prevents the beloved from being seen as he or she is; it stems from magic, it is a veil. "And I am not to snatch it from our eyes? That would be weakness … cowardice. Let us analyze her when the pleasure is over, this goddess who has just blinded me."[66] Love itself is an unscientific concept: "False definitions are always leading us astray," Dolmance declares in the memorable fifth dialogue of *La Philosophie dans le Boudoir*, "I don't know what it is—the heart. I simply use that term for weakness of mind."[67] "If we spend one moment in what Lucretius calls the 'background of life,'"—meaning, in cold analysis—"we find that neither the elevation of the beloved nor romantic feeling withstands analysis. . . . It is the body alone that I love, and it is the body alone that I lament, although I can have it again at any time."[68] What is true in all this is the insight into the dissociation of love, the work of progress. This dissociation, which mechanizes pleasure and distorts longing into a deception, attacks love at its core. By turning her praise of genital and perverted sexuality into condemnation of what is unnatural, immaterial, illusory, the libertine Juliette has thrown in her lot with the normality which belittles and restricts not only the utopian exaltation of love but physical pleasure, not only the loftiest joy but that which is nearest at hand. The cynical roué whose side she takes has metamorphosed, with the help of the sex educator, the psychoanalyst, and the hormone physiologist, into the open-minded practical man who extends his affirmation of sport and hygiene to include the sex life. Juliette's critique contains the same inner discord as the Enlightenment itself. In so far as the criminal violation of taboos, which once made common cause with the bourgeois revolution, has not been simply absorbed into the new matter-of-factness, it lives on, with sublime love, as fidelity to the utopia brought near by the availability of physical pleasure to all.

"The ridiculous enthusiasm" which attached us to a particular individual as the only one, the elevation of woman in love, can be traced back beyond Christianity to matriarchal stages. "It is certain that our spirit of chivalrous courtship, which comically offers our homage to an object made only to satisfy our need—it is certain, I say, that this spirit stems from the reverence our ancestors once had for women because of their profession as prophetesses in town and country. Through terror, aversion became worship, and chivalry was nurtured in the womb of superstition. But this reverence never existed in nature, and it would be a waste of time to seek it there. The inferiority of that sex to ours is too well founded ever to give us a sound motive to respect it, and the love which arises from that blind reverence is, like it, a prejudice."[69] It is on power, however legalistically veiled, that the social hierarchy ultimately rests. The mastery of nature is reproduced within humanity. Christian civilization, which used the idea of protecting the physically weak to justify exploitation of the strong bondsman, never entirely won the hearts of the converted peoples. The principle of love was too strongly disavowed by the sharp intellect and the still sharper weapons of the Christian masters, until Lutheranism abolished the antithesis between state and doctrine by making the sword and rod the Gospel's quintessence. It directly equated spiritual freedom with the affirmation of actual oppression. But woman bears the stigma of weakness; her weakness places her in a minority even when she is numerically superior to men. As with the subjugated original inhabitants in early forms of state, the indigenous population of colonies, who lack the organization and weapons of their conquerors, as with the Jews among Aryans, her defenselessness legitimizes her oppression. Sade expresses as formulae the reflections of Strindberg. "Let us not doubt that there is a difference between man and woman no less certain and important than that between man and the apes of the forest. We would have just as good reason to deny woman membership of our species as to refuse to acknowledge brotherhood with the apes. Examine carefully a naked woman beside a man of the same age, naked like her, and you will be readily convinced of the considerable difference (disregarding the sex) which exists between the two creatures and will clearly see that the woman is merely a lower degree of the man. The differences likewise exist within, and anatomical dissection of one and the other, if done with painstaking care, will bring this truth to light."[70] Christianity's attempt to compensate the suppression of sexuality ideologically by the veneration of woman, and thus to sublimate the memory of the archaic instead of merely repressing it, is annulled by its rancor against the woman thus elevated and against theoretically emancipated pleasure. The affect which corresponds to the practice of oppression is contempt, not veneration, and lurking behind the love of one's neighbor throughout the Christian centuries has been the forbidden, compulsive hatred of the object which continually brought to mind the futility of that exertion: woman. Women paid for the cult of the Madonna with the obsessive belief in witches, the revenge taken on the memory of the pre-Christian prophetess who secretly called into question the sanctified patriarchal system of power. The woman excites the savage rage of the half-converted man who is required to honor her, just as the weak in general can count on the mortal enmity of the superficially civilized strong who are supposed to spare them. Sade brings this hatred to consciousness. "I have never believed," says Count Ghigi, the Roman chief of police, "that the union of two bodies could ever give rise to the union of two hearts. I see in this physical union strong reasons for contempt . . . , for revulsion, but not a single one for love."[71] And when a girl terrorized by Saint-Fonds, the royal minister, bursts into tears, he exclaims: "That is how I like women. . . . Why cannot I reduce them all to such a state with a single word?"[72] Man as ruler refuses to do woman the honor of individualizing her. Socially, the individual woman is an example of the species, a representative of her sex, and thus, wholly encompassed by male logic, she stands for nature, the substrate of never-ending subsumption on the plane of ideas and of never-ending subjection on that of reality. Woman as an allegedly natural being is a product of history, which denatures her. But the desperate, destructive urge directed against everything which embodies the lure of nature, everything which is physiologically, biologically, nationally, or socially inferior, indicates that Christianity's attempt has failed. "*Que ne puis-je, d'un mot, les réduire toutes en cet état!*" To eradicate utterly the hated but overwhelming temptation to lapse back into nature—that is the cruelty which stems from failed civilization; it is barbarism, the other side of culture. "Them all!" For destruction tolerates no exceptions; the will to destroy is totalitarian, and totalitarianism springs from that will alone. "I have reached the point," Juliette tells the Pope, "where I can say with Tiberius: if only the whole of mankind had only one head, so that I could have the pleasure of cutting it off with a single blow!"[73] The signs of powerlessness, hasty uncoordinated movements, animal fear, swarming masses, provoke the lust for murder. The explanation for the hatred of woman as the weaker in mental and physical power, who bears the mark of domination on her brow, is the same as for the hatred of the Jews. Women and Jews show visible evidence of not having ruled for thousands of years. They live, although they could be eliminated, and their fear and weakness, the greater affinity to nature produced in them by perennial oppression, is the element in which they live. In the strong, who pay for their strength with their strained remoteness from nature and must forever forbid themselves fear, this incites blind fury. They identify themselves with nature by calling forth from their victims, multiplied a thousandfold, the cry they may not utter themselves. "These senseless creatures!" writes President Blammont of women in *Aline et Valcour*, "How I love to see them struggling in my hands! They are like lambs in the jaws of the lion."[74] And in the same letter: "It is the same as conquering a city. You must occupy the heights . . . establish yourself at all the commanding points and then launch your attack without any fear of resistance."[75] A creature which has fallen attracts predators: humiliation of those already visited by misfortune brings the keenest pleasure. The less the danger to the one on top, the more unhampered the joy in the torments he can now inflict: only through the hopeless despair of the victim can power become pleasure and triumphantly revoke its own principle, discipline. Fear averted from the self bursts out in hearty laughter, the expression of a hardening within the individual which can only be fully lived out through the collective. Ringing laughter has always denounced civilization. "Of all the lava spewed forth from the crater of the human mouth, the most calamitous is merriment," writes Victor Hugo in the chapter headed "Storms of men are worse than storms of oceans."[76] "It is on misfortune," Juliette teaches,[77] "that the full weight of our malice must fall. The tears wrung from wretchedness have a keenness which profoundly thrills our nervous substance."[78] Rather than with tenderness, pleasure makes its pact with cruelty, and sexual love becomes what according to Nietzsche[79] it always was: "in its means, war; and at its basis the mortal hatred of the sexes." "With both the male and the female," zoology teaches us, "'love', or sexual attraction, is originally and preeminently 'sadic'; it is positively gratified by the infliction of pain; it is as cruel as hunger."[80] Thus, as its final result, civilization leads back to the terrors of nature. The lethal love on which Sade's work is constantly focused, Nietzsche's impudently solicitous magnanimity in seeking to spare the victim humiliation at any price: cruelty and the idea of greatness deal no less harshly with human beings on the plane of play and imagination than German fascism* was to do on that of reality. However, whereas the unconscious colossus of real existence, subjectless capitalism, inflicts its destruction blindly, the deludedly rebellious subject is willing to see that destruction as its fulfillment, and, together with the biting cold it emits toward human beings misused as things, it also radiates the perverted love which, in the world of things, takes the place of love in its immediacy. Sickness becomes the symptom of recovery. In transfiguring the victims, delusion accepts their degradation. It makes itself resemble the monster of domination which it cannot physically overcome. Imagination seeks as horror to withstand horror. The Roman proverb that harshness is true pleasure expresses not merely the brutality of slave drivers but the indissoluble contradiction of order, which, when it sanctions happiness, turns it into self-parody and creates it only through proscribing it. While they perpetuated this contradiction, Sade and Nietzsche also contributed to its clarification.

To reason, devotion to the adored creature appears as idol worship. The demise of idolatry follows necessarily from the ban on mythology pronounced by Jewish monotheism and enforced against the changing objects of adoration in the history of thought by that monotheism's secularized form, enlightenment. The decay of economic reality, which has always been at the basis of superstition, released specific forces of negation. Christianity, however, propagated love: the pure adoration of Jesus. It sought to elevate the blind sexual drive by the hallowing of marriage, as it also tried to bring the crystalline radiance of law closer to earthly life by the idea of heavenly grace. The reconciliation of civilization with nature which it sought prematurely to purchase with the doctrine of the crucified God remained as alien to Judaism as to the rigorism of the Enlightenment. Neither Moses nor Kant proclaimed emotion; their icy law knew neither love nor sacrificial pyres. Nietzsche's attack on monotheism dealt a heavier blow to Christian than to Jewish doctrine. While he repudiated the Law he pledged himself to the "higher self,"[81] a self no longer natural but more-than-natural. He wanted to replace God by the "Overman" because monotheism, in its broken, Christian form, had transparently become mythology. But just as, in the service of this higher self, the old ascetic ideals are extolled by Nietzsche as self-overcoming in the interest of developing "dominant power,"[82] so the higher self turns out to be a desperate attempt to rescue the God who was dead. In this, Nietzsche renews Kant's endeavor to transform the divine law into an autonomous principle, to rescue European civilization from giving up the ghost in English skepticism. Kant's principle: "that everything be done from the maxim of one's will as a will that could at the same time have as its object itself as giving universal law,"[83] is also the secret of the Overman. His will is no less despotic than the categorical imperative. Both principles aim at independence from external powers, at the unconditional freedom from tutelage which defines the essence of enlightenment. However, as the fear of falsehood, a fear which even in his most "enlightened" moments Nietzsche decried as "a piece of Quixotism,"[84] replaced the Law with self-legislation, so that everything was made transparent as one great unmasked superstition, enlightenment itself, indeed, truth in any form, became an idol, and we realize that "even we knowing ones of today, the godless and antimetaphysical, still take *our* fire from the conflagration kindled by a belief millennia old, the Christian belief, which was also the belief of Plato, that God is truth, that the truth is divine."[85] Science itself, therefore, is open to the same criticism as metaphysics. The denial of God contains an irresolvable contradiction; it negates knowledge itself. Sade did not drive the idea of enlightenment to this point, where it turns against itself. The reflection of science on itself, the work of the Enlightenment's conscience, was left to philosophy, meaning German philosophy. For Sade, enlightenment was not so much an intellectual as a social phenomenon. He carried forward the dissolution of bonds—which Nietzsche idealistically believed could be overcome by the higher self—and the critique of solidarity with society, office, family[86] to the point of proclaiming anarchy. His work lays bare the mythological nature of the principles on which civilization was based after the demise of religion: those of the Decalogue, of paternal authority, of property. It is the exact inversion of the social theory elaborated by Le Play a hundred years later.[87] Each of the Ten Commandments is declared void before the tribunal of formal reason. They are revealed without exception as ideologies. At Juliette's request the Pope himself pleads the case for murder.[88] He finds it easier to rationalize un-Christian acts in the light of natural reason than it had ever been to justify the Christian principles according to which those acts were devilish. The "mitered philosopher" has less need of sophistry in advocating murder than Maimonides and St Thomas Aquinas in condemning it. Roman reason is even more inclined than the god of the Prussians to side with the bigger battalions. The Law, however, has been dethroned, and the love which was supposed to humanize it is unmasked as a reversion to idolatry. It is not just romantic sexual love which has been condemned as metaphysics by science and industry but love of any kind, for no love can withstand reason: neither that between wife and husband nor between lover and beloved, nor the love between parents and children. The Duc de Blangis announces to his subjects that those related to the rulers, daughters and wives, should be treated as harshly, indeed, still more harshly, than others, "in order to show you how deeply we despise the bonds by which you may think us fettered."[89] Woman's love is abolished like that of man. The rules of libertinage passed on by Saint-Fonds to Juliette are to apply to all women.[90] Dolmance voices the materialistic disenchantment of parental love. "These latter ties originate in the parents' fear of being abandoned in old age, and the self-interested concern they show for us in our childhood is intended to earn them the same consideration in old age."[91] Sade's argument is as old as the bourgeoisie. Democritus already denounced parental love as economic.[92] Sade, however, applies the same disenchantment even to exogamy, the foundation of civilization. According to him, there are no rational grounds to oppose incest,[93] and the hygienic argument formerly used has now been invalidated by advanced science, which ratifies Sade's cold judgment. "It has by no means been proved that children born of incest have a greater tendency than others to suffer from cretinism, deaf-muteness, rickets, etc."[94] The family, held together not by romantic sexual love but by maternal love, which forms the basis of all tenderness and social feelings,[95] conflicts with society itself. "Do not imagine you will make good republicans as long as you isolate children, who should belong only to the whole community, within your families. . . . Whereas there are great disadvantages in allowing children to be absorbed into family interests which often diverge strongly from those of the nation, very great benefits lie in separating them from them."[96] "Conjugal ties" must be destroyed for social reasons; children are to be "absolutely forbidden" knowledge of their fathers, since they are "*uniquement les enfants de la patrie*";[97] the anarchy and individualism which Sade proclaimed in the struggle against laws[98] culminate in the absolute rule of the generality, the republic. Just as the deposed god returns as a more repressive idol, the old, undemanding bourgeois state reappears in the violence of the fascist collective. Sade thought through to the end the state socialism whose first steps brought the downfall of Saint-Just and Robespierre. If the bourgeoisie sent them, its most loyal politicians, to the guillotine, it banished its most outspoken writer to the hell of the Bibliothèque Nationale. For the *chronique scandaleuse* of Justine and Juliette which, turned out as if on a production line, prefigured in the style of the eighteenth century the sensational literature of the nineteenth and the mass literature of the twentieth is the Homeric epic after it has discarded its last mythological veil: the story of thought as an instrument of power. In taking fright at the image in its own mirror, that thought opens to view what lies beyond it. It is not the harmonious social ideal, which even Sade glimpsed dimly in the future: "*gardez vos frontières et restez chez vous*";[99] it is not even the socialist utopia developed in the story of Zamé:[100] it is the fact that Sade did not leave it to its enemies to be horrified by the Enlightenment which makes his work pivotal to its rescue.

The dark writers of the bourgeoisie, unlike its apologists, did not seek to avert the consequences of the Enlightenment with harmonistic doctrines. They did not pretend that formalistic reason had a closer affinity to morality than to immorality. While the light-bringing writers protected the indissoluble alliance of reason and atrocity, bourgeois society and power, by denying that alliance, the bearers of darker messages pitilessly expressed the shocking truth. "Into hands stained by the murder of spouses and children, sodomy, killing, prostitution, and infamy, heaven has placed these riches to reward me for such abominations," says Clairwil in her summary of her brother's life.[101] She exaggerates. The justice of bad domination is not quite so consistent as to reward only infamy. But only exaggeration is true. The essential character of prehistory* is the appearance of utmost horror in the individual detail. A statistical compilation of those slaughtered in a pogrom, which also includes mercy killings, conceals its essence, which emerges only in an exact description of the exception, the most hideous torture. A happy life in a world of horror is ignominiously refuted by the mere existence of that world. The latter therefore becomes the essence, the former negligible. No doubt, the ruling group in the bourgeois era did not engage in killing their own children and spouses, or in prostitution and sodomy, as frequently as their subjects, who took over the morals of the rulers of earlier times. However, when power was at stake, the rulers have piled up mountains of corpses even in recent centuries. Compared to the mentality and actions of the rulers under fascism, in which power has come fully into its own, the enthusiastic description of the life of Brisa-Testa—although those rulers are recognizable in it—pales to harmless banality. In Sade as in Mandeville, private vices are the anticipatory historiography of public virtues in the totalitarian era. It is because they did not hush up the impossibility of deriving from reason a fundamental argument against murder, but proclaimed it from the rooftops, that Sade and Nietzsche are still vilified, above all by progressive thinkers. In a different way to logical positivism, they both took science at its word. In pursuing the implications of reason still more resolutely than the positivists their secret purpose was to lay bare the utopia which is contained in every great philosophy, as it is in Kant's concept of reason: the utopia of a humanity which, itself no longer distorted, no longer needs distortion. In proclaiming the identity of power and reason, their pitiless doctrines are more compassionate than those of the moral lackeys of the bourgeoisie. "Where are thy greatest dangers?," Nietzsche once asked,[102] "In pity." With his denial he redeemed the unwavering trust in humanity which day by day is betrayed by consoling affirmation.

The Culture Industry:
Enlightenment as Mass Deception

The sociological view that the loss of support from objective religion and the disintegration of the last precapitalist residues, in conjunction with technical and social differentiation and specialization, have given rise to cultural chaos is refuted by daily experience. Culture today is infecting everything with sameness. Film, radio, and magazines form a system. Each branch of culture is unanimous within itself and all are unanimous together. Even the aesthetic manifestations of political opposites proclaim the same inflexible rhythm. The* decorative administrative and exhibition buildings of industry differ little between authoritarian and other countries. The bright monumental structures shooting up on all sides show off the systematic ingenuity of the state-spanning combines, toward which the unfettered entrepreneurial system, whose monuments are the dismal residential and commercial blocks in the surrounding areas of desolate cities, was already swiftly advancing. The older buildings around the concrete centers already look like slums, and the new bungalows on the outskirts, like the flimsy structures at international trade fairs, sing the praises of technical progress while inviting their users to throw them away after short use like tin cans. But the town-planning projects, which are supposed to perpetuate individuals as autonomous units in hygienic small apartments, subjugate them only more completely to their adversary, the total power of capital.* Just as the occupants of city centers are uniformly summoned there for purposes of work and leisure, as producers and consumers, so the living cells crystallize into homogenous, well-organized complexes. The conspicuous unity of macrocosm and microcosm confronts human beings with a model of their culture: the false identity of universal and particular. All mass culture under monopoly is identical, and the contours of its skeleton, the conceptual armature fabricated by monopoly, are beginning to stand out. Those in charge no longer take much trouble to conceal the structure, the power of which increases the more bluntly its existence is admitted. Films and radio no longer need to present themselves as art. The truth that they are nothing but business is used as an ideology to legitimize the trash they intentionally produce. They call themselves industries, and the published figures for their directors' incomes quell any doubts about the social necessity of their finished products.

Interested parties like to explain the culture industry in technological terms. Its millions of participants, they argue, demand reproduction processes which inevitably lead to the use of standard products to meet the same needs at countless locations. The technical antithesis between few production centers and widely dispersed reception necessitates organization and planning by those in control. The standardized forms, it is claimed, were originally derived from the needs of the consumers: that is why they are accepted with so little resistance. In reality, a cycle of manipulation and retroactive need is unifying the system ever more tightly. What is not mentioned is that the basis on which technology is gaining power over society is the power of those whose economic position in society is strongest.* Technical rationality today is the rationality of domination. It is the compulsive character of a society alienated from itself. Automobiles, bombs, and films hold the totality together until their leveling element demonstrates its power against the very system of injustice it served. For the present the technology of the culture industry confines itself to standardization and mass production and sacrifices what once distinguished the logic of the work from that of society. These adverse effects, however, should not be attributed to the internal laws of technology itself but to its function within the economy today.* Any need which might escape the central control is repressed by that of individual consciousness. The step from telephone to radio has clearly distinguished the roles. The former liberally permitted the participant to play the role of subject. The latter democratically makes everyone equally into listeners, in order to expose them in authoritarian fashion to the same programs put out by different stations. No mechanism of reply has been developed, and private transmissions are condemned to unfreedom. They confine themselves to the apocryphal sphere of "amateurs," who, in any case, are organized from above. Any trace of spontaneity in the audience of the official radio is steered and absorbed into a selection of specializations by talent-spotters, performance competitions, and sponsored events of every kind. The talents belong to the operation long before they are put on show; otherwise they would not conform so eagerly. The mentality of the public, which allegedly and actually favors the system of the culture industry, is a part of the system, not an excuse for it. If a branch of art follows the same recipe as one far removed from it in terms of its medium and subject matter; if the dramatic denouement in radio "soap operas"* is used as an instructive example of how to solve technical difficulties—which are mastered no less in "jam sessions" than at the highest levels of jazz—or if a movement from Beethoven is loosely "adapted" in the same way as a Tolstoy novel is adapted for film, the pretext of meeting the public's spontaneous wishes is mere hot air. An explanation in terms of the specific interests of the technical apparatus and its personnel would be closer to the truth, provided that apparatus were understood in all its details as a part of the economic mechanism of selection.* Added to this is the agreement, or at least the common determination, of the executive powers to produce or let pass nothing which does not conform to their tables, to their concept of the consumer, or, above all, to themselves.

If the objective social tendency of this age is incarnated in the obscure subjective intentions of board chairmen, this is primarily the case in the most powerful sectors of industry: steel, petroleum, electricity, chemicals. Compared to them the culture monopolies are weak and dependent. They have to keep in with the true wielders of power, to ensure that their sphere of mass society, the specific product of which still has too much of cozy liberalism and Jewish intellectualism about it, is not subjected to a series of purges.* The dependence of the most powerful broadcasting company on the electrical industry, or of film on the banks, characterizes the whole sphere, the individual sectors of which are themselves economically intertwined. Everything is so tightly clustered that the concentration of intellect reaches a level where it overflows the demarcations between company names and technical sectors. The relentless unity of the culture industry bears witness to the emergent unity of politics. Sharp distinctions like those between A and B films, or between short stories published in magazines in different price segments, do not so much reflect real differences as assist in the classification, organization, and identification of consumers. Something is provided for everyone so that no one can escape; differences are hammered home and propagated. The hierarchy of serial qualities purveyed to the public serves only to quantify it more completely. Everyone is supposed to behave spontaneously according to a "level" determined by indices and to select the category of mass product manufactured for their type. On the charts of research organizations, indistinguishable from those of political propaganda, consumers are divided up as statistical material into red, green, and blue areas according to income group.

The schematic nature of this procedure is evident from the fact that the mechanically differentiated products are ultimately all the same. That the difference between the models of Chrysler and General Motors is fundamentally illusory is known by any child, who is fascinated by that very difference. The advantages and disadvantages debated by enthusiasts serve only to perpetuate the appearance of competition and choice. It is no different with the offerings of Warner Brothers and Metro Goldwyn Mayer. But the differences, even between the more expensive and cheaper products from the same firm, are shrinking—in cars to the different number of cylinders, engine capacity, and details of the gadgets, and in films to the different number of stars, the expense lavished on technology, labor and costumes, or the use of the latest psychological formulae. The unified standard of value consists in the level of conspicuous production, the amount of investment put on show. The budgeted differences of value in the culture industry have nothing to do with actual differences, with the meaning of the product itself. The technical media, too, are being engulfed by an insatiable uniformity. Television aims at a synthesis of radio and film, delayed only for as long as the interested parties cannot agree. Such a synthesis, with its unlimited possibilities, promises to intensify the impoverishment of the aesthetic material so radically that the identity of all industrial cultural products, still scantily disguised today, will triumph openly tomorrow in a mocking fulfillment of Wagner's dream of the total art work. The accord between word, image, and music is achieved so much more perfectly than in *Tristan* because the sensuous elements, which compliantly document only the surface of social reality, are produced in principle within the same technical work process, the unity of which they express as their true content. This work process integrates all the elements of production, from the original concept of the novel, shaped by its sidelong glance at film,* to the last sound effect. It is the triumph of invested capital. To impress the omnipotence of capital on the hearts of expropriated job candidates as the power of their true master is the purpose of all films, regardless of the plot selected by the production directors.

Even during their leisure time, consumers must orient themselves according to the unity of production. The active contribution which Kantian schematism still expected of subjects—that they should, from the first, relate sensuous multiplicity to fundamental concepts—is denied to the subject by industry. It purveys schematism as its first service to the customer. According to Kantian schematism, a secret mechanism within the psyche preformed immediate data to fit them into the system of pure reason. That secret has now been unraveled. Although the operations of the mechanism appear to be planned by those who supply the data, the culture industry, the planning is in fact imposed on the industry by the inertia of a society irrational despite all its rationalization, and this calamitous tendency, in passing through the agencies of business,* takes on the shrewd intentionality peculiar to them. For the consumer there is nothing left to classify, since the classification has already been preempted by the schematism of production. This dreamless art for the people fulfils the dreamy idealism which went too far for idealism in its critical form. Everything comes from consciousness—from that of God for Malebranche and Berkeley, and from earthly production management for mass art. Not only do hit songs, stars, and soap operas conform to types recurring cyclically as rigid invariants, but the specific content of productions, the seemingly variable element, is itself derived from those types. The details become interchangeable. The brief interval sequence which has proved catchy in a hit song, the hero's temporary disgrace which he accepts as a "good sport," the wholesome slaps the heroine receives from the strong hand of the male star, his plain-speaking abruptness toward the pampered heiress, are, like all the details, ready-made clichés, to be used here and there as desired and always completely defined by the purpose they serve within the schema. To confirm the schema by acting as its constituents is their sole *raison d'être*. In a film, the outcome can invariably be predicted at the start—who will be rewarded, punished, forgotten—and in light music the prepared ear can always guess the continuation after the first bars of a hit song and is gratified when it actually occurs. The average choice of words in a short story must not be tampered with. The gags and effects are no less calculated than their framework. They are managed by special experts, and their slim variety is specifically tailored to the office pigeonhole. The culture industry has developed in conjunction with the predominance of the effect, the tangible performance, the technical detail, over the work, which once carried the idea and was liquidated with it. By emancipating itself, the detail had become refractory; from Romanticism to Expressionism it had rebelled as unbridled expression, as the agent of opposition, against organization. In music, the individual harmonic effect had obliterated awareness of the form as a whole; in painting the particular detail had obscured the overall composition; in the novel psychological penetration had blurred the architecture. Through totality, the culture industry is putting an end to all that. Although operating only with effects, it subdues their unruliness and subordinates them to the formula which supplants the work. It crushes equally the whole and the parts. The whole confronts the details in implacable detachment, somewhat like the career of a successful man, in which everything serves to illustrate and demonstrate a success which, in fact, it is no more than the sum of those idiotic events. The so-called leading idea is a filing compartment which creates order, not connections. Lacking both contrast and relatedness, the whole and the detail look alike. Their harmony, guaranteed in advance, mocks the painfully achieved harmony of the great bourgeois works of art. In Germany even the most carefree films of democracy were overhung already by the graveyard stillness of dictatorship.

The whole world is passed through the filter of the culture industry. The familiar experience of the moviegoer, who perceives the street outside as a continuation of the film he has just left, because the film seeks strictly to reproduce the world of everyday perception, has become the guideline of production. The more densely and completely its techniques duplicate empirical objects, the more easily it creates the illusion that the world outside is a seamless extension of the one which has been revealed in the cinema. Since the abrupt introduction of the sound film, mechanical duplication has become entirely subservient to this objective. According to this tendency, life is to be made indistinguishable from the sound film. Far more strongly than the theatre of illusion, film denies its audience any dimension in which they might roam freely in imagination—contained by the film's framework but unsupervised by its precise actualities—without losing the thread; thus it trains those exposed to it to identify film directly with reality. The withering of imagination and spontaneity in the consumer of culture today need not be traced back to psychological mechanisms. The products themselves, especially the most characteristic, the sound film, cripple those faculties through their objective makeup. They are so constructed that their adequate comprehension requires a quick, observant, knowledgeable cast of mind but positively debars the spectator from thinking, if he is not to miss the fleeting facts. This kind of alertness is so ingrained that it does not even need to be activated in particular cases, while still repressing the powers of imagination. Anyone who is so absorbed by the world of the film, by gesture, image, and word, that he or she is unable to supply that which would have made it a world in the first place, does not need to be entirely transfixed by the special operations of the machinery at the moment of the performance. The required qualities of attention have become so familiar from other films and other culture products already known to him or her that they appear automatically. The power of industrial society* is imprinted on people once and for all. The products of the culture industry are such that they can be alertly consumed even in a state of distraction. But each one is a model of the gigantic economic machinery,* which, from the first, keeps everyone on their toes, both at work and in the leisure time which resembles it. In any sound film or any radio broadcast something is discernible which cannot be attributed as a social effect to any one of them, but to all together. Each single manifestation of the culture industry inescapably reproduces human beings as what the whole has made them. And all its agents, from the producer to the women's organizations, are on the alert to ensure that the simple reproduction of mind does not lead on to the expansion of mind.

The complaints of art historians and cultural attorneys over the exhaustion of the energy which created artistic style in the West are frighteningly unfounded. The routine translation of everything, even of what has not yet been thought, into the schema of mechanical reproducibility goes beyond the rigor and scope of any true style—the concept with which culture lovers idealize the precapitalist past as an organic era. No

Palestrina could have eliminated the unprepared or unresolved dissonance more puristically than the jazz arranger excludes any phrase which does not exactly fit the jargon. If he jazzes up Mozart, he changes the music not only where it is too difficult or serious but also where the melody is merely harmonized differently, indeed, more simply, than is usual today. No medieval patron of architecture can have scrutinized the subjects of church windows and sculptures more suspiciously than the studio hierarchies examine a plot by Balzac or Victor Hugo before it receives the imprimatur of feasibility. No cathedral chapter could have assigned the grimaces and torments of the damned to their proper places in the order of divine love more scrupulously than production managers decide the position of the torture of the hero or the raised hem of the leading lady's dress within the litany of the big film. The explicit and implicit, exoteric and esoteric catalog of what is forbidden and what is tolerated* is so extensive that it not only defines the area left free but wholly controls it. Even the most minor details are modeled according to this lexicon. Like its adversary, avantgarde art, the culture industry defines its own language positively, by means of prohibitions applied to its syntax and vocabulary. The permanent compulsion to produce new effects which yet remain bound to the old schema, becoming additional rules, merely increases the power of the tradition which the individual effect seeks to escape. Every phenomenon is by now so thoroughly imprinted by the schema that nothing can occur that does not bear in advance the trace of the jargon, that is not seen at first glance to be approved. But the true masters, as both producers and reproducers, are those who speak the jargon with the same free-and-easy relish as if it were the language it has long since silenced. Such is the industry's ideal of naturalness. It asserts itself more imperiously the more the perfected technology reduces the tension between the culture product and everyday existence. The paradox of routine travestied as nature is detectable in every utterance of the culture industry, and in many is quite blatant. A jazz musician who has to play a piece of serious music, Beethoven's simplest minuet, involuntarily syncopates, and condescends to start on the beat only with a superior smile. Such "naturalness," complicated by the ever more pervasive and exorbitant claims of the specific medium, constitutes the new style, "a system of nonculture to which one might even concede a certain 'unity of style' if it made any sense to speak of a stylized barbarism."[1]

The general influence of this stylization may already be more binding than the official rules and prohibitions; a hit song is treated more leniently today if it does not respect the thirty-two bars or the compass of the ninth than if it includes even the most elusive melodic or harmonic detail which falls outside the idiom. Orson Welles is forgiven all his offences against the usages of the craft because, as calculated rudeness, they confirm the validity of the system all the more zealously. The compulsion of the technically conditioned idiom which the stars and directors must produce as second nature, so that the nation may make it theirs, relates to nuances so fine as to be almost as subtle as the devices used in a work of the avant-garde, where, unlike those of the hit song, they serve truth. The rare ability to conform punctiliously to the obligations of the idiom of naturalness in all branches of the culture industry becomes the measure of expertise. As in logical positivism, what is said and how it is said must be verifiable against everyday speech. The producers are experts. The idiom demands the most prodigious productive powers, which it absorbs and squanders. Satanically, it has rendered cultural conservatism's distinction between genuine and artificial style obsolete. A style might possibly be called artificial if it had been imposed from outside against the resistance of the intrinsic tendencies of form. But in the culture industry the subject matter itself, down to its smallest elements, springs from the same apparatus as the jargon into which it is absorbed. The deals struck between the art specialists and the sponsor and censor over some all-too-unbelievable lie tell us less about internal, aesthetic tensions than about a divergence of interests. The reputation of the specialist, in which a last residue of actual autonomy still occasionally finds refuge, collides with the business policy of the church or the industrial combine producing the culture commodity. By its own nature, however, the matter has already been reified as negotiable even before the various agencies come into conflict. Even before Zanuck* acquired her, Saint Bernadette gleamed in the eye of her writer as an advert aimed at all the relevant consortia. To this the impulses of form have been reduced. As a result, the style of the culture industry, which has no resistant material to overcome, is at the same time the negation of style. The reconciliation of general and particular, of rules and the specific demands of the subject, through which alone style takes on substance, is nullified by the absence of tension between the poles: "the extremes which touch" have become a murky identity in which the general can replace the particular and vice versa.

Nevertheless, this caricature of style reveals something about the genuine style of the past. The concept of a genuine style becomes transparent in the culture industry as the aesthetic equivalent of power. The notion of style as a merely aesthetic regularity is a retrospective fantasy of Romanticism. The unity of style not only of the Christian Middle Ages but of the Renaissance expresses the different structures of social coercion in those periods, not the obscure experience of the subjects, in which the universal was locked away. The great artists were never those whose works embodied style in its least fractured, most perfect form but those who adopted style as a rigor to set against the chaotic expression of suffering, as a negative truth. In the style of these works expression took on the strength without which existence is dissipated unheard. Even works which are called classical, like the music of Mozart, contain objective tendencies which resist the style they incarnate. Up to Schönberg and Picasso, great artists have been mistrustful of style, which at decisive points has guided them less than the logic of the subject matter. What the Expressionists and Dadaists attacked in their polemics, the untruth of style as such, triumphs today in the vocal jargon of the crooner, in the adept grace of the film star, and even in the mastery of the photographic shot of a farm laborer's hovel. In every work of art, style is a promise. In being absorbed through style into the dominant form of universality, into the current musical, pictorial, or verbal idiom, what is expressed seeks to be reconciled with the idea of the true universal. This promise of the work of art to create truth by impressing its unique contours on the socially transmitted forms is as necessary as it is hypocritical. By claiming to anticipate fulfillment through their aesthetic derivatives, it posits the real forms of the existing order as absolute. To this extent the claims of art are always also ideology. Yet it is only in its struggle with tradition, a struggle precipitated in style, that art can find expression for suffering. The moment in the work of art by which it transcends reality cannot, indeed, be severed from style; that moment, however, does not consist in achieved harmony, in the questionable unity of form and content, inner and outer, individual and society, but in those traits in which the discrepancy emerges, in the necessary failure of the passionate striving for identity. Instead of exposing itself to this failure, in which the style of the great work of art has always negated itself, the inferior work has relied on its similarity to others, the surrogate of identity. The culture industry has finally posited this imitation as absolute. Being nothing other than style, it divulges style's secret: obedience to the social hierarchy. Aesthetic barbarism today is accomplishing what has threatened intellectual formations since they were brought together as culture and neutralized. To speak about culture always went against the grain of culture. The general designation "culture" already contains, virtually, the process of identifying, cataloging, and classifying which imports culture into the realm of administration. Only what has been industrialized, rigorously subsumed, is fully adequate to this concept of culture. Only by subordinating all branches of intellectual production equally to the single purpose of imposing on the senses of human beings, from the time they leave the factory in the evening to the time they clock on in the morning, the imprint of the work routine which they must sustain throughout the day, does this culture mockingly fulfill the notion of a unified culture which the philosophers of the individual personality held out against mass culture.

The culture industry, the most inflexible style of all, thus proves to be the goal of the very liberalism which is criticized for its lack of style. Not only did its categories and contents originate in the liberal sphere, in domesticated naturalism no less than in the operetta and the revue, but the modern culture combines are the economic area in which a piece of the circulation sphere otherwise in the process of disintegration, together with the corresponding entrepreneurial types, still tenuously survives. In that area people can still make their way, provided they do not look too closely at their true purpose and are willing to be compliant. Anyone who resists can survive only by being incorporated. Once registered as diverging from the culture industry, they belong to it as the land reformer does to capitalism. Realistic indignation is the trademark of those with a new idea to sell. Public authority in the present society* allows only those complaints to be heard in which the attentive ear can discern the prominent figure under whose protection the rebel is suing for peace. The more immeasurable the gulf between chorus and leaders, the more certainly is there a place among the latter for anyone who demonstrates superiority by well-organized dissidence. In this way liberalism's tendency to give free rein to its ablest members survives in the culture industry. To open that industry to clever people is the function of the otherwise largely regulated market, in which, even in its heyday, freedom was the freedom of the stupid to starve, in art as elsewhere. Not for nothing did the system of the culture industry originate in the liberal industrial countries, just as all its characteristic media, especially cinema, radio, jazz, and magazines, also triumph there. Its progress, however, stems from the general laws of capital. Gaumont and Pathé,* Ullstein and Hugenberg* did not follow the international trend to their own disadvantage; Europe's economic dependence on the USA after the war and the inflation also made its contribution. The belief that the barbarism of the culture industry is a result of "cultural lag," of the backwardness of American consciousness in relation to the state of technology, is quite illusory. Prefascist Europe was backward in relation to the monopoly of culture. But it was precisely to such backwardness that intellectual activity owed a remnant of autonomy, its last exponents their livelihood, however meager. In Germany the incomplete permeation of life by democratic control had a paradoxical effect. Many areas were still exempt from the market mechanism which had been unleashed in Western countries. The German educational system, including the universities, the artistically influential theatres, the great orchestras, and the museums were under patronage. The political powers, the state and the local authorities who inherited such institutions from absolutism, had left them a degree of independence from the power of the market as the princes and feudal lords had done up to the nineteenth century. This stiffened the backbone of art in its late phase against the verdict of supply and demand, heightening its resistance far beyond its actual degree of protection. In the market itself the homage paid to not yet marketable artistic quality was converted into purchasing power, so that reputable literary and musical publishers could support authors who brought in little more than the respect of connoisseurs. Only the dire and incessant threat of incorporation into commercial life as aesthetic experts finally brought the artists to heel. In former times they signed their letters, like Kant and Hume, "Your most obedient servant," while undermining the foundations of throne and altar. Today they call heads of government by their first names and are subject, in every artistic impulse, to the judgment of their illiterate principals. The analysis offered by de Tocqueville a hundred years ago has been fully borne out in the meantime. Under the private monopoly of culture tyranny does indeed "leave the body free and sets to work directly on the soul. The ruler no longer says: 'Either you think as I do or you die.' He says: 'You are free not to think as I do; your life, your property—all that you shall keep. But from this day on you will

be a stranger among us.'"[2] Anyone who does not conform is condemned
to an economic impotence which is prolonged in the intellectual powerlessness of the eccentric loner. Disconnected from the mainstream, he is
easily convicted of inadequacy. Whereas the mechanism of supply and
demand is today disintegrating in material production, in the superstructure it acts as a control on behalf of the rulers. The consumers are the
workers and salaried employees, the farmers and petty bourgeois.
Capitalist production hems them in so tightly, in body and soul, that they
unresistingly succumb to whatever is proffered to them. However, just as
the ruled have always taken the morality dispensed to them by the rulers
more seriously than the rulers themselves, the defrauded masses today
cling to the myth of success still more ardently than the successful. They,
too, have their aspirations. They insist unwaveringly on the ideology by
which they are enslaved. The pernicious love of the common people for
the harm done to them outstrips even the cunning of the authorities. It
surpasses the rigor of the Hays Office,* just as, in great epochs, it has
inspired renewed zeal in greater agencies directed against it, the terror of
the tribunals. It calls for Mickey Rooney* rather than the tragic Garbo,
Donald Duck rather than Betty Boop. The industry bows to the vote it
has itself rigged. The incidental costs to the firm which cannot turn a profit from its contract with a declining star are legitimate costs for the system
as a whole. By artfully sanctioning the demand for trash, the system inau-
gurates total harmony. Connoisseurship and expertise are proscribed as the
arrogance of those who think themselves superior, whereas culture dis-
tributes its privileges democratically to all. Under the ideological truce
between them, the conformism of the consumers, like the shamelessness
of the producers they sustain, can have a good conscience. Both content
themselves with the reproduction of sameness.

Unending sameness also governs the relationship to the past. What
is new in the phase of mass culture compared to that of late liberalism is
the exclusion of the new. The machine is rotating on the spot. While it
already determines consumption, it rejects anything untried as a risk. In
film, any manuscript which is not reassuringly based on a best-seller is
viewed with mistrust. That is why there is incessant talk of ideas, novelty
and surprises, of what is both totally familiar and has never existed before.
Tempo and dynamism are paramount. Nothing is allowed to stay as it was,
everything must be endlessly in motion. For only the universal victory of

the rhythm of mechanical production and reproduction promises that nothing will change, that nothing unsuitable will emerge. To add anything to the proven cultural inventory would be too speculative. The frozen genres—sketch, short story, problem film, hit song—represent the average of late liberal taste threateningly imposed as a norm. The most powerful of the culture agencies, who work harmoniously with others of their kind as only managers do, whether they come from the ready-to-wear trade or* college, have long since reorganized and rationalized the objective mind. It is as if some omnipresent agency* had reviewed the material and issued an authoritative catalog tersely listing the products available. The ideal forms are inscribed in the cultural heavens where they were already numbered by Plato—indeed, were only numbers, incapable of increase or change.

Amusement and all the other elements of the culture industry existed long before the industry itself. Now they have been taken over from above and brought fully up to date. The culture industry can boast of having energetically accomplished and elevated to a principle the often inept transposition of art to the consumption sphere, of having stripped amusement of its obtrusive naiveties and improved the quality of its commodities. The more all-embracing the culture industry has become, the more pitilessly it has forced the outsider into either bankruptcy or a syndicate; at the same time it has become more refined and elevated, becoming finally a synthesis of Beethoven and the Casino de Paris.* Its victory is twofold: what is destroyed as truth outside its sphere can be reproduced indefinitely within it as lies. "Light" art as such, entertainment, is not a form of decadence. Those who deplore it as a betrayal of the ideal of pure expression harbor illusions about society.* The purity of bourgeois art, hypostatized as a realm of freedom contrasting to material praxis, was bought from the outset with the exclusion of the lower class; and art keeps faith with the cause of that class, the true universal, precisely by freeing itself from the purposes of the false. Serious art has denied itself to those for whom the hardship and oppression of life make a mockery of seriousness and who must be glad to use the time not spent at the production line in being simply carried along. Light art has accompanied autonomous art as its shadow. It is the social bad conscience of serious art. The truth which the latter could not apprehend because of its social premises gives the former an appearance of objective justification. The split between them is itself the truth: it expresses at least the negativity of the culture which is the sum of both spheres. The antithesis can be reconciled least of all by absorbing light art into serious or vice versa. That, however, is what the culture industry attempts. The eccentricity of the circus, the peep show, or the brothel in relation to society is as embarrassing to it as that of Schönberg and Karl Kraus. The leading jazz musician Benny Goodman therefore has to appear with the Budapest String Quartet, more pedantic rhythmically than any amateur clarinetist, while the quartet play with the saccharine monotony of Guy Lombardo.* What is significant is not crude ignorance, stupidity or lack of polish. The culture industry has abolished the rubbish of former times by imposing its own perfection, by prohibiting and domesticating dilettantism, while itself incessantly committing the blunders without which the elevated style cannot be conceived. What is new, however, is that the irreconcilable elements of culture, art, and amusement have been subjected equally to the concept of purpose and thus brought under a single false denominator: the totality of the culture industry. Its element is repetition. The fact that its characteristic innovations are in all cases mere improvements to mass production is not extraneous to the system. With good reason the interest of countless consumers is focused on the technology, not on the rigidly repeated, threadbare and half-abandoned content. The social power revered by the spectators manifests itself more effectively in the technically enforced ubiquity of stereotypes than in the stale ideologies which the ephemeral contents have to endorse.

Nevertheless, the culture industry remains the entertainment business. Its control of consumers is mediated by entertainment, and its hold will not be broken by outright dictate but by the hostility inherent in the principle of entertainment to anything which is more than itself. Since the tendencies of the culture industry are turned into the flesh and blood of the public by the social process as a whole, those tendencies are reinforced by the survival of the market in the industry. Demand has not yet been replaced by simple obedience. The major reorganization of the film industry shortly before the First World War, the material precondition for its expansion, was a deliberate adaptation to needs of the public registered at the ticket office, which were hardly thought worthy of consideration in the pioneering days of the screen. That view is still held by the captains of the film industry, who accept only more or less phenomenal box-office success as evidence and prudently ignore the counterevidence, truth. Their ideology is business. In this they are right to the extent that the power of the culture industry lies in its unity with fabricated need and not in simple antithesis to it—or even in the antithesis between omnipotence and powerlessness. Entertainment is the prolongation of work under late capitalism. It is sought by those who want to escape the mechanized labor process so that they can cope with it again. At the same time, however, mechanization has such power over leisure and its happiness, determines so thoroughly the fabrication of entertainment commodities, that the off-duty worker can experience nothing but after-images of the work process itself. The ostensible content is merely a faded foreground; what is imprinted is the automated sequence of standardized tasks. The only escape from the work process in factory and office is through adaptation to it in leisure time. This is the incurable sickness of all entertainment. Amusement congeals into boredom, since, to be amusement, it must cost no effort and therefore moves strictly along the well-worn grooves of association. The spectator must need no thoughts of his own: the product prescribes each reaction, not through any actual coherence—which collapses once exposed to thought—but through signals. Any logical connection presupposing mental capacity is scrupulously avoided. Developments are to emerge from the directly preceding situation, not from the idea of the whole. There is no plot which could withstand the screenwriters' eagerness to extract the maximum effect from the individual scene. Finally, even the schematic formula seems dangerous, since it provides some coherence of meaning, however meager, when only meaninglessness is acceptable. Often the plot is willfully denied the development called for by characters and theme under the old schema. Instead, the next step is determined by what the writers take to be their most effective idea. Obtusely ingenious surprises disrupt the plot. The product's tendency to fall back perniciously on the pure nonsense which, as buffoonery and clowning, was a legitimate part of popular art up to Chaplin and the Marx brothers, emerges most strikingly in the less sophisticated genres. Whereas the films of Greer Garson and Bette Davis can still derive some claim to a coherent plot from the unity of the socio-psychological case represented, the tendency to subvert meaning has taken over completely in the text of novelty songs,* suspense films, and cartoons. The idea itself, like objects in comic and horror films, is massacred and mutilated. Novelty songs have always lived on contempt for meaning, which, as both ancestors and descendants of psycho-analysis, they reduce to the monotony of sexual symbolism. In crime and adventure films the spectators are begrudged even the opportunity to witness the resolution. Even in nonironic examples of the genre they must make do with the mere horror of situations connected in only the most perfunctory way.

Cartoon and stunt films were once exponents of fantasy against rationalism. They allowed justice to be done to the animals and things electrified by their technology, by granting the mutilated beings a second life. Today they merely confirm the victory of technological reason over truth. A few years ago they had solid plots which were resolved only in the whirl of pursuit of the final minutes. In this their procedure resembled that of slapstick comedy. But now the temporal relations have shifted. The opening sequences state a plot motif so that destruction can work on it throughout the action: with the audience in gleeful pursuit the protagonist is tossed about like a scrap of litter. The quantity of organized amusement is converted into the quality of organized cruelty.* The self-elected censors of the film industry, its accomplices, monitor the duration of the* atrocity prolonged into a hunt. The jollity dispels the joy supposedly conferred by the sight of an embrace and postpones satisfaction until the day of the pogrom. To the extent that cartoons do more than accustom the senses to the new tempo, they hammer into every brain the old lesson that continuous attrition, the breaking of all individual resistance, is the condition of life in this society. Donald Duck in the cartoons and the unfortunate victim in real life receive their beatings so that the spectators can accustom themselves to theirs.

The enjoyment of the violence done to the film character turns into violence against the spectator; distraction becomes exertion. No stimulant concocted by the experts may escape the weary eye; in face of the slick presentation no one may appear stupid even for a moment; everyone has to keep up, emulating the smartness displayed and propagated by the production. This makes it doubtful whether the culture industry even still fulfils its self-proclaimed function of distraction. If the majority of radio stations and cinemas were shut down, consumers probably would not feel too much deprived. In stepping from the street into the cinema, they no longer enter the world of dream in any case, and once the use of these institutions was no longer made obligatory by their mere existence, the urge to use them might not be so overwhelming.* Shutting them down in this way would not be reactionary machine-wrecking. Those who suffered would not be the film enthusiasts but those who always pay the penalty in any case, the ones who had lagged behind. For the housewife, despite the films which are supposed to integrate her still further, the dark of the cinema grants a refuge in which she can spend a few unsupervised hours, just as once, when there were still dwellings and evening repose, she could sit gazing out of the window. The unemployed of the great centers find freshness in summer and warmth in winter in these places of regulated temperature. Apart from that, and even by the measure of the existing order, the bloated entertainment apparatus does not make life more worthy of human beings. The idea of "exploiting" the given technical possibilities,* of fully utilizing the capacities for aesthetic mass consumption, is part of an economic system which refuses to utilize capacities when it is a question of abolishing hunger.

The culture industry endlessly cheats its consumers out of what it endlessly promises. The promissory note of pleasure issued by plot and packaging is indefinitely prolonged: the promise, which actually comprises the entire show, disdainfully intimates that there is nothing more to come, that the diner must be satisfied with reading the menu. The desire inflamed by the glossy names and images is served up finally with a celebration of the daily round it sought to escape. Of course, genuine works of art were not sexual exhibitions either. But by presenting denial as negative, they reversed, as it were, the debasement of the drive and rescued by mediation what had been denied. That is the secret of aesthetic sublimation: to present fulfillment in its brokenness. The culture industry* does not sublimate: it suppresses. By constantly exhibiting the object of desire, the breasts beneath the sweater, the naked torso of the sporting hero, it merely goads the unsublimated anticipation of pleasure, which through the habit of denial has long since been mutilated as masochism. There is no erotic situation in which innuendo and incitement are not accompanied by the clear notification that things will never go so far. The Hays Office* merely confirms the ritual which the culture industry has staged in any case: that of Tantalus. Works of art are ascetic and shameless; the culture industry is pornographic and prudish. It reduces love to romance. And, once reduced, much is permitted, even libertinage as a marketable specialty, purveyed by quota with the trade description "daring." The mass production of sexuality automatically brings about its repression. Because of his ubiquity, the film star with whom one is supposed to fall in love is, from the start, a copy of himself. Every tenor now sounds like a Caruso record, and the natural faces of Texas girls already resemble those of the established models by which they would be typecast in Hollywood. The mechanical reproduction of beauty—which, admittedly, is made only more inescapable by the reactionary culture zealots with their methodical idolization of individuality—no longer leaves any room for the unconscious idolatry with which the experience of beauty has always been linked. The triumph over beauty is completed by humor, the malicious pleasure elicited by any successful deprivation. There is laughter because there is nothing to laugh about. Laughter, whether reconciled or terrible, always accompanies the moment when a fear is ended.* It indicates a release, whether from physical danger or from the grip of logic. Reconciled laughter resounds with the echo of escape from power; wrong laughter copes with fear by defecting to the agencies which inspire it. It echoes the inescapability of power. Fun is a medicinal bath which the entertainment industry never ceases to prescribe. It makes laughter the instrument for cheating happiness. To moments of happiness laughter is foreign; only operettas, and now films, present sex amid peals of merriment. But Baudelaire is as humorless as Hölderlin. In wrong society laughter is a sickness infecting happiness and drawing it into society's worthless totality. Laughter about something is always laughter at it, and the vital force which, according to Bergson, bursts through rigidity in laughter is, in truth, the irruption of barbarity, the self-assertion which, in convivial settings, dares to celebrate its liberation from scruple. The collective of those who laugh parodies humanity. They are monads, each abandoning himself to the pleasure—at the expense of all others and with the majority in support—of being ready to shrink from nothing. Their harmony presents a caricature of solidarity. What is infernal about wrong laughter is that it compellingly parodies what is best, reconciliation. Joy, however, is austere: *res severa verum gaudium.** The ideology of monasteries, that it is not asceticism but the sexual act which marks the renunciation of attainable bliss, is negatively confirmed by the gravity of the lover who presciently pins his whole life to the fleeting moment. The culture industry replaces pain, which is present in ecstasy no less than in asceticism, with jovial denial. Its supreme law is that its consumers shall at no price be given what they desire: and in that very deprivation they must take their laughing satisfaction. In each performance of the culture industry the permanent denial imposed by civilization is once more inflicted on and unmistakably demonstrated to its victims. To offer them something and to withhold it is one and the same. That is what the erotic commotion achieves. Just because it can never take place, everything revolves around the coitus. In film, to allow an illicit relationship without due punishment of the culprits is even more strictly tabooed than it is for the future son-in-law of a millionaire to be active in the workers' movement. Unlike that of the liberal era, industrial no less than nationalist culture can permit itself to inveigh against capitalism, but not to renounce the threat of castration. This threat constitutes its essence.* It outlasts the organized relaxation of morals toward the wearers of uniforms, first in the jaunty films produced for them and then in reality. What is decisive today is no longer Puritanism, though it still asserts itself in the form of women's organizations, but the necessity, inherent in the system,* of never releasing its grip on the consumer, of not for a moment allowing him or her to suspect that resistance is possible. This principle requires that while all needs should be presented to individuals as capable of fulfillment by the culture industry, they should be so set up in advance that individuals experience themselves through their needs only as eternal consumers, as the culture industry's object. Not only does it persuade them that its fraud is satisfaction; it also gives them to understand that they must make do with what is offered, whatever it may be. The flight from the everyday world, promised by the culture industry in all its branches, is much like the abduction of the daughter in the American cartoon: the father is holding the ladder in the dark. The culture industry presents that same everyday world as paradise. Escape, like elopement, is destined from the first to lead back to its starting point. Entertainment fosters the resignation which seeks to forget itself in entertainment.

Amusement, free of all restraint, would be not only the opposite of art but its complementary extreme. Absurdity in the manner of Mark Twain, with which the American culture industry flirts from time to time, could be a corrective to art. The more seriously art takes its opposition to existence, the more it resembles the seriousness of existence, its antithesis: the more it labors to develop strictly according to its own formal laws, the more labor it requires to be understood, whereas its goal had been precisely to negate the burden of labor. In some revue films, and especially in grotesque stories and "funnies,"* the possibility of this negation is momentarily glimpsed. Its realization, of course, cannot be allowed. Pure amusement indulged to the full, relaxed abandon to colorful associations and merry nonsense, is cut short by amusement in its marketable form: it is disrupted by the surrogate of a coherent meaning with which the culture industry insists on endowing its products while at the same time slyly misusing them as pretexts for bringing on the stars. Biographies and other fables stitch together the scraps of nonsense into a feeble-minded plot. It is not the bells on the fool's cap that jingle but the bunch of keys of capitalist reason, which even in its images harnesses joy to the purpose of getting ahead. Every kiss in the revue film must contribute to the career of the boxer or hit-song expert whose success is being glorified. The deception is not that the culture industry serves up amusement but that it spoils the fun by its business-minded attachment to the ideological clichés of the culture which is liquidating itself. Ethics and taste suppress unbridled amusement as "naïve"—naivety being rated no more highly than intellectualism—and even restrict its technical possibilities. The culture industry is corrupt, not as a sink of iniquity but as the cathedral of higher gratification. At all its levels, from Hemingway to Emil Ludwig,* from Mrs. Miniver* to the Lone Ranger,* from Toscanini to Guy Lombardo,* intellectual products drawn ready-made from art and science are infected with untruth. Traces of something better persist in those features of the culture industry by which it resembles the circus—in the stubbornly purposeless expertise of riders, acrobats, and clowns, in the "defense and justification of physical as against intellectual art."[3] But the hiding places of mindless artistry, which represents what is human against the social mechanism, are being relentlessly ferreted out by organizational reason, which forces everything to justify itself in terms of meaning and effect. It is causing meaninglessness to disappear at the lowest level of art just as radically as meaning is disappearing at the highest.

The fusion of culture and entertainment is brought about today not only by the debasement of culture but equally by the compulsory intellectualization of amusement. This is already evident in the fact that amusement is now experienced only in facsimile, in the form of cinema photography or the radio recording. In the age of liberal expansion amusement was sustained by an unbroken belief in the future: things would stay the same yet get better. Today, that belief has itself been intellectualized, becoming so refined as to lose sight of all actual goals and to consist only in a golden shimmer projected beyond the real. It is composed of the extra touches of meaning—running exactly parallel to life itself—applied in the screen world to the good guy, the engineer, the decent girl, and also to the ruthlessness disguised as character, to the sporting interest, and finally to the cars and cigarettes, even where the entertainment does not directly serve the publicity needs of the manufacturer concerned but advertises the system as a whole. Amusement itself becomes an ideal, taking the place of the higher values it eradicates from the masses by repeating them in an even more stereotyped form than the advertising slogans paid for by private interests. Inwardness, the subjectively restricted form of truth, was always more beholden to the outward rulers than it imagined. The culture industry is perverting it into a barefaced lie. It appears now only as the high-minded prattle tolerated by consumers of religious bestsellers, psychological films, and women's serials* as an embarrassingly agreeable ingredient, so that they can more reliably control their own human emotions. In this sense entertainment is purging the affects in the manner once attributed by Aristotle to tragedy and now by Mortimer Adler* to film. The culture industry reveals the truth not only about style but also about catharsis.

The more strongly the culture industry entrenches itself, the more it can do as it chooses with the needs of consumers—producing, controlling, disciplining them; even withdrawing amusement altogether: here, no limits are set to cultural progress. But the tendency is immanent in the principle of entertainment itself, as a principle of bourgeois enlightenment. If the need for entertainment was largely created by industry, which recommended the work to the masses through its subject matter, the oleograph through the delicate morsel it portrayed and, conversely, the pudding mix through the image of a pudding, entertainment has always borne the trace of commercial brashness, of sales talk, the voice of the fairground huckster. But the original affinity between business and entertainment reveals itself in the meaning of entertainment itself: as society's apologia. To be entertained means to be in agreement. Entertainment makes itself possible only by insulating itself from the totality of the social process, making itself stupid and perversely renouncing from the first the inescapable claim of any work, even the most trivial: in its restrictedness to reflect the whole. Amusement always means putting things out of mind, forgetting suffering, even when it is on display. At its root is powerlessness. It is indeed escape, but not, as it claims, escape from bad reality but from the last thought of resisting that reality. The liberation which amusement promises is from thinking as negation. The shamelessness of the rhetorical question "What do people want?" lies in the fact that it appeals to the very people as thinking subjects whose subjectivity it specifically seeks to annul. Even on those occasions when the public rebels against the pleasure industry it displays the feebleness systematically instilled in it by that industry. Nevertheless, it has become increasingly difficult to keep the public in submission. The advance of stupidity must not lag behind the simultaneous advance of intelligence. In the age of statistics the masses are too astute to identify with the millionaire on the screen and too obtuse to deviate even minutely from the law of large numbers. Ideology hides itself in probability calculations. Fortune will not smile on all—just on the one who draws the winning ticket or, rather, the one designated to do so by a higher power—usually the entertainment industry itself, which presents itself as ceaselessly in search of talent. Those discovered by the talent scouts and then built up by the studios are ideal types of the new, dependent middle classes. The female starlet is supposed to symbolize the secretary, though in a way which makes her seem predestined, unlike the real secretary, to wear the flowing evening gown. Thus she apprises the female spectator not only of the possibility that she, too, might appear on the screen but still more insistently of the distance between them. Only one can draw the winning lot, only one is prominent, and even though all have mathematically the same chance, it is so minimal for each individual that it is best to write it off at once and rejoice in the good fortune of someone else, who might just as well be oneself but never is. Where the culture industry still invites naïve identification, it immediately denies it. It is no longer possible to lose oneself in others. Once, film spectators saw their own wedding in that of others. Now the happy couple on the screen are specimens of the same species as everyone in the audience, but the sameness posits the insuperable separation of its human elements. The perfected similarity is the absolute difference. The identity of the species prohibits that of the individual cases. The culture industry* has sardonically realized man's species being. Everyone amounts only to those qualities by which he or she can replace everyone else: all are fungible, mere specimens. As individuals they are absolutely replaceable, pure nothingness, and are made aware of this as soon as time deprives them of their sameness. This changes the inner composition of the religion of success, which they are sternly required to uphold. The path *per aspera ad astra*, which presupposes need and effort, is increasingly replaced by the prize. The element of blindness in the routine decision as to which song is to be a hit, which extra a heroine, is celebrated by ideology. Films emphasize chance. By imposing an essential sameness on their characters, with the exception of the villain, to the point of excluding any faces which do not conform—for example, those which, like Garbo's, do not look as if they would welcome the greeting "Hello, sister"—the ideology does, it is true, make life initially easier for the spectators. They are assured that they do not need to be in any way other than they are and that they can succeed just as well without having to perform tasks of which they know themselves incapable. But at the same time they are given the hint that effort would not help them in any case, because even bourgeois success no longer has any connection to the calculable effect of their own work. They take the hint. Fundamentally, everyone recognizes chance, by which someone is sometimes lucky, as the other side of planning.* Just because society's energies have developed so far on the side of rationality that anyone might become an engineer or a manager, the choice of who is to receive from society the investment and confidence to be trained for such functions becomes entirely irrational. Chance and planning become identical since, given the sameness of people, the fortune or misfortune of the individual, right up to the top, loses all economic importance. Chance itself is planned; not in the sense that it will affect this or that particular individual but in that people believe in its control. For the planners it serves as an alibi, giving the impression that the web of transactions and measures into which life has been transformed* still leaves room for spontaneous, immediate relationships between human beings. Such freedom is symbolized in the various media of the culture industry by the arbitrary selection of average cases. In the detailed reports on the modestly luxurious pleasure trip organized by the magazine for the lucky competition winner—preferably a shorthand typist who probably won through contacts with local powers-that-be—the powerlessness of everyone is reflected. So much are the masses mere material that those in control* can raise one of them up to their heaven and cast him or her out again: let them go hang with their justice and their labor. Industry* is interested in human beings only as its customers and employees and has in fact reduced humanity as a whole, like each of its elements, to this exhaustive formula. Depending on which aspect happens to be paramount at the time, ideology stresses plan or chance, technology or life, civilization or nature. As employees people are reminded of the rational organization and must fit into it as common sense requires. As customers they are regaled, whether on the screen or in the press, with human interest stories demonstrating freedom of choice and the charm of not belonging to the system. In both cases they remain objects.

The less the culture industry has to promise and the less it can offer a meaningful explanation of life, the emptier the ideology it disseminates necessarily becomes. Even the abstract ideals of the harmony and benevolence of society are too concrete in the age of the universal advertisement. Abstractions in particular are identified as publicity devices. Language which appeals to mere truth only arouses impatience to get down to the real business behind it. Words which are not a means seem meaningless, the others seem to be fiction, untruth. Value judgments are perceived either as advertisements or as mere chatter. The noncommittal vagueness of the resulting ideology does not make it more transparent, or weaker. Its very vagueness, the quasiscientific reluctance to be pinned down to anything which cannot be verified, functions as an instrument of control. Ideology becomes the emphatic and systematic proclamation of what is. Through its inherent tendency to adopt the tone of the factual report, the culture industry makes itself the irrefutable prophet of the existing order. With consummate skill it maneuvers between the crags of demonstrable misinformation and obvious truth by faithfully duplicating appearances, the density of which blocks insight. Thus the omnipresent and impenetrable world of appearances is set up as the ideal. Ideology is split between the photographing of brute existence and the blatant lie about its meaning, a lie which is not articulated directly but drummed in by suggestion. The mere cynical reiteration of the real is enough to demonstrate its divinity. Such photological proof* may not be stringent, but it is overwhelming. Anyone who continues to doubt in face of the power of monotony is a fool. The culture industry sweeps aside objections to itself along with those to the world it neutrally duplicates. One has only the choice of conforming or being consigned to the backwoods: the provincials who oppose cinema and radio by falling back on eternal beauty and amateur theatricals have already reached the political stance toward which the members of mass culture are still being driven. This culture is hardened enough either to poke fun at the old wishful dreams, the paternal ideal no less than unconditional feeling, or to invoke them as ideology, as the occasion demands. The new ideology has the world as such as its subject. It exploits the cult of fact by describing bad existence with utmost exactitude in order to elevate it into the realm of facts. Through such elevation existence itself becomes a surrogate of meaning and justice. Beauty is whatever the camera reproduces. The disappointed hope that one might oneself be the employee who won the world trip is matched by the disappointing appearance of the exactly photographed regions through which the journey might have led. What is offered is not Italy but evidence that it exists. The film can permit itself to show the Paris in which the young American woman hopes to still her longing as a desolately barren place, in order to drive her all the more implacably into the arms of the smart American boy she might equally well have met at home. That life goes on at all, that the system, even in its most recent phase, reproduces the lives of those who constitute it instead of doing away with them straight away, is even credited to the system as its meaning and value. The ability to keep going at all becomes the justification for the blind continuation of the system, indeed, for its immutability. What is repeated is healthy—the cycle in nature as in industry. The same babies grin endlessly from magazines, and endlessly the jazz machine pounds. Despite all the progress in the techniques of representation, all the rules and specialties, all the gesticulating bustle, the bread on which the culture industry feeds humanity, remains the stone of stereotype. It lives on the cyclical, on the admittedly well-founded amazement that, in spite of everything, mothers still give birth to children, that the wheels have not yet come completely to a halt. All this consolidates the immutability of the existing circumstances. The swaying cornfields at the end of Chaplin's film on Hitler give the lie to the antifascist speech about freedom. They resemble the blond tresses of the German maidens whose outdoor life in the summer wind is photographed by Ufa. Nature, in being presented by society's control mechanism as the healing antithesis of society, is itself absorbed into that incurable society and sold off. The solemn pictorial affirmation that the trees are green, the sky is blue, and the clouds are sailing overhead already makes them cryptograms for factory chimneys and gasoline stations. Conversely, wheels and machine parts are made to gleam expressively, debased as receptacles of that leafy, cloudy soul. In this way both nature and technology are mobilized against the alleged stuffiness, the faked recollection of liberal society as a world in which people idled lasciviously in plush-lined rooms instead of taking wholesome open-air baths as they do today, or suffered breakdowns in antediluvian Benz models instead of traveling at rocket speed from where they are in any case to where it is no different. The triumph of the giant corporation* over entrepreneurial initiative is celebrated by the culture industry as the perpetuity of entrepreneurial initiative. The fight is waged against an enemy who has already been defeated, the thinking subject.* The resurrection of *Hans Sonnenstößer,** the enemy of bourgeois philistines, in Germany, and the smug coziness of *Life with Father** have one and the same meaning.

On one matter, however, this hollow ideology is utterly serious: everyone is provided for. "No one must be hungry or cold. Anyone failing to comply goes to a concentration camp." The joke from Hitler's Germany might well shine out as a maxim above all the portals of the culture industry. With naïve shrewdness it anticipates the situation characteristic of the latest society:* that it knows how to identify its true supporters. Formal freedom is guaranteed for everyone. No one has to answer officially* for what he or she thinks. However, all find themselves enclosed from early on within a system of churches, clubs, professional associations, and other relationships which amount to the most sensitive instrument of social control. Anyone who wants to avoid ruin must take care not to weigh too little in the scales of this apparatus. Otherwise he will fall behind in life and finally go under. The fact that in every career, and especially in the liberal professions, specialist knowledge as a rule goes hand in hand with a prescribed set of attitudes easily gives the misleading impression that expert knowledge is all that counts. In reality, it is a feature of the irrationally systematic nature of this society that it reproduces, passably, only the lives of its loyal members. The gradations in the standard of living correspond very precisely to the degree by which classes and individuals inwardly adhere to the system. Managers can be relied on; even the minor employee Dagwood,* who lives in reality no less than in the comic strip, is reliable. But anyone who goes hungry and suffers from cold, especially if he once had good prospects, is a marked man. He is an outsider, and—with the occasional exception of the capital crime—to be an outsider is the gravest guilt. In films such a person is, at best, an eccentric, an object of maliciously indulgent humor; but mostly he is a villain and is identified as such on his very first appearance, long before the action requires it, to forestall even the momentary misapprehension that society turns against those of good will. In fact, a kind of welfare state on a higher level is being established* today. To assert their positions people keep in motion an economy in which the extreme development of technology has made the masses in principle superfluous as producers in their own country. According to the ideological illusion, the workers, the true providers, are fed by the leaders of industry,* whom they feed. Thus the position of the individual becomes precarious. Under liberalism the poor were regarded as lazy; today they are automatically suspect. Anyone who is not provided for outside the concentration camp belongs inside it, or at any rate in the hell of the most demeaning labor and the slums. The culture industry, however, reflects society's positive and negative provision* for those it administers as direct human solidarity in the world of honest folk. No one is forgotten, everywhere are neighbors, social welfare officers, Dr Gillespies, and armchair philosophers with their hearts in the right place who, with their kindly man-to-man interventions, turn the socially perpetuated wretchedness into remediable individual cases, unless even that is ruled out by the personal depravity of those concerned. The managed provision of friendly care, administered by every factory as a means of increasing production, brings the last private impulse under social control; by being given the appearance of immediacy, the relationships of people within production are returned to the private sphere. Such "winter aid"* casts its conciliatory shadow over the films and broadcasts of the culture industry long before such care is transferred in totalitarian style from the factory to society itself. The great helpers and benefactors of humanity, whose scholarly and scientific achievements have to be embellished by scriptwriters as simple acts of compassion to wring from them a fictitious human interest, function as stand-ins for the leaders of nations, who ultimately decree the abolition of compassion and succeed in preventing all infections by exterminating the last of the sick.

The emphasis on the heart of gold is society's way of admitting the suffering it creates: everyone knows that they are helpless within the system, and ideology must take account of this. Far from merely concealing the suffering under the cloak of improvised comradeship, the culture industry stakes its company pride on looking it manfully in the eye and acknowledging it with unflinching composure. This posture of steadfast endurance justifies the world which that posture makes necessary. Such is the world—so hard, yet therefore so wonderful, so healthy. The lie does not shrink back even from tragedy. Just as totalitarian society does not abolish the suffering of its members, but registers and plans it, mass culture does the same with tragedy. Hence the persistent borrowings from art. Art supplies the tragic substance which pure entertainment cannot provide on its own yet which it needs if it is to adhere to its principle of meticulously duplicating appearance. Tragedy, included in society's calculations and affirmed as a moment of the world, becomes a blessing. It deflects the charge that truth is glossed over, whereas in fact it is appropriated with cynical regret. It imparts an element of interest to the insipidity of censored happiness and makes that interest manageable. To the consumer who has seen culturally better days it offers the surrogate of long-abolished depth, and to regular moviegoers the veneer of culture they need for purposes of prestige. To all it grants the solace that human fate in its strength and authenticity is possible even now* and its unflinching depiction inescapable. The unbroken surface of existence, in the duplication of which ideology consists solely today, appears all the more splendid, glorious, and imposing the more it is imbued with necessary suffering. It takes on the aspect of fate. Tragedy is leveled down to the threat to destroy anyone who does not conform, whereas its paradoxical meaning once lay in hopeless resistance to mythical threat. Tragic fate becomes the just punishment into which bourgeois aesthetics has always longed to transform it. The morality of mass culture has come down to it from yesterday's children's books. In the first-class production the villain is dressed up as the hysteric who, in a study of ostensibly clinical exactitude, seeks to trick her more realistic rival out of her life's happiness and who herself suffers a quite untheatrical death. To be sure, only at the top are things managed as scientifically as this. Further down, the resources are scarcer. There tragedy has its teeth drawn without social psychology. Just as any honest Hungarian-Viennese operetta must have its tragic finale in the second act, leaving nothing for the third but the righting of misunderstandings, mass culture gives tragedy permanent employment as routine. The obvious existence of a formula is enough in itself to allay the concern that tragedy might still be untamed. The housewife's description of the recipe for drama as "getting into trouble and out again" encompasses the whole of mass culture from the weak-minded women's serial* to its highest productions. Even the worst outcome, which once had better intentions, still confirms the established order and corrupts tragedy, whether because the irregular lover pays for her brief happiness with death or because the sad end in the picture makes the indestructibility of actual life shine all the more brightly. Tragic cinema is becoming truly a house of moral correction. The masses, demoralized by existence under the pressure of the system* and manifesting civilization only as compulsively rehearsed behavior in which rage and rebelliousness everywhere show through, are to be kept in order by the spectacle of implacable life and the exemplary conduct of those it crushes. Culture has always contributed to the subduing of revolutionary as well as of barbaric instincts. Industrial culture does something more. It inculcates the conditions on which implacable life is allowed to be lived at all. Individuals must use their general satiety as a motive for abandoning themselves to the collective power of which they are sated. The permanently hopeless situations which grind down filmgoers in daily life are transformed by their reproduction, in some unknown way, into a promise that they may continue to exist. One needs only to become aware of one's nullity, to subscribe to one's own defeat, and one is already a party to it. Society is made up of the desperate and thus falls prey to rackets. In a few of the most significant German novels of the prefascistic era, such as *Berlin Alexanderplatz* and *Kleiner Mann, was nun?*, this tendency was as vividly evident as in the mediocre film and in the procedures of jazz. Fundamentally, they all present the self-mockery of man. The possibility of becoming an economic subject, an entrepreneur, a proprietor, is entirely liquidated. Right down to the small grocery, the independent firm on the running and inheriting of which the bourgeois family and the position of its head were founded, has fallen into hopeless dependence. All have become employees, and in the civilization of employees the dignity of the father, dubious in any case, ceases to be. The behavior of the individual toward the racket, whether commercial, professional, or political, both before and after admittance to it; the gestures of the leader before the masses, of the lover before the woman he woos, are taking on peculiarly masochistic traits. The attitude all are forced to adopt in order to demonstrate ever again their moral fitness for this society is reminiscent of that of boys during admission to a tribe; circling under the blows of the priest, they wear stereotypical smiles. Existence in late capitalism is a permanent rite of initiation. Everyone must show that they identify wholeheartedly with the power which beats them. This is inherent in the principle of syncopation in jazz, which mocks the act of stumbling while elevating it to the norm. The eunuch-like voice of the radio crooner, the handsome suitor of the heiress, who falls into the swimming pool wearing his tuxedo, are models for those who want to make themselves into that to which the system* breaks them. Everyone can be like the omnipotent society, everyone can be happy if only they hand themselves over to it body and soul and relinquish their claim to happiness. In their weakness society recognizes its own strength and passes some of it back to them. Their lack of resistance certifies them as reliable customers. Thus is tragedy abolished. Once, the antithesis between individual and society made up its substance. Tragedy glorified "courage and freedom of feeling in face of a mighty foe, sublime adversity, a problem which awakened dread."[4] Today tragedy has been dissipated in the void of the false identity of society and subject, the horror of which is still just fleetingly visible in the vacuous semblance of the tragic. But the miracle of integration, the permanent benevolence of those in command,* who admit the unresisting subject while he chokes down his unruliness—all this signifies fascism. Fascism lurks in the humaneness with which Döblin allows his protagonist Biberkopf to find refuge, no less than in films with a social slant. The ability to slip through, to survive one's own ruin, which has superseded tragedy, is ingrained in the new generation; its members are capable of any work, since the work process allows them to become attached to none. One is reminded of the sad pliability of the soldier returning home, unaffected by the war, of the casual laborer who finally joins the clandestine groups and the paramilitary organizations. The liquidation of tragedy confirms the abolition of the individual.

It is not only the standardized mode of production of the culture industry which makes the individual illusory in its products. Individuals are tolerated only as far as their wholehearted identity with the universal is beyond question. From the standardized improvisation in jazz to the original film personality who must have a lock of hair straying over her eyes so that she can be recognized as such, pseudoindividuality reigns. The individual trait is reduced to the ability of the universal so completely to mold the accidental that it can be recognized as accidental. The sulky taciturnity or the elegant walk of the individual who happens to be on show is serially produced like the Yale locks which differ by fractions of a millimeter. The peculiarity of the self is a socially conditioned monopoly commodity misrepresented as natural. It is reduced to the moustache, the French accent, the deep voice of the prostitute, the "Lubitsch touch"—like a fingerprint on the otherwise uniform identity cards to which the lives and faces of all individuals, from the film star to the convict, have been reduced by the power of the universal. Pseudoindividuality is a precondition for apprehending and detoxifying tragedy: only because individuals are none but mere intersections of universal tendencies is it possible to reabsorb them smoothly into the universal. Mass culture thereby reveals the fictitious quality which has characterized the individual throughout the bourgeois era and is wrong only in priding itself on this murky harmony between universal and particular. The principle of individuality was contradictory from the outset. First, no individuation was ever really achieved. The class-determined form of self-preservation maintained everyone at the level of mere species being. Every bourgeois* character expressed the same thing, even and especially when deviating from it: the harshness of competitive society. The individual, on whom society was supported, itself bore society's taint; in the individual's apparent freedom he was the product of society's economic and social apparatus. Power has always invoked the existing power relationships when seeking the approval of those subjected to power. At the same time, the advance of bourgeois society has promoted the development of the individual. Against the will of those controlling it, technology has changed human beings from children into persons. But all such progress of individuation has been at the expense of the individuality in whose name it took place, leaving behind nothing except individuals' determination to pursue their own purposes alone. The citizens whose lives are split between business and private life, their private life between ostentation and intimacy, their intimacy between the sullen community of marriage and the bitter solace of being entirely alone, at odds with themselves and with everyone, are virtually already Nazis, who are at once enthusiastic and fed up, or the city dwellers of today, who can imagine friendship only as "social contact" between the inwardly unconnected. The culture industry can only manipulate individuality so successfully because the fractured nature of society has always been reproduced within it. In the ready-made faces of film heroes and private persons fabricated according to magazine-cover stereotypes, a semblance of individuality—in which no one believes in any case—is fading, and the love for such hero-models is nourished by the secret satisfaction that the effort of individuation is at last being replaced by the admittedly more breathless one of imitation. The hope that the contradictory, disintegrating person could not survive for generations, that the psychological fracture within it must split the system itself, and that human beings might refuse to tolerate the mendacious substitution of the stereotype for the individual—that hope is vain. The unity of the personality has been recognized as illusory since Shakespeare's Hamlet. In the synthetically manufactured physiognomies of today the fact that the concept of human life ever existed is already forgotten. For centuries society has prepared for Victor Mature and Mickey Rooney.* They come to fulfill the very individuality they destroy.

The heroizing of the average forms part of the cult of cheapness. The highest-paid stars resemble advertisements for unnamed merchandise. Not for nothing are they often chosen from the ranks of commercial models. The dominant taste derives its ideal from the advertisement, from commodified beauty. Socrates' dictum that beauty is the useful has at last been ironically fulfilled. The cinema publicizes the cultural conglomerate* as a totality, while the radio advertises individually the products for whose sake the cultural system exists. For a few coins you can see the film which cost millions, for even less you can buy the chewing gum behind which stand the entire riches of the world, and the sales of which increase those riches still further. Through universal suffrage the vast funding of armies is generally known and approved, if *in absentia*, while prostitution behind the lines is not permitted. The best orchestras in the world, which are none, are delivered free of charge to the home. All this mockingly resembles the land of milk and honey as the national community apes the human one. Something is served up for everyone.* A provincial visitor's comment on the old Berlin Metropoltheater that "it is remarkable what can be done for the money" has long since been adopted by the culture industry and elevated to the substance of production itself. Not only is a production always accompanied by triumphant celebration that it has been possible at all, but to a large extent it is that triumph itself. To put on a show means to show everyone what one has and can do. The show is still a fairground, but one incurably infected by culture. Just as people lured by the fairground crier overcame their disappointment inside the booths with a brave smile, since they expected it in any case, the movie-goer remains tolerantly loyal to the institution. But the cheapness of mass-produced luxury articles, and its complement, universal fraud, are changing the commodity character of art itself. That character is not new: it is the fact that art now dutifully admits to being a commodity, abjures its autonomy and proudly takes its place among consumer goods, that has the charm of novelty. Art was only ever able to exist as a separate sphere in its bourgeois form. Even its freedom, as negation of the social utility which is establishing itself through the market, is essentially conditioned by the commodity economy. Pure works of art, which negated the commodity character of society by simply following their own inherent laws, were at the same time always commodities. To the extent that, up to the eighteenth century, artists were protected from the market by patronage, they were subject to the patrons and their purposes instead. The purposelessness of the great modern work of art is sustained by the anonymity of the market. The latter's demands are so diversely mediated that the artist is exempted from any particular claim, although only to a certain degree, since his autonomy, being merely tolerated, has been attended throughout bourgeois history by a moment of untruth, which has culminated now in the social liquidation of art. The mortally sick Beethoven, who flung away a novel by Walter Scott with the cry: "The fellow writes for money," while himself proving an extremely experienced and tenacious businessman in commercializing the last quartets—works representing the most extreme repudiation of the market—offers the most grandiose example of the unity of the opposites of market and autonomy in bourgeois art. The artists who succumb to ideology are precisely those who conceal this contradiction instead of assimilating it into the consciousness of their own production, as Beethoven did: he improvised on "Rage over a Lost Penny" and derived the metaphysical injunction "It must be," which seeks aesthetically to annul the world's compulsion by taking that burden onto itself, from his housekeeper's demand for her monthly wages. The principle of idealist aesthetics, purposiveness without purpose,* reverses the schema socially adopted by bourgeois art: purposelessness for purposes dictated by the market. In the demand for entertainment and relaxation, purpose has finally consumed the realm of the purposeless. But as the demand for the marketability of art becomes total, a shift in the inner economic composition of cultural commodities* is becoming apparent. For the use which is made of the work of art in antagonistic society is largely that of confirming the very existence of the useless, which art's total subsumption under usefulness has abolished. In adapting itself entirely to need, the work of art defrauds human beings in advance of the liberation from the principle of utility which it is supposed to bring about. What might be called use value in the reception of cultural assets is being replaced* by exchange value; enjoyment is giving way to being there and being in the know, connoisseurship by enhanced prestige. The consumer becomes the ideology of the amusement industry, whose institutions he or she cannot escape.* One has to have seen Mrs. Miniver,* just as one must subscribe to *Life* and *Time*. Everything is perceived only from the point of view that it can serve as something else, however vaguely that other thing might be envisaged. Everything has value only in so far as it can be exchanged, not in so far as it is something in itself. For consumers the use value of art, its essence, is a fetish, and the fetish—the social valuation which they mistake for the merit of works of art—becomes its only use value, the only quality they enjoy. In this way the commodity character of art disintegrates just as it is fully realized. Art becomes a species of commodity, worked up and adapted to industrial production, saleable and exchangeable; but art as the species of commodity which exists in order to be sold yet not for sale becomes something hypocritically unsaleable as soon as the business transaction is no longer merely its intention but its sole principle. The Toscanini performance on the radio is, in a sense, unsaleable. One listens to it for nothing, and each note of the symphony is accompanied, as it were, by the sublime advertisement that the symphony is not being interrupted by advertisements—"This concert is brought to you as a public service." The deception* takes place indirectly *via* the profit of all the united automobile and soap manufacturers, on whose payments the stations survive, and, of course, *via* the increased sales of the electrical industry as the producer of the receiver sets. Radio, the progressive latecomer to mass culture, is drawing conclusions which film's pseudomarket at present denies that industry. The technical structure of the commercial radio system* makes it immune to liberal deviations of the kind the film industry can still permit itself in its own preserve. Film is a private enterprise which already represents the sovereign whole,* in which respect it has some advantages over the other individual combines.* Chesterfield is merely the nation's cigarette, but the radio is its mouthpiece. In the total assimilation of culture products into the commodity sphere radio makes no attempt to purvey its products as commodities. In America it levies no duty from the public. It thereby takes on the deceptive form of a disinterested, impartial authority, which fits fascism like a glove. In fascism radio becomes the universal mouthpiece of the *Führer*; in the loudspeakers on the street his voice merges with the howl of sirens proclaiming panic, from which modern propaganda is hard to distinguish in any case. The National Socialists knew that broadcasting gave their cause stature as the printing press did to the Reformation. The *Führer's* metaphysical charisma, invented by the sociology of religion,* turned out finally to be merely the omnipresence of his radio addresses, which demonically parodies that of the divine spirit. The gigantic fact that the speech penetrates everywhere replaces its content, as the benevolent act of the Toscanini broadcast supplants its content, the symphony. No listener can apprehend the symphony's true coherence, while the *Führer's* address is in any case a lie. To posit the human word as absolute, the false commandment, is the immanent tendency of radio. Recommendation becomes command. The promotion of identical commodities under different brand names, the scientifically endorsed praise of the laxative in the slick voice of the announcer between the overtures of *La Traviata* and *Rienzi*, has become untenable if only for its silliness. One day the *Diktat* of production, the specific advertisement, veiled by the semblance of choice, can finally become the *Führer's* overt command. In a society of large-scale fascistic rackets which agree among themselves on how much of the national product is to be allocated to providing for the needs of the people, to invite the people to use a particular soap powder would, in the end, seem anachronistic. In a more modern, less ceremonious style, the *Führer* directly orders both the holocaust and the supply of trash.

Today works of art, suitably packaged like political slogans, are pressed on a reluctant public at reduced prices by the culture industry; they are opened up for popular enjoyment like parks. However, the erosion of their genuine commodity character does not mean that they would be abolished in the life of a free society but that the last barrier to their debasement as cultural assets has now been removed. The abolition of educational privilege by disposing of culture at bargain prices does not admit the masses to the preserves from which they were formerly exclud- ed but, under the existing social conditions, contributes to the decay of education and the progress of barbaric incoherence. Someone who in the nineteenth or early twentieth century spent money to attend a drama or a concert, paid the performance at least as much respect as the money spent. The citizen who wanted a return for his outlay might occasionally try to establish some connection to the work. The guidebooks to Wagner's music dramas or the commentaries on *Faust* bear witness to this. They form a transition to the biographical glaze applied to works of art and the other practices to which works of art are subjected today. Even when the art business was in the bloom of youth, use value* was not dragged along as a mere appendage by exchange value but was developed as a precondition of the latter, to the social benefit of works of art. As long as it was expen- sive, art kept the citizen within some bounds. That is now over. Art's un- bounded proximity to those exposed to it, no longer mediated by money, completes the alienation between work and consumer, which resemble each other in triumphant reification. In the culture industry respect is van- ishing along with criticism: the latter gives way to mechanical expertise, the former to the forgetful cult of celebrities. For consumers, nothing is expensive any more. Nevertheless, they are dimly aware that the less some- thing costs, the less it can be a gift to them. The twofold mistrust of tra- ditional culture as ideology mingles with that of industrialized culture as fraud. Reduced to mere adjuncts, the degraded works of art are secretly rejected by their happy recipients along with the junk the medium has made them resemble. The public should rejoice that there is so much to see and hear. And indeed, everything is to be had. The "screenos"* and cinema vaudevilles, the competitions in recognizing musical extracts, the free magazines, rewards, and gift articles handed out to the listeners of cer- tain radio programs are not mere accidents, but continue what is happen- ing to the culture products themselves. The symphony is becoming the prize for listening to the radio at all, and if the technology had its way the film would already be delivered to the apartment on the model of the radio.* It is moving towards the commercial system. Television points the way to a development which easily enough could push the Warner broth-

ers* into the doubtless unwelcome position of little theatre performers and
cultural conservatives. However, the pursuit of prizes has already left its
imprint on consumer behavior. Because culture presents itself as a bonus,
with unquestioned private and social benefits, its reception has become a
matter of taking one's chances. The public crowds forward for fear of missing something. What that might be is unclear, but, at any rate, only those
who join in have any chance. Fascism, however, hopes* to reorganize the
gift-receivers trained by the culture industry into its enforced adherents.

   Culture is a paradoxical commodity. It is so completely subject to the
law of exchange that it is no longer exchanged; it is so blindly equated with
use that it can no longer be used. For this reason it merges with the advertisement. The more meaningless the latter appears under monopoly, the
more omnipotent culture becomes. Its motives are economic enough.
That life could continue without the whole culture industry is too certain;
the satiation and apathy it generates among consumers are too great. It can
do little to combat this from its own resources. Advertising is its elixir of
life. But because its product ceaselessly reduces the pleasure it promises as
a commodity to that mere promise, it finally coincides with the advertisement it needs on account of its own inability to please. In the competitive
society advertising performed a social service in orienting the buyer in the
market, facilitating choice and helping the more efficient but unknown
supplier to find customers. It did not merely cost labor time, but saved it.
Today, when the free market is coming to an end, those in control of the
system are entrenching themselves in advertising.* It strengthens the bond
which shackles consumers to the big combines. Only those who can keep
paying the exorbitant fees charged by the advertising agencies, and most
of all by radio itself, that is, those who are already part of the system or are
co-opted into it by the decisions of banks and industrial capital, can enter
the pseudomarket as sellers. The costs of advertising, which finally flow
back into the pockets of the combines,* spare them the troublesome task
of subduing unwanted outsiders; they guarantee that the wielders of influence remain among their peers, not unlike the resolutions of economic
councils* which control the establishment and continuation of businesses
in the totalitarian state. Advertising today is a negative principle, a blocking device: anything which does not bear its seal of approval is economically suspect. All-pervasive advertising is certainly not needed to acquaint

people with the goods on offer, the varieties of which are limited in any case. It benefits the selling of goods only directly. The termination of a familiar advertising campaign by an individual firm represents a loss of prestige, and is indeed an offence against the discipline which the leading clique imposes on its members. In wartime, commodities which can no longer be supplied continue to be advertised merely as a display of industrial power. At such times the subsidizing of the ideological media is more important than the repetition of names.* Through their ubiquitous use under the pressure of the system, advertising techniques have invaded the idiom, the "style" of the culture industry. So complete is their triumph that in key positions it is no longer even explicit: the imposing buildings of the big companies,* floodlit advertisements in stone, are free of advertising, merely displaying the illuminated company initials on their pinnacles, with no further need of self-congratulation. By contrast, the buildings surviving from the nineteenth century, the architecture of which still shamefully reveals their utility as consumer goods, their function as accommodation, are covered from basement to above roof level with hoardings and banners: the landscape becomes a mere background for signboards and symbols. Advertising becomes simply the art with which Goebbels presciently equated it, *l'art pour l'art*, advertising for advertising's sake, the pure representation of social power. In the influential American magazines *Life* and *Fortune* the images and texts of advertisements are, at a cursory glance, hardly distinguishable from the editorial section. The enthusiastic and unpaid picture story about the living habits and personal grooming of celebrities, which wins them new fans, is editorial, while the advertising pages rely on photographs and data so factual and lifelike that they represent the ideal of information to which the editorial section only aspires. Every film is a preview of the next, which promises yet again to unite the same heroic couple under the same exotic sun: anyone arriving late cannot tell whether he is watching the trailer or the real thing. The montage character of the culture industry, the synthetic, controlled manner in which its products are assembled—factory-like not only in the film studio but also, virtually, in the compilation of the cheap biographies, journalistic novels, and hit songs—predisposes it to advertising: the individual moment, in being detachable, replaceable, estranged even technically from any coherence of meaning, lends itself to purposes outside the work. The special effect, the trick, the isolated and repeatable individual performance have always conspired with the exhibition of commodities for advertising purposes, and today every close-up of a film actress is an advert for her name, every hit song a plug for its tune. Advertising and the culture industry are merging technically no less than economically. In both, the same thing appears in countless places, and the mechanical repetition of the same culture product is already that of the same propaganda slogan. In both, under the dictate of effectiveness, technique is becoming psychotechnique, a procedure for manipulating human beings. In both, the norms of the striking yet familiar, the easy but catchy, the worldly wise but straightforward hold good; everything is directed at overpowering a customer conceived as distracted or resistant.

Through the language they speak, the customers make their own contribution to culture as advertising. For the more completely language coincides with communication, the more words change from substantial carriers of meaning to signs devoid of qualities; the more purely and transparently they communicate what they designate, the more impenetrable they become. The demythologizing of language, as an element of the total process of enlightenment, reverts to magic. In magic word and content were at once different from each other and indissolubly linked. Concepts like melancholy, history, indeed, life, were apprehended in the word which both set them apart and preserved them. Its particular form constituted and reflected them at the same time. The trenchant distinction which declares the word itself fortuitous and its allocation to its object arbitrary does away with the superstitious commingling of word and thing. Anything in a given sequence of letters which goes beyond the correlation to the event designated is banished as unclear and as verbal metaphysics. As a result, the word, which henceforth is allowed only to designate something and not to mean it, becomes so fixated on the object that it hardens to a formula. This affects language and subject matter equally. Instead of raising a matter to the level of experience, the purified word exhibits it as a case of an abstract moment, and everything else, severed from now defunct expression by the demand for pitiless clarity, therefore withers in reality also. The outside-left in football, the blackshirt,* the Hitler Youth member, and others of their kind are no more than what they are called. If, before its rationalization, the word had set free not only longing but lies, in its rationalized form it has become a straightjacket more for longing than for lies. The blindness and muteness of the data to which positivism reduces the world passes over into language itself, which is limited to registering those data. Thus relationships themselves become impenetrable, taking on an impact, a power of adhesion and repulsion which makes them resemble their extreme antithesis, spells. They act once more like the practices of a kind of sorcery, whether the name of a diva is concocted in the studio on the basis of statistical data, or welfare government is averted by the use of taboo-laden words such as "bureaucracy" and "intellectuals," or vileness exonerates itself by invoking the name of a homeland. The name, to which magic most readily attaches, is today undergoing a chemical change. It is being transformed into arbitrary, manipulable designations, the power of which, although calculable, is for that reason as willful as that of archaic names. First names, the archaic residues, have been brought up to date either by stylizing them into advertising brands—film stars' surnames have become first names—or by standardizing them collectively. By contrast, the bourgeois, family name which, instead of being a trademark, individualized its bearers by relating them to their own prehistory, sounds old-fashioned. In Americans it arouses a curious unease. To conceal the uncomfortable distance existing between particular people* they call themselves Bob and Harry, like replaceable members of teams. Such forms of interaction reduce human beings to the brotherhood of the sporting public, which protects them from true fraternity. Signification, the only function of the word admitted by semantics, is consummated in the sign. Its character as sign is reinforced by the speed with which linguistic models are put into circulation from above. Whether folksongs are rightly or wrongly called upper-class culture which has come down in the world, their elements have at least taken on their popular form in a long, highly mediated process of experience. The dissemination of popular songs, by contrast, is practically instantaneous. The American term "fad" for fashions which catch on epidemically—inflamed by the action of highly concentrated economic powers—referred to this phenomenon long before totalitarian advertising bosses had laid down the general lines of culture in their countries. If the German fascists launch a word like "intolerable" [*Untragbar*] over the loudspeakers one day, the whole nation is saying "intolerable" the next. On the same pattern, the nations against which the German *Blitzkrieg* was directed have adopted it in their own jargon. The universal repetition of the term denoting such measures makes the measures, too, familiar, just as, at the time of the free market, the brand name on everyone's lips increased sales. The blind and rapidly spreading repetition of designated words links advertising to the totalitarian slogan. The layer of experience which made words human like those who spoke them has been stripped away, and in its prompt appropriation language takes on the coldness which hitherto was peculiar to billboards and the advertising sections of newspapers. Countless people use words and expressions which they either have ceased to understand at all or use only according to their behavioral functions, just as trademarks adhere all the more compulsively to their objects the less their linguistic meaning is apprehended. The Minister of Public Education speaks ignorantly of "dynamic forces," and the hit songs sing endlessly of "reverie" and "rhapsody," hitching their popularity to the magic of the incomprehensible as if to some deep intimation of a higher life. Other stereotypes, such as "memory," are still partly comprehended, but become detached from the experience which might fulfill them. They obtrude into the spoken language like enclaves. On the German radio of Flesch and Hitler they are discernible in the affected diction of the announcer, who pronounces phrases like "Goodnight, listeners," or "This is the Hitler Youth speaking," or even "the *Führer*" with an inflection which passes into the mother tongue of millions. In such turns of phrase the last bond between sedimented experience and language, which still exerted a reconciling influence in dialect in the nineteenth century, is severed. By contrast, in the hands of the editor whose supple opinions have promoted him to the status of *Schriftleiter*,* German words become petrified and alien. In any word one can distinguish how far it has been disfigured by the fascist "folk" community. By now, of course, such language* has become universal, totalitarian. The violence done to words is no longer audible in them. The radio announcer does not need to talk in an affected voice; indeed, he would be impossible if his tone differed from that of his designated listeners. This means, however, that the language and gestures of listeners and spectators are more deeply permeated by the patterns of the culture industry than ever before, in nuances still beyond the reach of experimental methods. Today the culture industry has taken over the civilizing inheritance of the frontier and entrepreneurial democracy, whose receptivity to intellectual deviations was never too highly developed. All are free to dance and amuse themselves, just as, since the historical neutralization of religion, they have been free to join any of the countless sects. But freedom to choose an ideology, which always reflects economic coercion, everywhere proves to be freedom to be the same. The way in which the young girl accepts and performs the obligatory date, the tone of voice used on the telephone and in the most intimate situations, the choice of words in conversation, indeed, the whole inner life compartmentalized according to the categories of vulgarized depth psychology, bears witness to the attempt to turn oneself into an apparatus meeting the requirements of success, an apparatus which, even in its unconscious impulses, conforms to the model presented by the culture industry. The most intimate reactions of human beings have become so entirely reified, even to themselves, that the idea of anything peculiar to them survives only in extreme abstraction: personality means hardly more than dazzling white teeth and freedom from body odor and emotions. That is the triumph of advertising in the culture industry: the compulsive imitation by consumers of cultural commodities which, at the same time, they recognize as false.*

Elements of Anti-Semitism:
Limits of Enlightenment

I

Anti-Semitism today is for some a question affecting human destiny and for others a mere pretext. For the fascists the Jews are not a minority but the antirace, the negative principle as such; on their extermination the world's happiness depends. Diametrically opposed to this is the thesis that the Jews, free of national or racial features, form a group through religious belief and tradition and nothing else. Jewish traits relate to Eastern Jews, and only to those not yet assimilated. Both doctrines are true and false at the same time.

The first is true in the sense that fascism has made it true. The Jews are today the group which, in practice and in theory, draws to itself the destructive urge which the wrong social order spontaneously produces. They are branded as absolute evil by absolute evil. In this sense they are indeed the chosen people. Now that power is no longer needed for economic reasons,* the Jews are designated as its absolute object, existing merely for the exercise of power. The workers,* who are the real target, are understandably not told as much to their faces; the blacks must be kept in their place, but the Jews are to be wiped from the face of the earth, and the call to exterminate them like vermin finds an echo among the prospective fascists of all countries. In the image of the Jew which the racial nationalists hold up before the world they express their own essence. Their craving is for exclusive ownership, appropriation,* unlimited power, and at any price. The Jew, burdened with his tormentors' guilt, mocked as their lord, they nail to the cross, endlessly repeating a sacrifice in whose power they are unable to believe.

The other, liberal thesis is true as an idea. It contains an image of the society in which rage would no longer reproduce itself or seek qualities on which to be discharged.* But by assuming the unity of humanity to have been already realized in principle, the liberal thesis serves as an apology for the existing order. The attempt to avert the direst threat by minority policies and other democratic measures is ambiguous as is the defensive strategy of the last liberal citizens. Their powerlessness attracts the enemy of powerlessness. The mode of life and appearance of the Jews compromise the existing universal by deficient adaptation. Their inflexible adherence to their own order of life has placed them in an insecure relationship to the prevailing one. They expected to be sustained by that order without subscribing to it. Their relationship to the dominant nations was one of greed and fear. Yet whenever they sacrificed their difference to the prevailing mode, the successfully adapted Jews took on in exchange the cold, stoical character which existing society* imposes on human beings. The dialectical intertwinement of enlightenment and power, the dual relationship of progress to both cruelty and liberation, which has been brought home to the Jews no less by the great exponents of enlightenment than by democratic popular movements, manifests itself in the makeup of the assimilated Jews themselves. The enlightened self-control with which adapted Jews effaced within themselves the painful scars of domination by others, a kind of second circumcision, made them forsake their own dilapidated community and wholeheartedly embrace the life of the modern bourgeoisie, which was already advancing ineluctably toward a reversion to pure oppression and reorganization into an exclusively racial entity. Race is not, as the racial nationalists claim, an immediate, natural peculiarity. Rather, it is a regression to nature as mere violence, to the hidebound particularism which, in the existing order,* constitutes precisely the universal. Race today is the self-assertion of the bourgeois individual, integrated into the barbaric collective. The harmonious society to which the liberal Jews declared their allegiance has finally been granted to them in the form of the national community. They believed that only anti-Semitism disfigured this order, which in reality cannot exist without disfiguring human beings.

The persecution of the Jews, like any persecution, cannot be separated from that order.* Its essence, however it may hide itself at times, is the violence which today is openly revealed.

II

Anti-Semitism as a popular movement has always been driven by the urge of which its instigators accuse the social democrats: to make everyone the same. Those without the power to command must fare no better than ordinary people. From the German civil servant to the Negroes in Harlem, those avidly emulating their betters have always known that they would really gain nothing but the satisfaction of seeing others no better off than themselves. The Aryanization of Jewish property, which in any case primarily benefited those at the top, enriched the masses in the Third Reich hardly more than the wretched booty pillaged from Jewish quarters enriched the Cossacks. The real benefit it brought was a half-understood ideology. That the demonstration of its economic futility heightened rather than moderated the attraction of the racialist panacea points to its true nature: it does not help human beings but assuages their urge to destroy. The actual advantage enjoyed by the racialist comrade is that his rage will be sanctioned by the collective. The less he gains in any other way, the more obstinately, against better knowledge, he clings to the movement. Anti-Semitism has proved immune to the charge of inadequate profitability. For the common people it is a luxury.

Its usefulness for the rulers is evident. It serves as a distraction, a cheap means of corruption, a terrorist warning. The respectable rackets condone it, the disreputable ones* carry it out. But the form of the mentality, both social and individual, which manifests itself in anti-Semitism, the primeval-historical entrapment from which it is a desperate attempt to escape, remains wholly obscure. If a malady so deeply embedded in civilization is not properly accounted for by knowledge, the individual, too, though he may be as well intentioned as the victim himself, cannot mitigate it through understanding. The plausibly rational, economic, and political explanations and counterarguments—however correct their individual observations—cannot appease it, since rationality itself, through its link to power, is submerged in the same malady. Whether blindly dealing out blows or blindly fending them off, persecutors and victims form part of the same calamitous cycle. Anti-Semitic behavior is unleashed in situations in which blinded people, deprived of subjectivity, are let loose as subjects. Their actions—for those involved—are lethal yet meaningless reactions, of the kind which behaviorists register but fail to interpret. Anti-Semitism is a well-rehearsed pattern, indeed, a ritual of civilization, and the pogroms are the true ritual murders. They demonstrate the impotence of what might have restrained them—reflection, meaning, ultimately truth. The mindless pastime of beating people to death confirms the drab existence to which one merely conforms.

The blindness of anti-Semitism, its lack of intention, lends a degree of truth to the explanation of the movement as a release valve. Rage is vented on those who are both conspicuous and unprotected. And just as, depending on the constellation, the victims are interchangeable: vagrants,* Jews, Protestants, Catholics, so each of them can replace the murderer, in the same blind lust for killing, as soon as he feels the power of representing the norm. There is no authentic anti-Semitism, and certainly no born anti-Semite. The older adults to whom the call for Jewish blood has become second nature are as ignorant of the reason as the young people who have to shed it. The high-placed instigators, who know the reason, neither hate the Jews nor love their own followers. The latter, however, who always go short, economically and sexually, hate without end; they find relaxation unbearable because they do not know fulfillment. Indeed, the organized robbers and murderers are animated by a kind of dynamic idealism. Setting out on their pillages, they construct a grandiose ideology for what they do, with fatuous talk of saving the family, the fatherland, humanity. But as they remain the dupes they secretly suspect themselves to be, their pitiful rational motive, the theft which was supposed to rationalize the deed, is finally discarded entirely, and the rationalization becomes truthful against its will. The obscure impulse which was always more congenial to them than reason takes them over completely. The rational island sinks beneath the flood, and those desperately floundering now appear only as defenders of truth, restorers of the earth, which has to be reformed to its farthest corners. All living things become material for their ghastly duty, which now flinches at nothing. Action becomes a purpose in itself, cloaking its own purposelessness. Anti-Semitism always starts with an appeal to complete the task. Anti-Semitism and totality have always been profoundly connected. Blindness encompasses everything because it comprehends nothing.

Liberalism had granted the Jews property, but without the authority to command. The purpose of human rights was to promise happiness even where power was lacking. Because the cheated masses are dimly aware that this promise, being universal, remains a lie as long as classes exist, it arouses their anger; they feel themselves scorned. They must constantly repress the thought of that happiness, even as a possibility, an idea, and they deny it all the more fiercely the more its time has come. Wherever it appears to be realized amid the systematic deprivation, they must reenact the suppression which has been applied to their own longing. Whatever that reenactment is directed against, however unhappy it may itself be—Ahasuerus and Mignon, exoticism which evokes the promised land, beauty which summons the thought of sex, the animal whose hint of promiscuity condemns it as repulsive—draws down on itself the destructive fury of the civilized, who can never fully complete the painful process of civilization. To those who compulsively control it, tormented nature provocatively reflects back the appearance of powerless happiness. The idea of happiness without power is unendurable because it alone would be happiness. The fantasy of the conspiracy of lascivious Jewish bankers who finance Bolshevism is a sign of innate powerlessness, the good life an emblem of happiness. These are joined by the image of the intellectual, who appears to enjoy in thought what the others deny themselves and is spared the sweat of toil and bodily strength. The banker and the intellectual, money and mind, the exponents of circulation, are the disowned wishful image of those mutilated by power, an image which power uses to perpetuate itself.

III

The present society, in which primitive religious feelings, new cults, and the legacy of revolutions are peddled in the market, in which the fascist leaders barter the land and lives of nations behind locked doors while the public lulled by their radio sets calculate the cost; this society in which even the word which unmasks it doubles as an invitation to join a political racket; in which no longer is politics merely business but business is the whole of politics—this society is scandalized by the Jew with his obsolete shopkeeper's mannerisms, labeling him a materialist, a haggler, who should make way for the pioneering spirit of those who have elevated business to an absolute.

Bourgeois anti-Semitism has a specific economic purpose: to conceal domination in production. If in earlier epochs the rulers were directly repressive, so that they not only left work exclusively to the lower orders but declared it the ignominy it always was under domination, in the age of mercantilism the absolute monarch transformed himself into the supreme master of manufactories. Production became presentable at court. Finally, as bourgeois, the masters replaced their colorful robes with civilian dress. Work is no disgrace, they said—the more rationally to take possession of* that of others. Aligning themselves with the productive elements, they remained the parasites of old.* The factory owner ventured and raked in like a great merchant or banker. He calculated, procured, bought, sold. In the market he competed with the merchants and bankers for the profit due to his capital. But he grabbed not merely from the market but from the source: as a functionary of the class system he took care not to go short of the fruits of his workers' labor. The workers had to deliver as much as possible. Like a true Shylock he insisted on his contract. By virtue of owning the machines and materials, he forced the others to produce. He called himself the producer, but he and everyone secretly knew the truth. The productive work of the capitalist, whether he justified his profit as the reward of enterprise, as under liberalism, or as the director's salary, as today, was the ideology which concealed the nature of the labor contract and the rapacity of the economic system in general.*

That is why people shout: "Stop thief!"—and point at the Jew. He is indeed the scapegoat, not only for individual maneuvers and machinations but in the wider sense that the economic injustice of the whole class is attributed to him. The factory owner has his debtors, the workers, under observation in his factory and can check their performance before he parts with his money. They only find out the true nature of the exchange only when they see what they can buy with it: the smallest magnate has access to a quantity of services and goods available to no ruler before him; but the workers receive what is called the cultural minimum. Not content with letting the market tell them how few goods can be theirs, the salesman sings the praises of those they cannot afford. Only the relationship of wages to prices expresses what is withheld* from the workers. With their wages they have accepted the principle of just remuneration. The merchant presents them with the promissory note they have signed on behalf of the manufacturer. The merchant is the bailiff for the whole system, taking upon himself the odium due to the others. That the circulation sphere is responsible for exploitation is a socially necessary illusion.

The Jews had not been the only people active in the circulation sphere. But they had been locked up in it too long not to reflect in their makeup something of the hatred so long directed at that sphere. Unlike their Aryan colleagues, they were largely denied access to the source of added value. Only at a late stage and with difficulty were they allowed to gain ownership of the means of production. To be sure, in the history of Europe, and even in imperial Germany, baptized Jews had reached high positions in administration and industry. But they always had to justify this with redoubled devotion and diligence, and stubborn self-denial. They were only admitted if, through their behavior, they tacitly adopted and confirmed the verdict on the other Jews: that is the purpose of baptism. All the great achievements of their prominent members were not enough to allow Jews to be admitted to the peoples of Europe; having been prevented from putting down roots they were then criticized as rootless. They always remained the protected Jews, dependent on emperors, princes, or the absolutist state. These patrons were economically more advanced than the rest of the population. To the extent that they could make use of the Jew as an intermediary, they protected him against the masses who had to foot the bill for progress. The Jews were the colonizers of progress. Having helped as merchants to disseminate Roman civilization throughout Gentile Europe, they became, in keeping with their patriarchal religion, representatives of urban, civic, and finally industrial conditions. As bearers of capitalist modes of existence from country to country they earned the hatred of those who suffered under that system. For the sake of the economic progress which today is their downfall the Jews were from the first a thorn in the side of the craftsmen and farmers whose status capitalism undermined. Now it is their turn to bear the brunt of its exclusive, particularist character. They, who always wanted to be first, are left far behind. Even the Jewish head of an American entertainment trust is hopelessly defensive amid his wealth. The caftan was the ghostly residue of ancient civic dress. Today it is a sign that its wearers have been flung to the margins of a society* which, now wholly enlightened, is exorcising the spirits of its prehistory. They who propagated individualism, abstract law, the concept of the person, have been debased to a species. They who were never allowed untroubled ownership of the civic right which should have granted them human dignity are again called "the Jews" without distinction. Even in the nineteenth century the Jew remained dependent on an alliance with the central authority. The general law, protected by the state, was the guarantor of his safety, and the exceptive law the specter which ensured his docility. He remained an object, dependent on grace and favor, even when claiming his rights. Trade was not his vocation, it was his fate. The Jews were the trauma of the knights of industry, who have to masquerade as productive creators.* In the Jewish jargon they detect what they secretly despise in themselves: their anti-Semitism is self-hate, the bad conscience of the parasite.

IV

Nationalist anti-Semitism seeks to disregard religion. It claims to be concerned with purity of race and nation. Its exponents notice that people have long ceased to trouble themselves about eternal salvation.* The average believer today is as crafty as only cardinals were in former times. To accuse the Jews of being obdurate unbelievers is no longer enough to incite the masses. But the religious hostility which motivated the persecution of the Jews for two millennia is far from completely extinguished. Rather, anti-Semitism's eagerness to deny its religious tradition indicates that that tradition is secretly no less deeply embedded in it than secular idiosyncrasy once was in religious zealotry. Religion has been incorporated as cultural heritage, not abolished. The alliance between enlightenment and power has debarred from consciousness the moment of truth in religion while conserving its reified forms. Both circumstances finally benefit fascism: the unchanneled longing is guided into racial-nationalist rebellion, while the descendants of the evangelistic zealots are converted into conspirators of blood communities and elite guards, on the model of the Wagnerian knights of the Grail. In this way religion as an institution is partly meshed directly into the system and partly transposed into the pomp of mass culture and parades. The fanatical faith on which leader and followers pride themselves is no other than the grim doctrine which was earlier used to discipline the desperate, except that its content has gone astray. That content lives on only as hatred of those who do not share the faith. Among the "German Christians,"* all that remained of the religion of love was anti-Semitism.

Christianity is not only a regression beyond Judaism. The latter's God, in passing from a henotheistic to a universal form, did not entirely shed the features of the nature demon. The terror originating in remote preanimist times passes from nature into the concept of the absolute self which, as its creator and ruler, entirely subjugates nature. Despite the ineffable power and splendor in which such alienation clothes it, that ruler is still attainable to thought, which becomes universal through this very relationship to something supreme, transcendental. God as spirit is the principle opposed to nature; it not only stands for nature's blind cycle as do all the mythical gods, but offers liberation from it. But in its remote abstractness, the incommensurable has at the same time become more terrible, and the pitiless statement: "I am who am," which tolerates nothing beside itself, surpasses in its inescapable power the blinder and therefore more ambiguous judgment of anonymous fate. The God of Judaism demands what he is owed and settles accounts with the defaulter. He enmeshes his creatures in a tissue of debt and credit, guilt and merit. In contrast, Christianity emphasized the moment of grace, although that, too, is contained in Judaism, in God's covenant with men and in the Messianic promise. It softened the terror of the absolute by allowing the creature to find itself reflected in the deity: the divine mediator is called by a human name and dies a human death. His message is: fear not; the law yields before faith; love becomes greater than any majesty, the only commandment.

But by virtue of the same moments by which it lifted the spell of nature religion, Christianity is producing ideology once again, in a spiritualized form. To the same degree as the absolute is brought closer to the finite, the finite is made absolute. Christ, the incarnated spirit, is the deified sorcerer. The human self-reflection in the absolute, the humanization of God through Christ, is the *proton pseudos* [first substitution]. The progress beyond Judaism is paid for with the assertion that the mortal Jesus was God. The harm is done precisely by the reflective moment of Christianity, the spiritualization of magic. A spiritual essence is attributed to something which mind identifies as natural. Mind consists precisely in demonstrating the contradiction inherent in such pretensions of the finite. Bad conscience is therefore obliged to present the prophet as a symbol, the magical practice as transubstantiation. It is that which makes Christianity a religion, and, in a sense, the only one: an intellectual link to something intellectually suspect, a special sphere of culture. Like the great Asiatic belief systems, pre-Christian Judaism was hardly separable from national life, from collective self-preservation. The reshaping of the heathen ritual of sacrifice not only took place in worship and in the mind but determined the form of the labor process. In providing the schema for the latter, sacrifice becomes rational. The taboo is transformed into the rational organization of the work process. It regulates administration in war and peace, sowing and harvesting, food preparation and slaughter. Although the rules may not arise from rational reflection, rationality arises from them. The effort of primitive peoples to free themselves from immediate fear engendered among them the institution of ritual; this was refined by Judaism into the sanctified rhythm of family and national life. The priests were appointed to watch over the proper observance of custom. Their function within the power structure was clearly displayed in theocratic practice; Christianity, however, wanted to remain spiritual even where it aspired to power. In ideology it repudiated self-preservation by the ultimate sacrifice, that of the man-god, but thereby relegated devalued life to the sphere of the profane: it abolished the law of Moses but rendered what was theirs unto both God and Caesar. Secular authority is either confirmed or usurped, while Christianity acquires a license to manage salvation. Self-preservation is to be conquered though the imitation of Christ—by order. In this way self-sacrificing love is stripped of its naivety, severed from natural love and turned to account as credit. The love mediated by ecclesiastical knowledge is presented as immediate love, in which nature and the supernatural are reconciled. Therein lies its untruth: in the fraudulently affirmative interpretation of self-forgetting.

That interpretation is fraudulent because the church depends for its existence on people's belief that they will attain salvation by following its teaching, whether that teaching demands works like the Catholic version or faith like the Protestant, yet cannot guarantee that goal. The nonbinding nature of the religious promise of salvation, the Jewish and negative moment in the Christian doctrine, by which magic and finally the church itself are relativized, is tacitly ignored by naive believers, for whom Christianity, supranaturalism, becomes a magic ritual, a nature religion. They believe only by forgetting their belief. They convince themselves of the certainty of their knowledge like astrologers or spiritualists. That is not necessarily worse than spiritualized theology. The old Italian lady who with devout simplicity consecrates a candle to St Gennaro to protect her grandson in the war may be closer to the truth than the high priests and pontiffs who, untainted by idolatry, bless the weapons against which St Gennaro is powerless. To the simple, however, religion itself becomes a substitute for religion. Christianity had some awareness of this from its earliest days, but it was only the paradoxical Christians, the antiofficial thinkers from Pascal through Lessing and Kierkegaard to Barth, who made it the keystone of their theology. In this awareness they were not only the radical Christians but the tolerant ones. The others, who repressed that knowledge and with bad conscience convinced themselves of Christianity as a secure possession, were obliged to confirm their eternal salvation by the worldly ruin of those who refused to make the murky sacrifice of reason. That is the religious origin of anti-Semitism. The adherents of the religion of the Son hated the supporters of the religion of the Father as one hates those who know better. This is the hostility of spirit hardened as faith in salvation for spirit as mind. What is vexatious for the Christian enemies of the Jews is the truth which withstands evil without rationalizing it, and clings to the idea of unearned beatitude in disregard of worldly actions and the order of salvation which allegedly bring it about. Anti-Semitism is supposed to confirm that the ritual of faith and history is justified by ritually sacrificing those who deny its justice.

V

"I simply can't abide you—so don't forget it," says Siegfried to Mime, who is trying to win his love. The stock reply of all anti-Semites is the appeal to idiosyncrasy. Society's emancipation from anti-Semitism depends on whether the content of that idiosyncrasy is raised to the level of a concept and becomes aware of its own senselessness. But idiosyncrasy attaches itself to the peculiar. The universal, that which fits into the context of social utility, is regarded as natural. But anything natural which has not been absorbed into utility by passing through the cleansing channels of conceptual order—the screech of stylus on slate which sets the teeth on edge, the *haut goût* which brings to mind filth and corruption, the sweat which appears on the brow of the diligent—whatever is not quite assimilated, or infringes the commands in which the progress of centuries has been sedimented, is felt as intrusive and arouses a compulsive aversion.

The motifs which trigger such idiosyncrasy are those which allude to origin. They recreate moments of biological prehistory: danger signs which made the hair stand on end and the heart stop. In the idiosyncratic aversion individual organs escape the subject's control, autonomously obeying fundamental biological stimuli. The self which experiences itself in such reactions—rigidity of the skin, muscles, and limbs—is not quite master of them. For a few moments they mimic the motionlessness of surrounding nature. But as what is mobile draws closer to the immobile, more highly developed life to mere nature, it is also estranged from it, since immobile nature, which living creatures, like Daphne, seek with utmost agitation to become, is capable only of the most external, spatial relationships. Space is absolute alienation. Where the human seeks to resemble nature, at the same time it hardens itself against it. Protection as petrified terror is a form of camouflage. These numb human reactions are archaic patterns of self-preservation: the tribute life pays for its continued existence is adaptation to death.

Civilization replaced the organic adaptation to otherness, mimetic behavior proper, firstly, in the magical phase, with the organized manipulation of mimesis, and finally, in the historical phase, with rational praxis, work. Uncontrolled mimesis is proscribed. The angel which, with fiery sword, drove humans out of paradise and on to the path of technical progress, is itself the symbol of that progress. The severity with which, over the centuries, the rulers have prevented both their own successors and the subjugated masses from relapsing into mimetic behavior—from the religious ban on graven images through the social ostracizing of actors and gypsies to the education which "cures" children of childishness—is the condition of civilization. Social and individual education reinforces the objectifying behavior required by work and prevents people from submerging themselves once more in the ebb and flow of surrounding nature. All distraction, indeed, all devotion has an element of mimicry. The ego has been forged by hardening itself against such behavior. The transition from reflecting mimesis to controlled reflection completes its formation. Bodily adaptation to nature is replaced by "recognition in a concept,"* the subsuming of difference under sameness. However, the constellation under which sameness is established, both the direct sameness of mimesis and the indirect sameness of synthesis, the adaptation of the self to the thing in the blind act of living no less than the comparison of reified elements in scientific conceptualization—that constellation remains terror. Society perpetuates the threat from nature as the permanent, organized compulsion which, reproducing itself in individuals as systematic self-preservation, rebounds against nature as society's control over it. Science is repetition, refined to observed regularity and preserved in stereotypes. The mathematical formula is consciously manipulated regression, just as the magic ritual was; it is the most sublimated form of mimicry. In technology the adaptation to lifelessness in the service of self-preservation is no longer accomplished, as in magic, by bodily imitation of external nature, but by automating mental processes, turning them into blind sequences. With its triumph human expressions become both controllable and compulsive. All that remains of the adaptation to nature is the hardening against it. The camouflage used to protect and strike terror today is the blind mastery of nature, which is identical to farsighted instrumentality.

In the bourgeois mode of production the ineradicable mimetic heritage present in all praxis is consigned to oblivion. The pitiless ban on regression appears like an edict of fate; the denial is so total that it is no longer registered consciously. Those blinded by civilization have contact with their own tabooed mimetic traits only through certain gestures and forms of behavior they encounter in others, as isolated, shameful residues in their rationalized environment. What repels them as alien is all too familiar.[1] It lurks in the contagious gestures of an immediacy suppressed by civilization: gestures of touching, nestling, soothing, coaxing. What makes such impulses repellent today is their outmodedness. In seeking to win over the buyer with flattery, the debtor with threats, the creditor with supplication, they appear to translate long-reified human relationships back into those of personal power. Any emotion is finally embarrassing; mere excitement is preferable. All unmanipulated expression appears like the grimace which the manipulated expression—of the film actor, the lynch mob, the *Führer*'s speech—always was. Undisciplined mimicry is the brand burned by the old domination into the living substance of the dominated, and is inherited through an unconscious process of imitation in early childhood from generation to generation, from the Jewish rags-and-bones man to the banker. Such mimicry provokes anger, because it puts on show, in face of the new relationships of production, the old fear which one has had to forget in order to survive them. It is the compulsive moment in behavior, the rage of the tormentor and of the tormented, reappearing indistinguishably in the grimace, that triggers the specific rage of civilized people. Impotent appearance is answered by deadly reality, play by seriousness.

The grimace seems like play-acting because, instead of performing serious work, it prefers to portray displeasure. It appears to evade the seriousness of life by admitting it without restraint: therefore it is false. But expression is the painful echo of overwhelming power, violence which finds utterance in complaint. It is always overdone, no matter how heartfelt it may be, because, as in each work of art, the whole world seems contained in every plaintive sound. Only activity is proportionate. It, and not mimesis, can bring an end to suffering. But its consequence is the rigid, unmoved visage, culminating, at the end of this age, in the baby faces of the practical men, the politicians, priests, managing directors, racketeers. The strident voices of fascist rabble-rousers and camp commanders show the reverse side of the same social condition. The screaming is as cold-blooded as business. Even the plaintive sounds of nature are appropriated as an element of technique. The bellowing of these orators is to the pogrom what its howling klaxon is to the German flying bomb: the cry of terror which announces terror is mechanically switched on. The screamers deliberately use the wail of the victim, which first called violence by its name, and even the mere word which designates the victim—Frenchman, Negro, Jew—to induce in themselves the desperation of the persecuted who have to hit out. They are the false likeness of the terrified mimesis. They reproduce within themselves the insatiability of the power of which they are afraid. Everything must be used, everything must belong to them. The mere existence of the other is a provocation. Everyone else "gets in the way" and must be shown their limits—the limits of limitless horror. No one who seeks shelter shall find it; those who express what everyone craves—peace, homeland, freedom—will be denied it, just as nomads and traveling players have always been refused rights of domicile. Whatever someone fears, that is done to him. Even the last resting place shall be none. The despoiling of graveyards is not an excess of anti-Semitism; it is anti-Semitism itself. Those evicted compulsively arouse the lust to evict them even here. The marks left on them by violence endlessly inflame violence. Anything which merely wants to vegetate must be rooted out. The chaotically regular flight reactions of the lower animals, the patterns of swarming crowds, the convulsive gestures of the tortured—all these express what wretched life can never quite control: the mimetic impulse. In the death throes of the creature, at the furthest extreme from freedom, freedom itself irresistibly shines forth as the thwarted destiny of matter. It is against this freedom that the idiosyncratic aversion, the purported motive of anti-Semitism, is ultimately directed.

The psychic energy harnessed by political anti-Semitism is this rationalized idiosyncrasy. All the gesticulations devised by the *Führer* and his followers are pretexts for giving way to the mimetic temptation without openly violating the reality principle—with honor, as it were. They detest the Jews and imitate them constantly. There is no anti-Semite who does not feel an instinctive urge to ape what he takes to be Jewishness. The same mimetic codes are constantly used: the argumentative jerking of the hands, the singing tone of voice, which vividly animates a situation or a feeling independently of judgment, and the nose, that physiognomic *principium individuationis*, which writes the individual's peculiarity on his face. In the ambiguous partialities of the sense of smell the old nostalgia for what is lower lives on, the longing for immediate union with surrounding nature, with earth and slime. Of all the senses the act of smelling, which is attracted without objectifying, reveals most sensuously the urge to lose oneself in identification with the Other. That is why smell, as both the perception and the perceived—which are one in the act of olfaction—is more expressive than other senses. When we see we remain who we are, when we smell we are absorbed entirely. In civilization, therefore, smell is regarded as a disgrace, a sign of the lower social orders, lesser races, and baser animals. The civilized person is allowed to give way to such desires only if the prohibition is suspended by rationalization in the service of practical purposes, real or apparent. One is allowed to indulge the outlawed drive if acting with the unquestionable aim of expunging it. This is manifested in the practical joke. It is a wretched parody of fulfillment. The mimetic function is sneeringly enjoyed as something despised and self-despising. Anyone who sniffs out "bad" smells in order to extirpate them may imitate to his heart's content the snuffling which takes its unrationalized pleasure in the smell itself. Disinfected by the civilized sniffer's absolute identification with the prohibiting agency, the forbidden impulse eludes the prohibition. If it crosses the threshold, the response is laughter. That is the schema of the anti-Semitic reaction. The anti-Semites gather to celebrate the moment when authority lifts the ban; that moment alone makes them a collective, constituting the community of kindred spirits. Their ranting is organized laughter. The more dreadful the accusations and threats, the greater the fury, the more withering is the scorn. Rage, mockery, and poisoned imitation are fundamentally the same thing. The purpose of the fascist cult of formulae, the ritualized discipline, the uniforms, and the whole allegedly irrational apparatus, is to make possible mimetic behavior. The elaborate symbols proper to every counterrevolutionary movement, the death's heads and masquerades, the barbaric drumming, the monotonous repetition of words and gestures, are so many organized imitations of magical practices, the mimesis of mimesis. The *Führer*, with his ham-actor's facial expressions and the hysterical charisma turned on with a switch, leads the dance. In his performance he acts out by proxy and in effigy what is denied to everyone else in reality. Hitler can gesticulate like a clown, Mussolini risk false notes like a provincial tenor, Goebbels talk as glibly as the Jewish agent whose murder he is recommending, Coughlin* preach love like the Savior himself, whose crucifixion he impersonates for the sake of yet more bloodshed. Fascism is also totalitarian in seeking to place oppressed nature's rebellion against domination directly in the service of domination.

This mechanism needs the Jews. Their artificially heightened visibility acts on the legitimate son of Gentile civilization like a kind of magnetic field. In being made aware, through his very difference from the Jew, of the humanity they have in common, the rooted Gentile is overcome by a feeling of something antithetical and alien. In this way the tabooed impulses which run counter to work in its dominant form are converted into conforming idiosyncrasies. Against this the economic position of the Jews, the last defrauded fraudsters of the liberal ideology, offers no reliable protection. Because they are so eminently suited to generating these inductive psychic currents they are unresistingly allocated to such functions. They share the fate of the rebellious nature for which fascism substitutes them, being put to use with the perspicuity of the blind. It makes little difference whether the Jews as individuals really display the mimetic traits which cause the malign infection or whether those traits are merely imputed. If the holders of economic power have once overcome their fear of employing fascist agents, in face of the Jews the harmony of the national community is automatically established. They are sacrificed by the dominant order when, through its increasing estrangement from nature, it has reverted to mere nature. The Jews as a whole are charged with practicing forbidden magic and bloody rituals. Disguised as an accusation, the subliminal craving of the indigenous population to revert to mimetic sacrificial practices is joyously readmitted to their consciousness. Once the horror of the primeval age, sent packing by civilization, has been rehabilitated as a rational interest through projection onto the Jews, there is no holding back. It can be acted out in reality, and the evil which is acted out surpasses even the evil content of the projection. The popular nationalist fantasies of Jewish crimes, of infanticide and sadistic excesses, of racial poisoning and international conspiracy, precisely define the anti-Semitic dream, and fall short of its realization. Once things have gone so far, the mere word Jew appears like the bloody grimace whose image—skull and mangled cross in one—is unfurled on the swastika flag; the fact that someone is called a Jew acts as a provocation to set about him until he resembles that image.

Civilization is the triumph of society over nature—a triumph which transforms everything into mere nature. The Jews themselves, over the millennia, have played their part in this, with enlightenment no less than with cynicism. As the oldest surviving patriarchy, the incarnation of monotheism, they converted taboos into maxims of civilization while the others were still enmeshed in magic. The Jews appeared to have successfully achieved what Christianity had attempted in vain: the disempowerment of magic by means of its own strength, which, as worship of God, is turned against itself. They have not so much eradicated the adaptation to nature as elevated it to the pure duties of ritual. In this way they have preserved its reconciling memory, without relapsing through symbols into mythology. They are therefore regarded by advanced civilization as both backward and too advanced, like and unlike, shrewd and stupid. They are pronounced guilty of what, as the first citizens, they were the first to subdue in themselves: the susceptibility to the lure of base instincts, the urge toward the beast and the earth, the worship of images. Because they invented the concept of the kosher, they are persecuted as swine. The anti-Semites appoint themselves executors of the Old Testament: they see to it that the Jews, having eaten of the Tree of Knowledge, unto dust shall return.

VI

Anti-Semitism is based on false projection. It is the reverse of genuine mimesis and has deep affinities to the repressed; in fact, it may itself be the pathic character trait in which the latter is precipitated. If mimesis makes itself resemble its surroundings, false projection makes its surroundings resemble itself. If, for the former, the outward becomes the model to which the inward clings, so that the alien becomes the intimately known, the latter displaces the volatile inward into the outer world, branding the intimate friend as foe. Impulses which are not acknowledged by the subject and yet are his, are attributed to the object: the prospective victim. For the ordinary paranoiac the choice of victim is not free; it obeys the laws of his illness. In fascism this behavior is adopted by politics; the object of the illness is declared true to reality, the system of delusions the reasonable norm in a world which makes deviation neurosis. The mechanism which the totalitarian order takes into its service is as old as civilization. The sexual impulses suppressed by humanity survived in both individuals and peoples and asserted themselves in the imaginary transformation of the surrounding world into a diabolic system. Those impelled by blind murderous lust have always seen in the victim the pursuer who has driven them to desperate self-defense, and the mightiest of the rich have experienced their weakest neighbor as an intolerable threat before falling upon him. The rationalization was both a ruse and a compulsion. The person chosen as foe is already perceived as foe. The disorder lies in the subject's faulty distinction between his own contribution to the projected material and that of others.

In a certain sense, all perception is projection. The projection of sense impressions is a legacy of animal prehistory, a mechanism for the purposes of defense and obtaining food, an extension of the readiness for combat with which higher species reacted actively or passively to movements, regardless of the intention of the object. Projection has been automated in man like other forms of offensive or defensive behavior which have become reflexes. In this way his objective world has been constituted as a product of "an art concealed in the depths of the human soul, whose real modes of activity nature is hardly likely ever to allow us to discover, and to have open to our gaze."[2] The system of things, the fixed universal order of which science is merely an abstract expression, is, if Kant's

critique of knowledge is applied anthropologically, the unconscious product of the animal tool in the struggle for existence—it is the automatic
projection. In human society, however, where both the affective and the
intellectual life grow complex with the formation of the individual, projection must be increasingly controlled; individuals must learn both to
refine and to inhibit it. As economic compulsion teaches them to distinguish between their own thoughts and feelings and those of others, a distinction emerges between outer and inner, the possibility of detachment
and of identification, self-consciousness and conscience. More precise
reflection is needed to understand this controlled form of projection and
its degeneration into the false projection which is essential to anti-
Semitism.

The physiological theory of perception, which has been despised by
philosophers since Kant as naively realistic and as a circular argument,
holds the world of perception to be a reflection, guided by the intellect, of
the data received from real objects by the brain. According to this view,
punctual indices, or impressions, are registered physiologically and then
ordered by the mind. Although the Gestalt people may insist that the
physiological substance receives not merely points but structure, Schopenhauer and Helmholtz, despite or even because of the circularity of their
view, knew more about the intermeshed relationship of subject and object
than is reflected in the official logical consistency of the schools, whether
neopsychological or neo-Kantian: the perceptual image does indeed contain concepts and judgments. Between the actual object and the indu-
bitable sense datum, between inner and outer, yawns an abyss which the
subject must bridge at its own peril. To reflect the thing as it is, the subject must give back to it more than it receives from it. From the traces the
thing leaves behind in its senses the subject recreates the world outside it:
the unity of the thing in its manifold properties and states; and in so
doing, in learning how to impart a synthetic unity not only to the outward
impressions but to the inward ones which gradually separate themselves
from them, it retroactively constitutes the self. The identical ego is the
most recent constant product of projection. In a process which could only
be accomplished historically when the powers of the human physiological
constitution were fully developed, this self has emerged as a unified and,
at the same time, an eccentric function. But even as an autonomously
objectified subject it is only what the objective world is for it. The inner

depth of the subject consists in nothing other than the delicacy and rich-
ness of the outer perceptual world. If this intermeshing is broken, the self
petrifies. If it is confined, positivistically, to registering the given without
itself giving, it shrinks to a point, and if, idealistically, it projects the world
out of the bottomless origin or its own self, it exhausts itself in monotonous repetition. In both cases it gives up the ghost—in this case the mind
or spirit. Only mediation, in which the insignificant sense datum raises
thought to the fullest productivity of which it is capable, and in which,
conversely, thought gives itself up without reservation to the overwhelming impression—only mediation can overcome the isolation which ails the
whole of nature. Neither the certainty untroubled by thought, nor the pre-
conceptual unity of perception and object, but only their self-reflective
antithesis contains the possibility of reconciliation. The antithesis is perceived in the subject, which has the external world within its own consciousness and yet recognizes it as other. Reflection on that antithesis,
therefore, the life of reason, takes place as conscious projection.

The pathic element in anti-Semitism is not projective behavior as
such but the exclusion of reflection from that behavior. Because the subject is unable to return to the object what it has received from it, it is not
enriched but impoverished. It loses reflection in both directions: as it no
longer reflects the object, it no longer reflects on itself, and thereby loses
the ability to differentiate. Instead of the voice of conscience, it hears voices; instead of inwardly examining itself in order to draw up a protocol of
its own lust for power, it attributes to others the Protocol of the Elders of
Zion. It overflows at the same time as it dries up. It invests the outside
world boundlessly with what is within itself; but what it invests is something utterly insignificant, an inflated accumulation of mere means, relationships, machinations, a grim praxis unilluminated by thought. Domination itself which, even as absolute power, is inherently only a means,
becomes in untrammeled projection the purpose both of oneself and of
others, purpose as such. In the sickness of the individual, humanity's
sharpened intellectual apparatus is turned once more against humanity,
regressing to the blind instrument of hostility it was in animal prehistory, and as which, for the species, it has never ceased to operate in relation
to the rest of nature. Just as, since its rise, the human species has manifested itself toward others as developmentally the highest, capable of the
most terrible destruction; and just as, within humanity, the more ad-

vanced races have confronted the more primitive, the technically superior nations the more backward, so the sick individual confronts the other individual, in megalomania as in persecution mania. In both cases the subject is at the center, the world a mere occasion for its delusion; it becomes the impotent or omnipotent quintessence of what is projected on to it. The opposition of which the paranoiac complains indiscriminately at every step is the result of the lack of resistance, of the emptiness which the encapsulated subject generates around itself. The paranoiac cannot stop. The idea, having no firm hold on reality, insists all the more and becomes the fixation.

Because paranoiacs perceive the outside world only in so far as it corresponds to their blind purposes, they can only endlessly repeat their own self, which has been alienated from them as an abstract mania. This naked schema of power as such, equally overwhelming toward others and toward a self at odds with itself, seizes whatever comes its way and, wholly disregarding its peculiarity, incorporates it in its mythic web. The closed circle of perpetual sameness becomes a surrogate for omnipotence. It is as if the serpent which told the first humans "Ye shall be as gods" had kept his promise in the paranoiac. He creates everything in his own image. He seems to need no living thing yet demands that all shall serve him. His will permeates the whole universe; nothing may be unrelated to him. His systems know of no gaps. As astrologer, he endows the stars with powers which bring about the ruin of the unsuspecting, whether it is the ruin of others in the preclinical stage or of his own ego in the clinical stage. As philosopher, he makes world history the executor of inescapable catastrophes and downfalls. As completely insane or absolutely rational, he annihilates those marked down as victims either by the individual act of terror or by the well-considered strategy of extermination. In this way he succeeds. Just as women adore the unmoved paranoid man, nations fall to their knees before totalitarian fascism. The paranoid element in the devotees responds to the paranoiac as to the evil spirit, their fear of conscience to his utter lack of scruples, for which they feel gratitude. They follow the man who looks past them, who does not treat them as subjects but hands them over to the operations of his many purposes. Like everyone else, these women have made the occupation of greater or lesser positions of power their religion, and themselves the malign creatures society takes them for. And so the gaze which reminds them of freedom must strike them as that of the over-naive seducer. Their world is inverted. But at the same time they know, like the ancient gods who shunned the gaze of the faithful, that something lifeless resides behind their veil. In the trusting look of the nonparanoid they are reminded of the spirit which has died in them, because they see outside them only the cold means of their self-preservation. To be touched in this way awakens in them shame and rage. Yet the madman does not reach them, even though he may stare them in the face like the *Führer*. He merely inflames them. His proverbial gaze straight into the eyes, unlike the free gaze, does not preserve individuality. It fixates. It binds others to one-sided loyalty, by confining them to the windowless monadic fortress of their own person. It does not awaken conscience, but prematurely imposes responsibility. The penetrating look and the one that goes past you, the hypnotic and the disregarding gaze, are of the same kind: in both, the subject is extinguished. Because in both looks reflection is absent, the unreflecting are electrified by them. They are betrayed: the women cast away, the nation incinerated. Thus, the self-encapsulated figure remains a caricature of divine power. Just as his lordly gesture is entirely without creative power in reality, so, like the devil, he lacks the attributes of the principle he usurps: mindful love and freedom secure within itself. He is malignant, driven by compulsion, and as weak as he is strong. If divine omnipotence is said to draw creation unto itself, this satanic, imagined omnipotence draws everything into its impotence. That is the secret of its rule. The compulsively projecting self can project nothing except its own unhappiness, from the cause of which, residing in itself, it is yet cut off by its lack of reflection. For this reason the products of false projection, the stereotyped schemata of both thought and reality, bring calamity. For the ego, sinking into the meaningless abyss of itself, objects become allegories of ruin, which harbor the meaning of its own downfall.

The psychoanalytic theory of pathic projection has identified the transference of socially tabooed impulses from the subject to the object as the substance of that projection. Under the pressure of the superego, the ego projects aggressive urges emanating from the id which, through their strength, are a danger to itself, as malign intentions onto the outside world, and succeeds in ridding itself of them as reactions to that outside world, either in fantasy by identification with the alleged malefactor or in reality by ostensible self-defense. The proscribed material converted into aggression is usually homosexual in nature. Through fear of castration, obedience toward the father preempts castration by adapting the conscious emotional life to that of a little girl, and hatred of the father is repressed as endless rancor. In paranoia, this hatred is intensified to a castration wish expressed as a universal urge to destroy. The sick subject regresses to an archaic confusion between love and dominance. It is concerned with physical closeness, with taking possession, finally with relationship at any price. Because it cannot acknowledge desire within itself, it assails the other with jealousy or persecution, as the repressed sodomite hounds the animal as hunter or driver. The attraction stems from excessive attachment or develops at first sight; it can emanate from great figures, as in the case of malcontents and murderers of presidents, or from the most wretched as in the pogrom itself. The objects of the fixation are replaceable like father figures in childhood; whatever it hits on fits its purpose; the delusion of relatedness strikes out unrelatedly. Pathic projection is a desperate exertion by an ego which, according to Freud has a far weaker resistance to internal than to external stimuli: under the pressure of pent-up homosexual aggression the psychic mechanism forgets its most recent phylogenetic attainment, the perception of self, and experiences that aggression as an enemy in the world, the better to master it.

This pressure acts also, however, on the healthy cognitive process as a moment of its unreflecting naivety, which tends toward violence. Wherever intellectual energies are concentrated on an external intention, wherever it is a matter of pursuing, ascertaining, grasping—of exerting those functions which have been sublimated from the primitive overpowering of animals into the scientific methods of controlling nature—the subjective process is easily overlooked in the schematization, and the system is posited as the thing itself. Objectifying thought, like its pathological counterpart, has the arbitrariness of a subjective purpose extraneous to the matter itself and, in forgetting the matter, does to it in thought the violence which later will be done in practice. The unconditional realism of civilized humanity, which culminates in fascism, is a special case of paranoid delusion which depopulates nature and finally nations themselves. In the abyss of uncertainty, which every objectifying act must bridge, paranoia installs itself. Because there is no absolutely compelling argument against materially false judgments, the distorted perception in which they lurk cannot be healed. Every percept unconsciously contains conceptual elements, just as every judgment contains unclarified phenomenalistic ones. Because imagination is involved in truth, it can always appear to this damaged imagination that truth is fantastic and its illusion the truth. The maimed subject lives on the element of imagination immanent in truth by ceaselessly putting it on show. Democratically, he insists on equal rights for his delusion, because, in fact, not even truth is stringent. While the citizen may admit that the anti-Semite is in the wrong, he requires the victim to be guilty too. Thus Hitler demands the right to practice mass murder in the name of the principle of sovereignty under international law, which tolerates any act of violence in another country.* Like every paranoiac he takes advantage of the hypocritical identity of truth and sophistry; the distinction between them is as uncompelling as it nevertheless is strict. Perception is only possible in so far as the thing is already apprehended as determinate—for example, as a case of a genus or type. It is a mediated immediacy, thought infused with the seductive power of sensuality. It blindly transfers subjective elements to the apparent givenness of the object. Only the self-conscious work of thought—that is, according to Leibnizian and Hegelian idealism, only philosophy—can escape this hallucinatory power. As, in the course of cognition, thought identifies the conceptual moments which are immediately posited in perception and are therefore compelling, it progressively takes them back into the subject and strips them of their intuitive power. In this process every earlier stage, including science, turns out to be, in comparison to philosophy, a kind of percept, an estranged phenomenon permeated with unrecognized intellectual elements; persistence at this stage, without negation, forms part of the pathology of cognition. The subject which naively postulates absolutes, no matter how universally active it may be, is sick, passively succumbing to the dazzlement of false immediacy.

Such blindness is, however, a constitutive element of all judgment, a necessary illusion. Every judgment, even negative, is reassuring. However much a judgment may stress its own isolation and relativity for the purpose of self-correction, it must assert its own content, no matter how cautiously formulated, as something not merely isolated and relative. That constitutes its nature as judgment, whereas the clause merely entrenches a claim. Truth, unlike probability, has no gradations. The negating step beyond the individual judgment, which rescues its truth, is possible only in so far as it takes itself to be truth and in that sense is paranoid. True derangement lies only in the immovable, in thought's incapacity for the negation in which, unlike the fixed judgment, thought actually consists. The paranoid over-consistency, the bad infinity of never-changing judgment, is a lack of consistency in thought; instead of conceptually carrying through the failure of the absolute claim and thereby continuing to qualify his or her judgment, the paranoiac clings obdurately to the claim which has caused the judgment to fail. Instead of going further by penetrating its subject matter more deeply, thought places itself entirely in the hopeless service of the particular judgment. The latter's irresistibility is the same as its intact positivity, and the paranoiac's weakness is that of thought itself. For reflection, which in the healthy subject breaks the power of immediacy, is never as compelling as the illusion it dispels. As a negative, reflective movement not directed straight ahead, it lacks the brutality inherent in the positive. If the psychic energy of paranoia stems from the libidinal dynamic laid bare by psychoanalysis, its objective impregnability is founded on the ambiguity inseparable from the objectifying act; indeed, the latter's hallucinatory power will have been originally decisive. To clarify, it can be said in the language of natural selection theory that during the formative period of the human sensorium those individuals survived in whom the power of the projective mechanisms extended most deeply into their rudimentary logical faculties, or was least moderated by the premature onset of reflection. Just as, even today, practically fruitful scientific enterprises call for an unimpaired capacity for definition, for shutting down thought at a point designated by social need, for demarcating a field which is then investigated in the minutest detail without passing outside it, paranoiacs cannot step outside a complex of interests designated by their psychological fate. Their mental acuteness consumes itself within the circle drawn by their fixed idea, as human ingenuity is liquidating itself under the spell of technical civilization. Paranoia is the shadow of cognition.

So calamitous is the mind's tendency to false projection that, as the isolated schema of self-preservation, such projection threatens to dominate everything which goes beyond self-preservation: culture. False projection is the usurper in the realm of freedom as of culture; paranoia is the symptom of the half-educated. For such people, all words become a system of delusion, an attempt mentally to occupy the regions to which their experience does not extend, violently to give meaning to a world which makes them meaningless, but at the same time to denigrate the intellect and the experience from which they are excluded and to burden them with the guilt really borne by the society which has brought about that exclusion. The half-educated who, unlike the merely uneducated, hypostatize limited knowledge as truth, cannot endure the breach between inward and outward, individual fate and social law, appearance and essence, which for them is heightened to unbearable levels. To be sure, their suffering does contain an element of truth, compared to the mere acceptance of the given to which superior understanding has sworn allegiance. Nevertheless, the half-educated reach out stereotypically in their fear for the formula which suits their need, now to justify the disaster which has happened, now to predict the catastrophe still to come, which is sometimes disguised as a regeneration. The explanation, in which their own desires appear as an objective power, is always as external and meaningless as the isolated event itself, at once feeble-minded and sinister. The obscurantist systems of today bring about what the devil myth of the official religion enabled people to do in the Middle Ages: to imbue the outside world with an arbitrary meaning, which the lone paranoiac now constructs according to a private schema shared by no one, and which only for that reason appears actually mad. Relief is provided by the dire conventicles and panaceas which put on scientific airs while cutting off thought: theosophy, numerology, naturopathy, eurhythmy, teetotalism, Yoga, and countless other sects, competing and interchangeable, all with academies, hierarchies and specialist jargon, the fetishized officialese of science and religion. When confronted by an educated public, they remained apocryphal and disreputable. But today, when education itself is withering for economic reasons, unprecedented conditions are created for the paranoia of the masses. The belief systems of the past, which were embraced by the populace as self-contained paranoid forms, had wider meshes. Just because they were so rationally elaborated and specific, they left room, at least above them, for culture and mind, which, conceived as spirit, were their true medium. Indeed, to an extent they counteracted paranoia. Freud calls neuroses— even rightly in this instance—"asocial formations"; "they endeavor to achieve by private means what is affected in society by collective effort."[3] Those belief systems retain something of the collectivity which preserves individuals from pathological symptoms. The sickness is socialized: in the intoxication of the communal ecstasy—indeed, as itself a community— blindness becomes a relationship and the paranoid mechanism is made controllable, without losing the power to strike terror. Perhaps that was one of the major contributions of religions to the survival of the species. Paranoid forms of consciousness tend to give rise to leagues, factions, rackets. Their members are afraid to believe their madness on their own. Projecting it, they everywhere see proselytizing and conspiracy. The established group has always taken a paranoid stance toward others; in this the great empires, indeed, organized humanity as a whole, are no better than headhunters. Those who were excluded from humanity against their will, like those who excluded themselves from it out of longing for humanity, knew that the pathological cohesion of the established group was strengthened by persecuting them. Its normal members relieve their paranoia by participating in the collective one, and cling passionately to the objectified, collective, approved forms of delusion. The *horror vacui* with which they devote themselves to their confederacies welds them together and gives them their almost irresistible power.

With bourgeois property, education and culture spread, driving paranoia into the dark corners of society and the psyche. But as the real emancipation of humanity did not coincide with the enlightenment of the mind, education itself became sick. The less social reality kept pace with educated consciousness, the more that consciousness itself succumbed to a process of reification. Culture was entirely commoditized, disseminated as information which did not permeate those who acquired it. Thought becomes short-winded, confines itself to apprehending isolated facts. Intellectual connections are rejected as an inconvenient and useless exertion. The developmental moment in thought, its whole genetic and intensive dimension, is forgotten and leveled down to what is immediately present, to the extensive. The present order of life allows the self no scope to draw intellectual or spiritual conclusions. Thought, stripped down to knowledge, is neutralized, harnessed merely to qualifying its practitioner for specific labor markets and heightening the commodity value of the personality. In this way the self-reflection of the mind, which counteracts paranoia, is disabled. Finally, under the conditions of late capitalism, the half-educated condition has become the objective spirit. In the totalitarian phase of government its exponents reinstate the provincial charlatans of politics, and with them the system of delusion, as the *ultima ratio*, imposing it on the majority of the administered, who have already been softened up by big politics and the culture industry.* The absurdity of the present system of rule is so transparent to healthy consciousness that it needs sick consciousness to keep itself alive. Only those suffering from persecution mania can tolerate the persecution which domination inevitably becomes, provided they are allowed to persecute others.

In fascism, where the responsibility for wife and child painfully inculcated by bourgeois civilization is being obscured by the individual's insistent conformity to regulations, conscience is being liquidated in any case. Contrary to the ideas of Dostoievski and the German apostles of inwardness, conscience consisted in the self's devotion to something substantial outside itself, in the ability to make the true concerns of others one's own. This ability involves reflection as an interpenetration of receptivity and imagination. Because the abolition of the independent economic subject by big industry*—partly by absorbing free entrepreneurs and partly by transforming the workers* into objects of trades unions—is irresistibly eroding the basis of moral decisions, reflection, too, must wither. The soul, as the possibility of guilt aware of itself, decays. Conscience is deprived of objects, since individuals' responsibility for themselves and their dependents is replaced—although still under the old moral title—by their mere performance for the apparatus. The internal conflict of drives, in which the agency of conscience is formed, can no longer be worked through. If internalized, the social injunctions would not only be made both more binding and more open but also would be emancipated from society and even turned against it; instead, the individual identifies himself or herself promptly and directly with the stereotyped scales of values. The exemplary German woman, who has a monopoly on femininity as the true German man has on masculinity, and their counterparts elsewhere, are conformist, asocial human types. Despite and because of its obvious deficiency, the system of power has become so preponderant that powerless individuals can avert their fate only through blind compliance.

In face of such power, it is left to chance—guided by the Party—to decide where despairing self-preservation is to project the guilt for its terror. The Jews are the predestined target of this guided chance. The circulation sphere, in which they once held positions of economic power, is vanishing. The liberal form of commercial enterprise once endowed fragmented wealth with political influence. Now, no sooner emancipated, its owners are merged with the state apparatus and placed at the mercy of capital powers which have outgrown competition. No matter what the makeup of the Jews may be in reality, their image, that of the defeated, has characteristics which must make totalitarian rule their mortal enemy: happiness without power, reward without work, a homeland without frontiers, religion without myth. These features are outlawed by the ruling powers because they are secretly coveted by the ruled. The former can survive only as long as the latter turn what they yearn for into an object of hate. They do so through pathic projection, since even hatred leads to union with the object—in destruction. It is the negative of reconciliation. Reconciliation is Judaism's highest concept, and expectation its whole meaning. The paranoid reaction stems from the incapacity for expectation. The anti-Semites are realizing their negative absolute through power, by transforming the world into the hell they have always taken it to be. A radical change would depend on whether the ruled, in face of absolute madness, could master themselves and hold the madness back. Only the liberation of thought from power, the abolition of violence, could realize the idea which has been unrealized until now*: that the Jew is a human being. This would be a step away from the anti-Semitic society, which drives both Jews and others into sickness, and toward the human one. Such a step would fulfill the fascist lie by contradicting it: the Jewish question would indeed prove the turning-point of history.* By conquering the sickness of the mind which flourishes on the rich soil of self-assertion unhampered by reflection, humanity would cease to be the universal antirace and become the species which, as nature, is more than mere nature, in that it is aware of its own image. The individual and social emancipation from domination is the countermovement to false projection, and no longer would Jews seek, by resembling it, to appease the evil senselessly visited on them as on all the persecuted, whether animals or human beings.

VII*

But there are no longer any anti-Semites. The last of them were liberals who wanted to express their antiliberal opinions. By the end of the nineteenth century the old-style conservative aloofness of the nobility and the officer corps toward the Jews was merely reactionary. The people abreast of the times were the Ahlwardts and the Knüppelkunzes.* They drew their followers from the same groups as the *Führer*, but their support came from troublemakers and malcontents throughout the country. When people voiced anti-Semitic attitudes, they felt they were being bourgeois and rebellious at the same time. Their nationalistic grumbling was still a distorted form of civil freedom. The beer hall politics of the anti-Semites exposed the lie of German liberalism, on which it fed and whose demise it finally brought about. Even though they used their own mediocrity as a license to subject the Jews to beatings in which universal murder was already latent, they were economically farsighted enough to weigh the risks of the Third Reich against the advantages of a hostile form of tolerance. Anti-Semitism was still a competing motif within a range of subjective choices. But the outcome related specifically to it. The whole chauvinistic vocabulary was implied from the start in the adoption of the *völkisch* thesis. Anti-Semitic views always reflected stereotyped thinking. Today only that thinking is left. People still vote, but only between totalities. The anti-Semitic psychology has largely been replaced by mere acceptance of the whole fascist ticket,* which is an inventory of the slogans of belligerent big business. Just as, on the ballot paper of the mass party, voters are present-ed with the names of people remote from their experience for whom they can only vote *en bloc*, the central ideological concepts have been codified into a small number of lists. One has to opt for one of them *en bloc* if one's own position is not to seem as futile as splinter votes on polling day in face of the statistical mammoths. Anti-Semitism has practically ceased to be an independent impulse and has become a plank in the platform: anyone who gives fascism its chance subscribes to the settlement of the Jewish question along with the breaking of the unions and the crusade against Bolshevism. The anti-Semite's conviction, however mendacious it may be, has been absorbed into the preconditioned reflexes of the subjectless expo-nents of a particular standpoint. When the masses accept the reactionary ticket containing the clause against the Jews, they are obeying social mech-anisms in which individual people's experiences of Jews play no part. It has been shown, in fact, that anti-Semitism's prospects are no less good in "Jew-free"* areas than in Hollywood itself. Experience is replaced by cliché, the imagination active in experience by diligent acceptance. The members of each class have to absorb their quota of guidelines on pain of rapid downfall. Just as they need to be instructed on the technical merits of a particular aircraft, so do they, too, on their allegiance to one of the prescribed agencies of power.

In the world of mass production, stereotypes replace intellectual cat-egories. Judgment is no longer based on a real act of synthesis but on blind subsumption. If, at an early historical stage, judgment consisted in the swift decision which immediately unleashed the poisoned arrow, in the meantime exchange and the institutions of law have taken their effect. The act of judgment passed through a stage of deliberation which afforded the judging subject some protection from brutal identification with the predicate. In late-industrial society there is a regression to judgment without judging. When, in fascism, the protracted legal process was replaced by an accelerated procedure in criminal trials, up-to-date people had been economically prepared for this development. They had learned to see things unreflectingly, through ready-made thought models, the *termini technici* which provide them with iron rations following the decay of language. The perceiver is no longer present in the process of perception. He or she is incapable of the active passivity of cognition, in which categorial elements are appropriately reshaped by preformed conventional schemata and vice versa, so that justice is done to the perceived object. In the field of the social sciences, as in that of individual experience, blind intuition and empty concepts are brought together rigidly and without mediation.* In the age of the "three hundred basic words" the ability to exercise judgment, and therefore to distinguish between true and false, is vanishing. Thinking, where it is not merely a highly specialized piece of professional equipment in this or that branch of the division of labor, is suspect as an old-fashioned luxury: "armchair thinking." It is supposed to "produce" something. The more superfluous physical labor is made by the development of technology, the more enthusiastically it is set up as a model for mental work, which must not be tempted, however, to draw any awkward conclusions. That is the secret of advancing stupidity, on which anti-Semitism thrives. If, even within the field of logic, the concept stands opposed to the particular as something merely external, anything which stands for difference within society itself must indeed tremble. Everyone is labeled friend or foe. The disregard for the subject makes things easy for the administration. Ethnic groups are transported to different latitudes; individuals labeled "Jew" are dispatched to the gas chambers.

The indifference to the individual expressed in logic draws its conclusions from the economic process. The individual had become an impediment to production. The lack of synchronicity between technical and human development, the "cultural lag" which used to exercise the minds of sociologists, is beginning to disappear. Economic rationality, the vaunted principle of the smallest necessary means, is unremittingly reshaping the last units of the economy: businesses and human beings. The most advanced form at a given time becomes the predominant one. Once, the department store expropriated the old-style specialist shop. The latter, having outgrown mercantilist regulation, had absorbed initiative, control, and organization within itself and become, like the old mill and smithy, a little factory, a free enterprise. Its mode of operation was complicated, expensive, risky. Competition therefore replaced it by the more efficient, centralized form of retail shop, the department store. The psychological small business—the individual—is meeting the same fate. It came into being as the power cell of economic activity. Emancipated from the tutelage of earlier economic stages, individuals fended for themselves alone: as proletarians by hiring themselves out through the labor market and by constant adaptation to new technical conditions, as entrepreneurs by tirelessly realizing of the ideal type of *homo oeconomicus*. Psychoanalysis has portrayed the internal small business which thus came into being as a complex dynamic of unconscious and conscious elements, of id, ego, and superego. In its negotiations with the superego, the ego, the agency of social control within the individual, keeps the drives within the limits set by self-preservation. The areas of friction are large and neuroses, the incidental expenses of such a drive economy, inevitable. Nevertheless, this complex psychical apparatus made possible the relatively free interplay of subjects which constituted the market economy. In the era of large combines and world wars, however, the mediation of the social process by innumerable monads is proving obsolete. The subjects of the drive economy are being psychologically expropriated, and the drive economy is being more rationally operated by society itself. The individual no longer has to decide what he or she is supposed to do in a given situation in a painful inner dialogue between conscience, self-preservation, and drives. For the human being as wage earner the decision is taken by a hierarchy extending from trade associations to the national administration; in the private sphere it is taken by the schema of mass culture, which appropriates even the most intimate impulses of its forced consumers. The committees and stars function as ego and superego, and the masses, stripped of even the semblance of personality, are molded far more compliantly by the catchwords and models than ever the instincts were by the internal censor. If, in liberalism, the individuation of a section of the population was necessary for the adaptation of society as a whole to the state of technology, today the functioning of the economic apparatus demands that the masses be directed without the hindrance of individuation. The economically determined direction of the whole society, which has always governed the mental and physical constitution of human beings, is causing the organs which enabled individuals to manage their lives autonomously to atrophy. Now that thinking has become a mere sector of the division of labor, the plans of the authorized experts and leaders have made individuals who plan their own happiness redundant. The irrationality of the unresisting and eager adaptation to reality becomes, for the individual, more reasonable than reason. If, previously, the bourgeois had introjected the compulsions of conscience and duty into themselves and the workers, now the entire human being has become at once the subject and the object of repression. In the progress of industrial society, which is supposed to have conjured away the law of increasing misery it had itself brought into being, the concept which justified the whole—the human being as person, as the bearer of reason—is going under. The dialectic of enlightenment is culminating objectively in madness.

This is also a madness of political reality. As a dense web of modern communications, the world has become so standardized that the differences between diplomatic breakfasts in Dumbarton Oaks and Persia have to be specially devised as an expression of national character, while actual national peculiarity is experienced primarily by the millions hungering for rice who have fallen through the narrow meshes. Although the abundance of goods which could be produced everywhere and simultaneously makes the struggle for raw materials and markets seem ever more anachronistic, humanity is nevertheless divided into a small number of armed power blocs. They compete more pitilessly than the firms involved in the anarchy of commodity production ever did, and strive toward mutual liquidation. The more senseless the antagonism, the more rigid the blocs. Only the total identification of the population with these monstrosities of power, so deeply imprinted as to have become second nature and stopping all the pores of consciousness, maintains the masses in the state of absolute apathy which makes them capable of their miraculous achievements. As far as any decisions are still left to individuals, they are effectively decided in advance. The irreconcilability of the ideologies trumpeted by the politicians from the different camps is itself just one more ideology of the blind constellation of power. Ticket thinking, a product of industrialization and its advertising, is being extended to international relations. Whether a citizen chooses the communist or the fascist ticket depends on whether he happens to be more impressed by the Red Army or the laboratories of the West. The reification by virtue of which the power structure, made possible solely by the passivity of the masses, appears to those same masses as an iron reality, has been consolidated to the point where any spontaneity, or even the ability to conceive of the true state of affairs, has necessarily become an eccentric utopia, an irrelevant sectarianism. Illusion has become so concentrated that to see through it objectively assumes the character of hallucination. To vote for a ticket, by contrast, means to practice adaptation to illusion petrified as reality, which endlessly reproduces itself through such adaptation. The reluctant voter is therefore ostracized as a deserter. Since Hamlet, hesitation was for modern people a sign of reflection and humanity. The wasted time at once represented and mediated the gap between individual and universal, as circulation does between consumption and production in the economy. Today individuals receive their tickets ready-made from the powers that be, as consumers receive their automobiles from the sales outlets of factories. Conformity to reality, adaptation to power, are no longer the result of a dialectical process between subject and reality but are produced directly by the cogs and levers of industry. The process is one of liquidation instead of sublation, of formal instead of determinate negation. The unleashed colossi of production have subdued the individual not by granting him or her full satisfaction, but by extinguishing the subject. Precisely therein lies their perfect rationality, which coincides with their insanity. The extreme disproportion between collective and individual eliminates tension, but the untroubled harmony between omnipotence and impotence is itself unmediated contradiction, the absolute antithesis of reconciliation.

For this reason the psychological determinants of the individual— which have always been the internal human agencies of wrong society— have not disappeared with the individual itself. However, these character types are now being assigned to their mathematically exact positions within the coordinates of power. Both their efficiency and their coefficient of friction are included in the calculation. The ticket acts as a gearwheel in this process. Anything in the old psychological mechanism which was compulsive, unfree, and irrational is precisely adjusted to it. The reactionary ticket which includes anti-Semitism is suited to the destructive-conventional syndrome. It is not so much that such people react originally against the Jews as that their drive-structure has developed a tendency toward persecution which the ticket then furnishes with an adequate object. The "elements of anti-Semitism" once derived from experience and now rendered inoperative by the loss of experience reflected in ticket thinking, are remobilized by the ticket. Being already corrupted, these elements also provide the neo-anti-Semite with the bad conscience and thus with the insatiability of evil. Just because the psychology of the individual can now construct itself and its content only from the synthetic schemata supplied by society, contemporary anti-Semitism takes on its empty but impenetrable character The Jewish middleman fully becomes the image of the devil only when economically he has ceased to exist. Victory is thus made easy, and the anti-Semitic family man becomes the spectator, exempt from responsibility, of an irresistible historical tendency, intervening only when called to do so by his role as an employee of the Party or the Zyklon gas factories. As they designate obsolete sections of the population for extermination, the administrations of totalitarian states are merely the executors of economic verdicts passed long ago. Members of other branches of the division of labor can look on with the indifference of people reading newspaper reports on clean-up operations at the scene of yesterday's catastrophe. The peculiarities for the sake of which the victims are killed have long been effaced. Those who fall within the terms of the decree as Jews have to be identified by means of elaborate questionnaires, now that the antagonistic religions which once differentiated them have been successfully remodeled and assimilated as cultural heritage under the leveling pressure of late-industrial society. The Jewish masses themselves are no more immune to ticket thinking than the most hostile youth organization. In this sense fascist anti-Semitism is obliged to invent its own object. Paranoia no longer pursues its goal on the basis of the individual case history of the persecutor; having become a vital component of society it must locate that goal within the delusive context of wars and economic cycles before the psychologically predisposed "national comrades" can support themselves on it, both inwardly and outwardly, as patients.

The tendency according to which anti-Semitism now exists only as one item on an interchangeable ticket gives irrefutable reason to hope for its end. The Jews are being murdered at a time when the leaders could replace the anti-Semitic plank in their platform just as easily as their followers can be transplanted from one location of wholly rationalized production to another. The development which leads to ticket thinking is based, in any case, on the universal reduction of every specific energy to the one, identical, abstract form of labor, from the battlefield to the studio. However, the transition from those conditions to a more human state cannot take place, because benign and malign tendencies suffer the same fate. The freedom on the progressive ticket is as far removed from the existing political power structures, to which progressive decisions necessarily lead, as hostility to the Jews is external to the chemical cartel. To be sure, the psychologically more humane are attracted to freedom, but the advancing loss of experience is finally turning even the supporters of the progressive ticket into enemies of difference. It is not just the anti-Semitic ticket which is anti-Semitic, but the ticket mentality itself. The rage against difference which is teleologically inherent in that mentality as the rancor of the dominated subjects of the domination of nature is always ready to attack the natural minority, even though it is the social minority which those subjects primarily threaten. The socially responsible elite is in any case far harder to pin down than other minorities. In the murky intertwinement of property, ownership, control, and management it successfully eludes theoretical definition. The ideology of race and the reality of class both equally reveal only an abstract difference from the majority. But although the progressive ticket tends to produce something worse than its content, the content of the fascist ticket is so vacuous that it can be maintained as a substitute for something better only by desperate efforts on the part of the deceived. Its horror is that of the blatant but insistent lie. While it admits no truth by which it might be measured, its absurdity is so monstrous as to bring truth negatively within reach, so that it can be kept apart from those deprived of judgment only by their total abstention from thought. Enlightenment itself, having mastered itself and assumed its own power, could break through the limits of enlightenment.

Notes and Sketches

AGAINST KNOWINGNESS

One of the lessons of the Hitler period is the stupidity of cleverness. How many were the expert arguments with which Jews dismissed the likelihood of Hitler's rise, when it was already as clear as daylight. I recall a conversation with an economist who demonstrated the impossibility of Germany's militarization from the interests of Bavarian brewers. And in any case, according to the clever people, fascism was impossible in the West. Clever people have always made things easy for barbarians, because they are so stupid. It is the well-informed, farsighted judgments, the prognoses based on statistics and experience, the observations which begin: "I happen to be an expert in this field," it is the well-founded, conclusive statements which are untrue.

Hitler was against intellect and humanity. But there is also an intellect which is against humanity: it is distinguished by well-informed superiority.

Postscript

That cleverness is becoming stupidity is inherent in the historical tendency. To be reasonable, in the sense used by Chamberlain when he called Hitler's demands at Bad Godesberg* unreasonable, means to insist that there be equivalence between giving and taking. Such reason is modeled on exchange. Objectives may be attained only through the mediation of a kind of market, in the little advantages that power can steal while respecting the rule by which one concession is exchanged for another. Cleverness is helpless as soon as power disregards that rule and simply appropriates directly. The medium of traditional bourgeois intelligence, discussion, is in decline. Even individuals can no longer converse, and know it; that is why they have turned card games into a serious, responsible institution that calls on all their powers, so that although there are no conversations, the silence goes unheard. It is no different on the big stage. A fascist does not like to be spoken to. When others have their say, he takes it as an impudent interruption. He is impervious to reason because he recognizes it only in concessions made by others.

The contradiction of the stupidity of cleverness is necessary. For bourgeois reason is obliged to claim universality while its own development curtails it. Just as, in an exchange, each party receives its due but social injustice nevertheless results, the exchange economy's form of reflection, the prevalent rationality, is just, universal, and particularistic, the instrument of privilege within equality. Fascism makes it pay the price. It openly represents the particular interest, thus unmasking reason, which wrongly flaunts its universality, as itself limited. That this turns clever people all at once into dunces convicts reason of its own unreason.

But the fascist, too, suffers under the contradiction. For bourgeois reason is not only particularistic but also, indeed, universal, and in denying its universality fascism defeats itself. Those who came to power in Germany were smarter than the liberals and more stupid. The "progress toward the new order" has been carried largely by people whose consciousness progress has left behind—bankrupts, sectarians, fools. They are exempt from error as long as their power precludes all competition. In the competition between states, however, the fascists not only are just as capable of making mistakes but—with qualities such as myopia, bigotry, ignorance of economic forces, and, above all, the inability to perceive the negative and include it in their assessment of the situation as a whole—are also impelled subjectively toward the catastrophe which, in their hearts, they have always expected.

TWO WORLDS

In this country* there is no difference between a person and that person's economic fate. No one is anything other than his wealth, his income, his job, his prospects. In the consciousness of everyone, including its wearer, the economic mask coincides exactly with what lies beneath it, even in its smallest wrinkles. All are worth as much as they earn, and earn as much as they are worth. They find out what they are through the ups and downs of their economic life. They know themselves as nothing else. If the materialist critique of society once opposed idealism by asserting that it is not consciousness which determines being but being consciousness, and that the truth about society is to be found not in its idealistic notions of itself but in its economy, up-to-date self-consciousness has meanwhile discarded such idealism. People judge their own selves by their market value and find out who they are from how they fare in the capitalist economy. Their fate, however sad it may be, is for them not something external: they acknowledge it. A Chinese, taking leave,

> Spoke with tear-dimmed tones: On me, my friend
> The smile of worldly fortune did not fall.
> And now I leave to wander mountain paths
> Seeking my heart's peace in their loneliness.*

"I am a failure," says the American—and that is that.

THE TRANSFORMATION OF THE IDEA
INTO POWER

Familiar tendencies from recent times are sometimes found prefigured in ancient, exotic history, where distance lends them a heightened clarity.

In his commentary on the Isa-Upanishad, Deussen[1] argues that in that work Indian thought took a step beyond what had gone before in the same way as Jesus in the Gospel according to St. Matthew[2] went beyond St. John the Baptist, and the Stoics beyond the Cynics. However, this observation is historically one-sided because the uncompromising ideas of John the Baptist and of the Cynics, no less than the views against which the first lines of the Isa-Upanishad are supposed to represent progress,[3] look much more like left-wing secessionist tendencies which have split off from powerful cliques and parties than central tendencies of historical movements, from which European philosophy, Christianity, and the living Vedic religion themselves branched off. Accordingly, as Deussen himself notes, the Isa-Upanishad is usually placed at the beginning of Indian collections, long before the writings it is said to have gone beyond. Yet this first work itself shows traces of a betrayal of youthful radicalism, of treachery against revolutionary opposition to the dominant reality.

Vedantism, Stoicism, and Christianity took the step which made them capable of organization when they began to participate in social reality and to construct unified theoretical systems. That step was mediated by the doctrine that an active role in life need not be harmful to the salvation of the soul, provided one has the right spiritual outlook. To be sure, Christianity reached this point only with St Paul. The idea which distances itself from the existing order turns into religion. Those who refused to compromise were censured. They stood aloof "from the desire for children, the desire for wealth, the desire for the world, and wandered about as beggars. For the desire for children is a desire for property, and the desire for property is a worldly desire; and both alike are vain."[4] Those who express such views may speak the truth according to the upholders of civilization, but they do not keep step with the course of social life. They therefore became madmen, and did indeed resemble John the Baptist. He "was clothed with camel's hair, and had a girdle of skin about his loins; and he did eat locusts and wild honey."[5] "The cynics," says Hegel, "have little philosophical training and never managed to produce a system, a science. Only later was their system made a philosophical discipline, by the Stoics."[6] "Swinish, shameless beggars,"[7] he called these successors.

The uncompromising figures of whom history has left some record did not entirely lack an organized following; otherwise not even their names would have come down to us. They set up at least some part of a systematic doctrine or a code of behavior. Even the more radical Upanishads, attacked by the Isa-Upanishad, were verses and sacrificial formulae used by priestly guilds;[8] John the Baptist may not have inaugurated a religion, but he did found an order.[9] The Cynics formed a school of philosophers; its founder, Antisthenes, even sketched the outlines of a theory of the state.[10] But the theoretical and practical systems of such historical outsiders were unstructured, without a center, and differed from the successful systems by a streak of anarchy. The idea and the individual mean more to them than administration and the collective. They therefore provoke anger. Plato, the champion of power, had the Cynics in his sights when he railed against equating the office of king with that of a common shepherd and compared a loose organization of humanity without national frontiers to a state of swine.[11] The uncompromising spirits may have been willing to unite and cooperate, but they lacked the skill to construct a solid hierarchy closed to those from below. Neither in their theory, which was without uniformity or consistency, nor in their practice, which lacked the cohesion to make an impact, did they themselves reflect the world as it actually was.

That was the formal difference between the radical and the conformist movements in religion and philosophy, which did not lie in their content in isolation. The sect of the ascetic Gautama conquered the Asiatic world. During his lifetime he showed a great talent for organization. Even if he did not, like the reformer Cankara, exclude the lower orders from the communication of his doctrine,[12] he expressly acknowledged property in human beings and prided himself on the "sons of noble families" who joined his order, in which pariahs, "if present at all, appear to have been rare exceptions."[13] From the first, his disciples were differentiated on the Brahmin model.[14] Cripples, the sick, criminals, and many others were denied admission.[15] Have you, applicants were asked, "leprosy, scrofula, white leprosy, consumption, epilepsy? Are you a human being? Are you a man? Are you your own master? Are you without debts? Are you not in the king's service?" and so on. Fully in keeping with India's brutal patriarchalism, women were admitted only reluctantly to the original Buddhist order. They had to subjugate themselves to the men and remained in effect minors.[16] The entire order enjoyed the patronage of the rulers and fitted admirably into Indian life.

Asceticism and materialism, those opposites, are ambiguous in the same way. Asceticism as a refusal to participate in the bad existing order coincides, in face of oppression, with the material demands of the masses, just as, conversely, asceticism as an agent of discipline, imposed by cliques, aims at adaptation to injustice. The materialistic acceptance of the status quo, individual egoism, has always been linked to renunciation, while the gaze of the unworldly zealot, roving beyond the existing order, rests materialistically on the land of milk and honey. Asceticism is sublated in true materialism, and materialism in true asceticism. The history of those ancient religions and schools, like that of the modern parties and revolutions, can teach us that the price of survival is practical complicity, the transformation of the idea into power.

THE THEORY OF GHOSTS

Freud's theory that the belief in ghosts comes from the evil thoughts of the living about the dead, from the memory of old death wishes, is too narrow. The hatred of the dead is jealousy as much as a feeling of guilt. Those left behind feel abandoned, and attribute their pain to the deceased who causes it. At the stages of humanity's development when death still appeared as a direct continuation of life, the abandonment of the living in death seemed necessarily like a betrayal, and even in enlightened times the old belief is not quite extinguished. It runs counter to consciousness to conceive of death as absolute nothingness; absolute nothingness cannot be thought. And as the burden of life falls back on those left behind, the situation of the dead can readily seem the better state. The way in which some bereaved people entirely reorganize their lives after the death of one close to them, the busy cult of the deceased or, inversely, the forgetting rationalized as tact, are the modern counterpart to the belief in ghosts which, in unsublimated form, continues unabated in spiritualism. Only when the horror of annihilation is raised fully into consciousness are we placed in the proper relationship to the dead: that of unity with them, since we, like them, are victims of the same conditions and of the same disappointed hope.

Postscript

The disturbed relationship to the dead—who are forgotten and embalmed—is one of the symptoms of the sickness of experience today. It might almost be said that the concept of human life itself, as the unity of a person's history, has become invalid: the individual's life is now defined merely by its opposite, annihilation, but has lost all concordance, all continuity between conscious remembrance and involuntary memory— meaning. Individuals are reduced to a mere succession of instantaneous presents, which leave behind no trace, or rather, the trace of which they hate as something irrational, superfluous, utterly obsolete. Just as any book which has not been published recently is suspect; just as the idea of history, outside the specialized activities of the academic discipline, makes up-to-date people nervous, the past of a human being makes them furious. What someone was and experienced earlier is annulled in face of what he is now, or of the purpose for which he can be used. The threateningly well-meaning advice frequently given to emigrants that they should forget the past because it cannot be transplanted, that they should write off their prehistory and start an entirely new life, merely inflicts verbally on the spectral intruders the violence they have long learned to do to themselves. They repress history in themselves and others, out of fear that it might remind them of the disintegration of their own lives, a disintegration which itself consists largely in the repression of history. The fate which befalls all feelings, the ostracizing of what has no market value, is applied most harshly to something which cannot even contribute to a psychological restoration of labor power, mourning. It is becoming the stigma of civilization, an asocial sentimentality which reveals that human beings have not yet been made to swear absolute allegiance to the realm of purposes. Therefore mourning, more than all else, is disfigured, deliberately turned into the social formality which, for the hardened survivors, the beautiful corpse has always been. In the funeral home and the crematorium, where the deceased are processed into transportable ashes, into a burdensome possession, it is indeed untimely to let oneself go, and the young girl who, proudly describing the first-class funeral of her grandmother, added: "A pity that Daddy lost control," because he had shed a few tears, precisely expresses the current state of affairs. The dead are in truth subjected to what for the ancient Jews was the most grievous curse: To thee shall no thoughts be turned. The living vent on the dead their despair that they no longer give thought to themselves.

QUAND MÊME

External pressure has forced human beings to overcome their own inertia, to produce material and intellectual works. Thinkers from Democritus to Freud are not wrong in believing this. The resistance of external nature, to which the pressure can finally be traced back, propagates itself in society through the classes, acting on all human beings from childhood onward as the callousness of their fellows. People are gentle when they want something from those who are stronger, and harsh when the weaker want something from them. That has been the key to the nature of the person in society up to now.

The conclusion drawn by conservatives, that terror and civilization are inseparable, is well founded. What could enable human beings to develop the ability to master complex stimuli, if not their own developmental exertions, which have to be spurred on by external resistance? The resistance which drives them is first embodied in the father; later it grows a thousand heads: teachers, superiors, customers, competitors, the representatives of social and state powers. Their brutality stimulates individual spontaneity.

That this harshness might be moderated in the future, that the bloody punishments by which humanity has been tamed in the course of centuries could be replaced by the establishment of sanatoria, seems no more than a dream. Simulated compulsion is powerless. Culture has evolved under the shadow of the executioner; Genesis, which tells of the expulsion from Paradise, and the *Soirées de Petersbourg** are in agreement on this. Work and pleasure take place under the shadow of the executioner. To contradict this is to fly in the face of all science, all logic. One cannot abolish terror and retain civilization. Even to relax the former means the beginning of disintegration. The most diverse conclusions can be drawn from this: from the worship of fascist barbarism to a flight into the circles of Hell.* There is one other possibility: to scorn logic, if it is against humanity.

ANIMAL PSYCHOLOGY*

A large dog stands beside the highway. If he walks trustfully onto it he will be run over. His peaceful expression indicates that normally he is better looked after—a pet which no one harms. But do the sons of the upper bourgeoisie, whom no one harms, have peaceful expressions on their faces? They have not been worse looked after than the dog, which is now run over.

FOR VOLTAIRE

Your reason is one-sided, whispers one-sided reason; you have done power an injustice. You have trumpeted the scandal of tyranny eloquently, tearfully, sarcastically, thunderously; but the good that power has brought about—on that you have kept silent. Without the security which only power could establish, that good would never have come into being. Beneath the wings of power, life and love have played; even your own happiness has been wrested from hostile nature by power. Thoughts inspired by apologetics are true and false at once. Despite its great accomplishments, only power can commit injustice, for only the executed judgment is unjust, not the lawyer's unexecuted plea. Only when discourse aims at oppression, defending power instead of powerlessness, does it contribute to the general wrong. But power, one-sided reason now whispers, is represented by human beings. By exposing the former, you make a target of the latter. And after them, worse perhaps will come. The lie speaks truth. When fascist murderers are waiting, one should not incite the people against the weak government. But even the alliance with the less brutal power does not imply that one should keep silent about infamies. The likelihood that good causes might be damaged by denunciation of the injustice which protects them from the devil has always been outweighed by the advantage the devil gains if the denunciation of injustice is left solely to him. How far must a society have sunk in which only scoundrels still speak the truth—and Goebbels reminds us that the lynch mob is still happily at work. Not the good but the bad is the subject matter of theory. Theory presupposes the reproduction of life in its existing forms. Its element is freedom, its theme oppression. Where language grows apologetic, it is already corrupted; by its nature it can be neither neutral nor practical.—Could you not portray the good sides of life and proclaim love as a principle, instead of endless bitterness?—There is only one expression for truth: the thought which repudiates injustice. If insistence on the good sides of life is not sublated in the negative whole, it transfigures its own opposite: violence. With words I can intrigue, propagate, suggest; that is the attribute which entangles them, as it entangles all activity in the world, and is the only one which is understood by the lie. It insinuates that even when one contradicts the existing order, one is acting in the service of other, emergent powers, competing bureaucracies, and rulers. In its nameless fear, it can and will see only what resembles itself. Anything which is absorbed into its medium, language as mere instrument, becomes identical to the lie as objects become indistinguishable in darkness. But although it is true that there is no word which could not ultimately be used by the lie, the word's temper never gleams in the lie but only in the thought hardened in the fight against power. Uncompromising hatred of the terror inflicted on the last of the earth's creatures legitimizes the gratitude of those who are spared. Invocation of the sun is idolatry. Only the spectacle of the tree withered in its heat gives a presentiment of the majesty of the day which will not scorch the world on which it shines.

CLASSIFICATION

General concepts coined by means of abstraction or axiomatically by individual sciences form the material of representation no less than the names of individual objects. Opposition to general concepts is absurd. There is more to be said, however, about the status of the general. What many individual things have in common, or what constantly recurs in one individual thing, needs not be more stable, eternal, or deep than the particular. The scale of categories is not the same as that of significance. That was precisely the error of the Eleatics and all who followed them, with Plato and Aristotle at their head.

The world is unique. The mere repetition in speech of moments which occur again and again in the same form bears more resemblance to a futile, compulsive litany than to the redeeming word. Classification is a condition of knowledge, not knowledge itself, and knowledge in turn dissolves classification.

AVALANCHE

The present time is without turning points. A turn of events is always for the better. But when, as today, calamity is at its height, the heavens open and hurl their fire on those who are lost in any case.

This impression is communicated first of all by what was commonly called the social and political sphere. At one time, the front pages of daily newspapers seemed strange and vulgar to happy women and children—newspapers reminded them of alehouse swagger—until the bold headline finally crossed their threshold as a real threat. Rearmament, overseas affairs, tension in the Mediterranean, and who knows what other grandiose phrases put genuine fear into people, until the First World War broke out. Then, with its ever more dizzying figures, came inflation.

When it paused in its course, that did not mean a turning point but still greater misfortune: rationalization, closures, demolition. When Hitler's vote went up, modestly at first but insistently, it was already clear that its motion was that of an avalanche. Voting figures are, indeed, characteristic of that phenomenon. When, on the evening of the prefascist election day, the first results came in from the districts an eighth, a sixteenth of the votes already anticipated the whole. If ten or twenty districts turn *en masse* in a certain direction, the remaining hundred will not oppose them. Already a uniform mentality exists. The essence of the world coincides with the statistical law by which its surface is classified.

In Germany, fascism triumphed under a crassly xenophobic, anti-cultural, collectivist ideology. Now that it has devastated the earth, nations must fight against it; there is no other way. But when all is over, a spirit of freedom need not spread across Europe; its nations may become as xenophobic, as hostile to culture, and as pseudocollectivist as the fascism against which they had to defend themselves. Even its defeat will not necessarily break the motion of the avalanche.

The fundamental principle of liberal philosophy was that of both/and. Today the principle of either/or seems to apply, but in such a way that the decision has already been taken for the worse.

ISOLATION BY COMMUNICATION

That communication media cause isolation is true not only in the intellectual sphere. Not only does the mendacious idiom of the radio announcer fix itself in the brain as an image of language itself, preventing people from speaking to one another; not only does the voice advertising Pepsi-Cola drown out the leveling of continents; not only does the ghostly image of the cinema hero model the embraces of adolescents, and later adultery. Progress keeps people literally apart. The little counter at the railroad station or the bank allowed the clerks to whisper to their colleagues and share their meager secrets; the glass partitions of modern offices, the huge rooms in which countless employees sitting together can be easily supervised both by the public and by their managers, no longer countenance private conversations and idylls. Even in offices, the taxpayer is now protected from wasting of time by wage earners, who are isolated in their collective. But the means of communication also isolate people physically.

The railroad has been supplanted by cars. The making of travel acquaintances is reduced by the private automobile to half-threatening encounters with hitchhikers. People travel on rubber tires in strict isolation from one another. What is talked about in one family automobile is the same as in another; in the nuclear family, conversation is regulated by practical interests. Just as every family with a certain income spends the same percentage on housing, cinema, cigarettes, exactly as statistics prescribe, the subject matter of conversations is schematized according to the class of automobile. When they meet on Sunday outings or in restaurants, the menus and décor of which are identical to others in the same price category, the guests find that with increasing isolation they have become more and more alike. Communication makes people conform by isolating them.

ON THE CRITIQUE OF THE PHILOSOPHY OF HISTORY

The human species is not, as has been asserted, a freak event in natural history, an incidental and abnormal formation produced by hypertrophy of the cerebral organ. That assertion is true only of reason in certain individuals, or perhaps even of a few countries over short periods, when the economy has allowed maneuvering space to such individuals. The cerebral organ, human intelligence, is firmly established enough to constitute a regular epoch of the earth's history. In this epoch, the human species, including its machines, chemicals, and organizational powers—for why should they not be seen as a part of it as teeth are a part of the bear, since they serve the same purpose and merely function better?—is the last word in adaptation. Humans have not only overtaken their immediate predecessors but have eradicated them more thoroughly than almost any other recent species, not excluding the carnivorous saurians.

In face of this it seems somewhat whimsical to try to construe world history, as did Hegel, in terms of categories such as freedom and justice. These categories do indeed originate in eccentric individuals, who are insignificant in relation to the general course of the whole, unless it be that they help to bring about transient historical conditions in which especially large quantities of machines and chemicals are produced to strengthen the species and subjugate others. According to this serious history, all ideas, prohibitions, religions, and political creeds are of interest only insofar as, arising from diverse conditions, they increase or decrease the natural survival prospects of the human species on the earth or within the universe. The liberation of citizens from the injustice of the feudal and absolutist past served, through liberalism, to unleash machinery, just as the emancipation of women has culminated in their being trained as a branch of the armed forces. The mind, and all that is good in its origins and existence, is hopelessly implicated in this horror. We owe the serum which the doctor administers to the sick child to the attack on defenseless creatures. In the endearments of lovers, as in the most sacred symbols of Christianity, we can detect the lust for the flesh of the kid, just as the ambiguous respect for the totem animal is discernible in that lust. Even our complex understanding of cooking, church, and theater is a consequence of the sophisticated division of labor, which exists at the expense of nature within and outside human society. The historical function of culture lies in retroactively heightening this form of organization. That is why genuine thought, which detaches itself from that function, reason in its pure form, takes on the trait of madness which down-to-earth people have never failed to observe. If that kind of reason were to win a decisive victory within humanity, the predominance of the species would be threatened. The "freak event" theory would finally turn out to be true. But that theory, which cynically sought to support a critique of the anthropocentric philosophy of history, is itself too anthropocentric to hold true. Reason acts as an instrument of adaptation and not as a sedative, as might appear from the use sometimes made of it by individuals. Its ruse consists in making humans into beasts with an ever-wider reach, and not in bringing about the identity of subject and object.

A philosophical interpretation of world history would have to show how, despite all the detours and resistances, the systematic domination over nature has been asserted more and more decisively and has integrated all internal human characteristics. Economic, political, and cultural forms* would have to be derived from this position. The idea of the superhuman can be applicable only in the sense of a transition from quantity to quality. Just as the airman with the toxic spray, who in a few flights can cleanse the last continents of the last free animals, might be called superman in comparison to the troglodyte,* a human super-amphibian might come into being for whom the airman of today would seem like a harmless swallow. But it is doubtful whether a species one stage higher than man can emerge as a genuine product of natural history. For anthropomorphism contains a measure of truth in that natural history did not reckon with the happy throw of the dice it accomplished in engendering the human being. The human capacity for destruction promises to become so great that—once this species has exhausted itself—a *tabula rasa* will have been created. Either the human species will tear itself to pieces or it will take all the earth's fauna and flora down with it, and if the earth is still young enough, the whole procedure—to vary a famous dictum*—will have to start again on a much lower level.

By attributing humane ideas as active powers to history, and presenting them as history's culmination, the philosophy of history stripped them of the naivety inherent in their content. The poor figure always cut by such ideas when the economy—that is, when power—was not with them* makes a mockery of everything weak, and in this way their authors have unwittingly identified themselves with the oppression they sought to abolish. The philosophy of history repeats what happened in Christianity: the good, which in reality remains at the mercy of suffering, is dressed up as a force which determines the course of history and finally triumphs. It is deified as the World Spirit or as an immanent law. But not only is history thereby turned into its direct opposite, but the idea, which was supposed to break the necessity, the logical course of events, is itself distorted. The danger of the "freak event" is averted. Impotence mistaken for power is denied a second time by such elevation, as if erased from memory. In this way, Christianity, idealism, and materialism, which in themselves contain truth, also bear guilt for the villainies committed in their name. In proclaiming power—even a benign power—they became themselves highly organized historical powers, and as such played their bloody role in the real history of the human species: as instruments of organization.

Because history as the correlative of unified theory, as something capable of interpretation, is not the good but, in fact, the horror, thought is in reality a negative element. The hope for better conditions, insofar as it is not merely an illusion, is founded less on the assurance that those conditions are guaranteed, sustainable, and final than on a lack of respect for what is so firmly ensconced amid the general suffering. The infinite patience, the tender, never-extinguished impulse of creaturely life toward expression and light, which seems to soften and pacify within itself the violence of creative evolution, does not, like the rational philosophies of history, prescribe a certain praxis as beneficial, not even that of nonresistance. The light of reason, which dawned in that impulse and is reflected in the recollecting thought of human beings, falls, even on the happiest day, on its irresolvable contradiction: the calamity which reason alone cannot avert.

MONUMENTS TO HUMANITY

Humanity has always been more at home in France than elsewhere. But the French were no longer aware of the fact. What their books contained was ideology recognized by all. The better qualities led a segregated existence of their own: in the inflection of voice, the turn of phrase, the artful cuisine, the existence of brothels, the cast-iron pissoirs. But the Blum government* already declared war on such respect for the individual, and even the conservatives did little to protect its monuments.

FROM A THEORY OF THE CRIMINAL*

. . . Like the criminal, imprisonment was a bourgeois affair. In the Middle Ages incarceration was reserved for the offspring of princes who symbolized an inconvenient hereditary claim. Criminals were tortured to death, to instill a respect for order and law in the mass of the population, since the example of severity and cruelty teaches the severe and cruel to love. Regular imprisonment presupposes a rising need for labor power.* It reflects the bourgeois mode of life as suffering. The rows of cells in a modern prison represent monads in the true Leibnizian sense. "The Monads have no windows, through which anything could come in or go out. Accidents cannot separate themselves from substances nor go about outside them, as the 'sensible species' of the Scholastics used to do. Thus neither substance nor accident can come into a Monad from outside."[17] The monads have no direct influence on one another; their lives are regulated and coordinated by God, or the prison administration.[18] The absolute loneliness, the enforced reliance on a self whose whole being consists in the mastering of material and the monotonous rhythm of work, spectrally prefigure human existence in the modern world. The radical isolation and the radical reduction to an unchanging, hopeless nothingness are identical. The human being in jail is the virtual image of the bourgeois type he has yet to make himself in reality. Those who fail to achieve this outside have it inflicted on them with terrible purity inside. The rationalization of prison life through the need to segregate the criminal from society, or even to improve him, does not go to the root of the matter. Prisons are the image of the bourgeois working world thought through to the end, set up as an emblem in the world by the hatred of human beings for what they are forced to make themselves become. The weak, the retarded, the brutalized must suffer in modified form the order of life to which others have lovelessly adapted themselves; the introverted violence of the latter is grimly repeated against the former. The criminal, in whose crime self-preservation was paramount, has in reality the weaker, more labile self; the habitual offender is an enfeebled being.

Prisoners are invalids. Their weakness has brought them into a situation which has undermined them in body and mind and continues to do so. Most were already sick when they committed the crime which put them in prison—sick through their constitution and their circumstances. Other acted as any healthy person would in the same constellation of stimuli and motives but were simply unlucky. A residue were more malevolent and cruel than most free people—as malevolent and cruel in their persons as the fascist world rulers are through their positions. The deed of the common criminal is petty, personal, directly destructive. The probability is that even in the case of the most extreme crimes the living substance, which is the same in everyone, could not, in any embodiment, have escaped the pressure of bodily constitution and individual fate from birth onward which led the criminal to the crime; and that you and I, but for the grace of the insight granted to us through a chain of circumstances, would have acted like the person who committed murder. And now, as prisoners, they are mere invalids, and the punishment meted out to them is blind, an alien event, a misfortune like cancer or the collapse of a house. Imprisonment is a lingering illness. This is revealed by prisoners' expressions, their cautious gait, their circumstantial way of thinking. Like the sick, they can talk only of their sickness.

When, as today, the boundaries between respectable and illegal rackets are objectively fluid, psychological figures also merge. But as long as criminals were still invalids, as in the nineteenth century, custody represented a reversal of their weakness. The strength to stand out as an individual against one's environment and, at the same time, to make contact with it through the approved forms of intercourse and thereby to assert oneself within it—in criminals this strength was eroded. They represented a tendency deeply inherent in living things, the overcoming of which is the mark of all development: the tendency to lose oneself in one's surroundings instead of actively engaging with them, the inclination to let oneself go, to lapse back into nature. Freud called this the death impulse, Caillois *le mimétisme*.[19] Addiction of this kind permeates anything which runs counter to unswerving progress, from crime, which cannot take the detour through the current forms of labor, to the sublime work of art. The yielding attitude to things without which art cannot exist is not so far removed from the clenched violence of the criminal. The inability to say No which causes the young girl to succumb to prostitution also tends to determine the career of the criminal. He is characterized by a negation which lacks the power of resistance. Against such deliquescence, which—without definite consciousness, timid and impotent even in its most brutal form—at the same time imitates and destroys pitiless civilization, the latter sets the solid walls of prisons and workhouses, its own stony ideal. Just as, according to de Tocqueville, bourgeois republics, unlike monarchies, do not violate the body but set to work directly on the soul, punishments of this kind attack the spirit. Those they torture no longer die broken on the wheel over long days and nights but perish mentally, as silent, invisible examples in the great prison buildings, which differ from lunatic asylums almost only in name.

Fascism absorbs both institutions. The concentration of command throughout production is causing society to revert to the stage of direct rule. As the detour of power via the internal markets of nations disappears, so, too, do intellectual mediations, including law. Thinking, which had developed though transactions, as a result of egoism's need to negotiate, is now given over wholly to the planning of violent appropriation. The fascist mass murderer has emerged as the pure essence of the German factory owner, no longer distinguished from the criminal by anything but power. The detour has become unnecessary. Civil law, which continued to function in regulating differences between entrepreneurs surviving in the shadow of big industry, has become a kind of tribunal against the lower orders, a justice which no longer upholds, however badly, the interests of victims—a mere instrument of terror. However, the legal protection which is now disappearing once defined property. Monopoly, as the consummation of private property, is annihilating the latter's concept. Of the international and social contract, which fascism* in its dealings with states is replacing by secret agreements, only the compulsion of the universal is allowed to apply in internal affairs, a compulsion its servants then liberally administer to the rest of humanity. In the totalitarian state* punishment and crime are being liquidated as superstitious residues, and a naked eradication of opponents, certain of its political goal, is spreading across Europe under the regime of criminals. Next to the concentration camp, the penitentiary seems like a memory of the good old days, much as the old-style advertiser, though it already betrayed truth, appears beside the glossy magazine, the literary content of which—even if it concerns Michelangelo—performs the function, still more than the advertisements, of business report, emblem of authority and publicity medium. The isolation once inflicted on prisoners from outside has by now implanted itself universally in the flesh and blood of individuals. Their well-trained souls and happiness are as bleak as the prison cells which the rulers can already do without, since the entire labor force of nations has fallen to them as spoils. The penal sentence pales beside the social reality.

LE PRIX DU PROGRÈS

In a recently discovered letter by the French physiologist Pierre Flourens, who once had the unhappy distinction of being elected to the Académie Française in preference to Victor Hugo, a curious passage occurs:

I still cannot bring myself to assent to the use of chloroform in general surgical practice. As you may know, I have devoted extensive study to this drug and as a result of animal experiments have been one of the first to describe its specific characteristics. My scruples are based on the simple fact that operations under chloroform, and probably also under the other known forms of narcosis, amount to a deception. The agents act only on certain motor and coordination centers and on the residual capacity of the nerve substance. Under the influence of chloroform it loses a significant part of its ability to record traces of impressions but not the capacity for feeling as such. On the contrary, my observations indicate that in conjunction with a general paralysis of innervation, pain is felt still more keenly than in the normal state. The deception of the public results from the inability of the patient to remember the events once the operation is completed. If we told our patients the truth, it is likely that none of them would opt for the drug, whereas now, as a result of our silence, they generally insist on its use.

But even disregarding the fact that the only, dubious benefit is a loss of memory regarding the time of the intervention, the spread of this practice seems to me to bring with it a far more serious danger. Given the increasing superficiality of the general academic training of our doctors, medicine might be encouraged by an unlimited use of the drug heedlessly to undertake ever more complicated and serious surgical interventions. Instead of carrying out such experiments on animals in the service of research, we should then make our patients the unwitting subjects of experiments. It is conceivable that the painful excitations which, in view of their specific nature, may exceed all known sensations of this kind, would cause lasting psychical damage to the patient, or might even lead to an indescribably agonizing death under narcosis, the peculiarities of which would remain for ever hidden from family members and the world. Would that not be altogether too great a price to pay for progress?

If Flourens were right in this letter, the obscure workings of the world's divine governance would at least for once be justified. The animal would be avenged by the sufferings of its executioner: each operation a vivisection. A suspicion would arise that our attitude toward human beings, and toward all creatures, is no different to that toward ourselves after a successful operation: blindness to torment. For cognition, the space separating us from others would mean the same thing as the time between us and the suffering in our own past: an insurmountable barrier. But the perennial dominion over nature, medical and nonmedical technology, derives its strength from such blindness; it would be made possible only by oblivion. Loss of memory as the transcendental condition of science. All reification is forgetting.*

VAIN TERROR

The gaze fixed on calamity has an element of fascination. But therefore of secret complicity. So strong are the social bad conscience of all who have a part in injustice, and the hatred of fulfilled life, that in critical situations they turn directly against self-interest as an immanent revenge. There was in the French bourgeois a fatal agency which ironically resembled the heroic ideal of the fascists: they rejoiced in the triumph of their likeness, as expressed in Hitler's rise, even though it threatened them with ruin; indeed, they took their own ruin as evidence of the justice of the order they represented. A precursor of this behavior is found in the attitude of many rich people to impoverishment, the image of which they conjure up under the rationalization of parsimony: it is their latent tendency, even while they fight tenaciously for every penny, suddenly to give up all their possessions without a fight or irresponsibly to gamble them away. In fascism they achieve the synthesis of power-craving and self-hate, and their vain terror is always accompanied by the qualification: I always saw it coming.

INTEREST IN THE BODY

Beneath the known history of Europe there runs a subterranean one. It consists of the fate of the human instincts and passions repressed and distorted by civilization. From the vantage point of the fascist present, in which the hidden is coming to light, the manifest history is also revealing its connection to that dark side, which is passed over in the official legend of nation states, and no less in its progressive critique.

Most mutilated of all is the relationship to the body. Under the division of labor, in which the benefits accrued to one side and labor to the other, brute strength was anathematized. The less the masters could do without the labor of the rest, the more base labor was declared to be. Like the slave, work received a stigma. Christianity celebrated labor but, in compensation, vilified the flesh as the source of all evil. In collusion with the unbeliever Machiavelli, it rang in the modern bourgeois order by extolling work, which in the Old Testament had been designated a curse. For the Desert Fathers, Dorotheus, Moses the Robber, Paul the Simple, and others of the poor in spirit, labor was still a direct means of entering the Kingdom of Heaven. For Luther and Calvin the link between work and salvation was already so convoluted that the relentless injunction to work seems almost like mockery, the boot grinding the worm into the dust.

The princes and patricians could console themselves for the religious gulf which had opened between their earthly days and their eternal vocation with the thought of the revenues they would derive from the labor time of others. For the irrationality of the doctrine of election left the possibility of redemption open to them. But on the others the pressure weighed all the more heavily. They were dimly aware that the mortification of the flesh by power was nothing other than the ideological reflection of the oppression practiced on them. The fate of the slaves of Antiquity was endured by victims up to the modern colonial peoples: they counted as inferior. There were by nature two races: the higher and the lower. The emancipation of the European individual took place in conjunction with a general cultural transformation by which the split within the emancipated penetrated more deeply the more the external physical compulsion abated. The exploited body was to be regarded by the lower orders as the bad and the mind, for which the others had leisure, as the highest good. This development made Europe capable of its most sublime cultural achievements, but, at the same time as the control over the body was increased, the hint of fraud which had been detectable from the first also intensified the obscene malice, the love-hate toward the body which permeated the mentality of the masses over the centuries and found its authentic expression in the language of Luther. In the relationship of individuals to the body, their own and that of others, is reenacted the irrationality and injustice of power as cruelty; and that irrationality is as far removed from judicious insight and serene reflection as power is from freedom. In Nietzsche's theory of cruelty, and still more in the work of Sade, the extent of this connection is recognized, while in Freud's doctrines of narcissism and the death impulse it is interpreted psychologically.

Love-hate for the body colors the whole of modern culture. The body is scorned and rejected as something inferior, enslaved, and at the same time is desired as forbidden, reified, estranged. Only culture treats the body as a thing that can be owned, only in culture has it been distinguished from mind, the quintessence of power and command, as the object, the dead thing, the *corpus*. In humanity's self-abasement to the *corpus* nature takes its revenge for the debasement of the human being to an object of power, to raw material. The compulsion toward cruelty and destruction stems from the organic repression of proximity to the body, much as, according to Freud's inspired intuition, disgust came into being when, with the adoption of the upright stance and the greater distance from the earth, the sense of smell, which attracted the male animal to the menstruating female, fell victim to organic repression. In Western civilization, and probably in any civilization, what pertains to the body is tabooed, a subject of attraction and revulsion. Among the Greek rulers, and in feudalism, the relationship to the body was also conditioned by power, through the need for personal physical prowess. The cultivation of the body had a naively social objective. The *kalos kagathos* was only partly an illusion; in part the gymnasium was needed for the actual maintenance of personal power, at least as training in the lordly posture. With the complete transition of power to the bourgeois form mediated by trade and communications, and still more with the rise of industry, a formal change occurred. Instead of to the sword, humanity has enslaved itself to the gigantic apparatus, which, to be sure, ultimately forges the sword. The rational purpose of enhancing the male body thereby disappeared; the Romantic attempts to achieve a renascence of the body in the nineteenth and twentieth centuries merely idealize something dead and mutilated. Nietzsche, Gauguin, George, and Klages recognized the nameless stupidity which is the result of progress. But they drew the wrong conclusion. They did not denounce the wrong as it is but transfigured the wrong as it was. The rejection of mechanization became an embellishment of industrial mass culture, which cannot do without the noble gesture. Against their will, artists reworked the lost image of the unity of body and mind for the advertising industry. The celebration of paragons of vitality, from the Blond Beast to the south-sea islanders, culminates ineluctably in the "sarong film," the advertisements for vitamins and skin cream, which are only stand-ins for the immanent goal of publicity: the new, big, beautiful, noble human type—the leaders and their troops. The fascist leaders again take the implements of murder into their hands, executing their prisoners with pistol and horsewhip, not as a result of their superior strength but because the gigantic apparatus and the real holders of power, who still abstain from such acts, deliver the victims of reason of state to the basement of their headquarters.

The body cannot be turned back into the envelope of the soul. It remains a cadaver, no matter how trained and fit it may be. The transformation into dead matter, indicated by the affinity of *corpus* to corpse, was a part of the perennial process which turned nature into stuff, material. The achievements of civilization are a product of sublimation, of the acquired love-hate for body and earth, from which domination has violently severed all human beings. The spirit's reaction to the corporealization of humanity is productive in medicine, while its reaction to the reification of the whole of nature is productive in technology. But the murderer, the killer, the brutalized colossi who are used by the ruling powers, legal and illegal, great and small, as their clandestine enforcers, the violent men who are always on hand when there is someone to be dispatched, the lynchers and clan members, the bruiser who steps in when someone answers back, the terrible figures to whom everyone is delivered up as soon as the protective hand of power is withdrawn from them, a soon as they lose wealth and position, all the werewolves lurking in the darkness of history and sustaining the fear without which there is no domination: in them the love-hate for the body is crude and direct; they desecrate what they touch, they destroy what they see in the light, and this destruction is a rancor against reification; in blind rage they repeat against the living thing what they cannot make undone: the splitting of life into mind and its object. The human being irresistibly attracts them, they want to reduce him or her to the body, nothing shall be allowed to live. This enmity of the lowest for the life withered within them, an enmity once carefully implanted and nurtured by those at the top, whether secular or clerical, and to which the lowest relate themselves, homosexually and paranoiacally, by killing, has always been an indispensable instrument of the art of government. The hostility of the enslaved to life is an inexhaustible source of history's dark side. Even the puritanical excess, hitting the booze, takes despairing revenge on life.

The love of nature and fate proclaimed by totalitarian propaganda is merely a superficial reaction to fixation at the level of the body, to the failure of civilization to fulfill itself. Being unable to escape it, one praises the body when not allowed to hit it. The "tragic" world-view of the fascists* is the ideological stag party on the eve of the real blood wedding. Those who extolled the body in Germany, the gymnasts and outdoor sports enthusiasts, always had an intimate affinity to killing, as nature lovers have to hunting. They see the body as a mobile mechanism, with its hinged links, the flesh upholstering the skeleton. They manipulate the body, actuating the limbs as if they were already severed. The Jewish tradition instills an aversion to measuring human beings with a yardstick, because the dead are measured—for the coffin. That is what gives the body-manipulators their enjoyment. Unaware, they measure the other with the eye of the coffin maker. The truth comes out when they state the result, calling the person tall [in German: long], short, fat, heavy. They are interested in illness, anticipating their fellow diner's death in what he eats, their interest being only thinly rationalized by concern for his health. Language keeps in step with them. It has converted the stroll into exercise and food into calories, just as in English and French the name for a throng of living trees is synonymous with "timber." Along with the mortality rate, society is reducing life to a chemical process.

In the fiendish humiliation of prisoners in the concentration camps, which—for no rational reason—the modern executioner adds to the death by torture, the unsublimated yet repressed rebellion of despised nature breaks out. Its full hideousness is vented on the martyrs of love, the alleged sexual offenders and libertines, for sexuality is the body unreduced; it is expression, that which the butchers secretly and despairingly crave. In free sexuality the murderer fears the lost immediacy, the original oneness, in which he can no longer exist. It is the dead thing which rises up and lives. He now makes everything one by making it nothing, because he has to stifle that oneness in himself. For him the victim represents life which has survived the schism; it must be broken and the universe must be nothing but dust and abstract power.

MASS SOCIETY

Complementing the cult of stars is the social mechanism of the notables, which levels anything that stands out; the stars and dignitaries are mere patterns for the ready-made world, and for the scissors of juridical and economic justice, which snip off the last loose ends.

Postscript

The view that the leveling and standardization of people in general, on the one hand, is matched, on the other, by a heightening of individuality in the so-called leader figures, in keeping with their power, is erroneous and itself a piece of ideology. The fascist masters of today are not so much supermen as functions of their own publicity apparatus, intersections of the identical reactions of countless people. If, in the psychology of the present-day masses, the leader no longer represents the father so much as the collective, monstrously enlarged projection of the impotent ego of each individual, then the leader figures do indeed correspond to what they represent. Not by accident do they resemble hairdressers, provincial actors, and gutter journalists. A part of their moral influence lies precisely in the fact that, while in themselves as powerless as all the rest, they embody on the latter's behalf the whole abundance of power without being anything more than the blank spaces which power has happened to occupy. It is not so much that they are exempt from the decay of individuality as that decayed individuals triumph in them and are in some way rewarded for their decay. The leaders have become fully what they always were slightly throughout the bourgeois era, actors playing leaders. The distance between the individuality of Bismarck and of Hitler is hardly less than that between the prose of *Gedanken und Erinnerungen* and the gibberish of *Mein Kampf.* In the struggle against fascism, not the least concern is to reduce the bloated leader images to the true scale of their insignificance. At least in the similarity between the ghetto barber and the dictator, Chaplin's film* hit on something essential.

CONTRADICTIONS

A moral system, with axioms, corollaries, and iron logic, and reliable application to every moral dilemma—that is what is demanded of philosophers. As a rule, they have fulfilled the expectation. Even when they have not set up a practical system or a fully developed casuistry, they have managed to derive obedience to authority from their theories. Usually they have justified once again the whole scale of values already sanctioned by public praxis, with all the comforts of sophisticated reasoning, demonstration, and evidence. "Honor the gods through the traditional native religion," said Epicurus,[20] and Hegel said it after him. A philosopher who hesitates to make such a profession is all the more energetically required to deliver a general principle. If thought does not simply reaffirm the prevalent rules, it must appear yet more self-assured, universal, and authoritative than if it had merely justified what was already in force. You consider the prevailing power unjust; would you rather have no power at all, but chaos? You criticize the standardization of life and progress; should we then light wax candles in the evening and have our cities filled with the stink of refuse, as in the Middle Ages? You do not like slaughterhouses; should society henceforth eat raw vegetables? The positive answers to such questions, however absurd, find willing listeners. Political anarchism, the reactionary arts and crafts movement, radical vegetarianism, eccentric sects and parties have "advertising appeal." The doctrine need only be general, self-assured, universal, and imperative. What people cannot endure is the attempt to evade the either/or, the mistrust of abstract principles, steadfastness without a doctrine.

Two young people are having a conversation:

A. You don't want to be a doctor?

B. By their profession doctors have a lot to do with dying people; that desensitizes them. Moreover, with advanced institutionalization the doctor represents business and its hierarchy vis-à-vis the patient. He is often tempted to act as an advocate of death. He becomes an agent of big business* against consumers. If one is selling automobiles it's not so bad, but if the commodity being administered is life and the consumers are the sick, that's a situation I'd prefer not to be in. The profession of family doctor may have been more innocuous, but that is in decline.

A. So you think there shouldn't be any doctors, or the old charlatans ought to come back?

B. I did not say that. I just have a horror of being a doctor myself, and especially a senior consultant with power of command over a mass hospital. Nevertheless, I do, of course, think it better to have doctors and hospitals than to leave sick people to die. I would not want to be a public prosecutor, yet giving a free run to armed robbers would seem to me a far greater evil than the existence of the body of people who put them in prison. Justice is reasonable. I am not against reason; I only want to investigate the form it has taken.

A. You are in contradiction with yourself. You yourself constantly make use of the advantages provided by doctors and judges. You are as guilty as they are. It is just that you don't want to be burdened with the work which others do for you. Your own life presupposes the principle you are trying to evade.

B. I do not deny it, but contradiction is necessary. It is a response to the objective contradiction of society. In a division of labor as complex as that of today, horror can manifest itself in one place and bring down guilt on everyone. If word of it got about, or if even a small proportion of people were aware of it, lunatic asylums and penal institutes might be humanized and courts of justice might finally be superfluous. But that is not the reason why I want to be a writer. I just want to be clearer about the terrible state in which everything is.

A. If everyone thought as you do, and no one wanted to get his hands dirty, there would be neither doctors nor judges, and the world would be even more dreadful.

B. That is just what I find questionable; for if everyone thought as I do, then I hope that not just the means of opposing evil would be reduced, but evil itself. Humanity has other possibilities. I am not the whole of humanity, and I cannot simply represent it in my thought. The moral precept that each of my actions ought to provide a general maxim is very problematic. It bypasses history. Why should my disinclination to be a doctor be equivalent to the view that there should be no doctors? In reality there are many people who would make good doctors and have a good chance of becoming one. If they behave morally within the limits to which their profession is subject today, they have my admiration. Perhaps they may even contribute to reducing the deficiencies I have pointed out to you; but perhaps they will deepen them, despite all their professional skill and morality. My life as I imagine it, my horror and my desire for knowledge, seem to me as justified as the profession of doctor, even though I cannot help anyone directly.

A. But if you knew that by studying medicine you might one day save the life of a loved person which would quite certainly be lost without you, would you not take it up at once?

B. Probably, but by now you can see for yourself that with your love of implacable logic you are forced to offer the most absurd examples, while I, with my impractical obstinacy and my contradictions, have remained within the bounds of common sense.

This conversation is repeated wherever someone refuses to give up thought in face of praxis. Such a person finds logic and consistency always on the other side. Anyone who is against vivisection ought not to draw a single breath which might cost the life of a bacillus. Logic places itself in the service of progress and of reaction, and at all events of reality. And yet, in an age when education is radically focused on reality, conversations have become rarer, and the neurotic interlocutor B needs superhuman strength in order not to become healthy.

MARKED

People in their forties are apt to make a curious observation. They discover that most of those with whom they have grown up and kept in contact show disorders in their habits and their consciousness. One allows his work to deteriorate so far that his business collapses; another destroys his marriage through no fault of his wife; another embezzles. But even those who escape such drastic changes bear signs of decomposition. Conversation with them becomes shallow, bombastic, fatuous. Whereas earlier the person growing older received intellectual stimulus from others, now he finds himself almost the only one who voluntarily displays objective interest.

To begin with he is inclined to regard the development of his coevals as an unpleasant accident. They have simply changed for the worse. Perhaps it has to do with their generation and its special outward fate. Finally he discovers that this experience is already familiar to him, but from a different perspective: that of his youth in relation to grown-ups. Was he not convinced then, too, that something was amiss with this or that teacher, with his uncles and aunts, the friends of his parents, and, later, with the university professors or the trainee's manager? It may have been that they displayed some ridiculous tic or that their presence was especially barren, oppressive, disappointing.

At that time he did not think further about it, accepting the inferiority of grown-ups as simply a fact of nature. But now he finds it confirmed that under the existing conditions the mere act of living while maintaining specific technical or intellectual skills leads even in the prime of life to cretinism. Not even the worldly-wise are exempt. It is as if human beings, as punishment for betraying the hopes of their youth and accommodating themselves to the world, are marked by premature decay.

Postscript

The decay of individuality today not only teaches us to regard that category as historical but also raises doubts concerning its positive nature. The inherent principle of the phase of competition was the wrong done to the individual. This relates, however, not only to the function of the individual and its particularistic interests in society but also to the inner composition of individuality itself. The tendency toward human emancipation emerged under the aegis of individuality but at the same time was the result of the very mechanism from which humanity was to be emancipated. In the autonomy and uniqueness of the individual, the resistance to the blind, repressive power of the irrational whole was crystallized. But that resistance was made historically possible only by the blindness and irrationality of the autonomous and unique individual. Conversely, however, that which, as particularistic, was absolutely opposed to the whole remains perniciously and opaquely attached to the existing order. The radically individual, unassimilated features of a human being are always both at once: residues not fully encompassed by the prevailing system and still happily surviving, and marks of the mutilation inflicted on its members by that system. In these traits, basic determinants of the system are repeated in exaggerated form: miserliness, for example, magnifies the principle of fixed property, hypochondria that of unreflecting self-preservation. Because the individual seeks desperately, through such traits, to assert itself against the compulsions of nature and society—sickness and bankruptcy—the traits themselves necessarily take on a compulsive quality. Within its innermost cell the individual encounters the same power from which it has fled within itself. This makes its flight a hopeless chimera. Molière's comedies show awareness of this curse no less than Daumier's caricatures; but the National Socialists, who are abolishing the individual, feed contentedly on it and set up Spitzweg as their classical painter.

Only in relation to hardened society, and not absolutely, does the hardened individual represent something better. Its hardness bears witness to the shame called forth by what the collective ceaselessly does to the individual and by what ensues when there are no longer individuals. The acolytes of today, bereft of self, are the necessary consequence of the splenetic apothecaries, the passionate rose growers and political cripples of yesterday.

PHILOSOPHY AND THE DIVISION OF LABOR

The place of science in the social division of labor is readily identified. Its task is to accumulate facts and functional connections between facts in the largest possible quantities. The storage system must be easily surveyed. It must enable individual industries immediately to locate the desired intellectual commodity in the required variety. Already the compilation is largely made with an eye for certain industrial contracts.

Historical works, too, are required to contribute material. Its utility is to be sought not directly in industry but indirectly in administration. Just as Machiavelli wrote for the purposes of princes and republics, historians of today work for economic and political committees. Admittedly, the historical form has become an impediment to such use; the material is better arranged straight away in terms of a specific administrative task: to manipulate commodity prices or the emotions of the masses. In addition to administration and industrial consortia, trade unions and political parties are potential customers.

Official philosophy serves the science which functions in this way. It is supposed, like a kind of intellectual Taylorism, to improve scientific production methods, to rationalize the accumulation of knowledge, and prevent the waste of mental energy. It has its allotted place in the division of labor, like chemistry or bacteriology. The few philosophical residues which hark back to the divine worship of the Middle Ages or the contemplation of eternal essentialities are still tolerated at secular universities because they are so reactionary. In addition, a few historians of philosophy continue to propagate themselves by tirelessly expounding Plato and Descartes while pointing out their obsoleteness. They are accompanied here and there by a veteran of sensualism or an expert personalist who keeps the field of science free of any dialectical weeds that might otherwise spring up.

Unlike its custodians, philosophy refers, among other things, to thinking which refuses to capitulate to the prevailing division of labor and does not accept prescribed tasks. The existing order coerces people not merely by physical force and material interests but by overwhelming suggestion. Philosophy is not a synthesis, a basic science, or an overarching science but an effort to resist suggestion, a determination to protect intellectual and actual freedom.

In this effort, the division of labor which has emerged under domination is not ignored. Philosophy detects the lie which domination inescapably brings with it. Refusing to be hypnotized by the preponderant power, it pursues it into all its hiding-places in the social machinery, which by its nature cannot be taken by storm, or placed under different control, but must be understood in freedom from the spell which it casts. When the officials which industry maintains in its intellectual departments—the universities, churches, and newspapers—challenge philosophy to produce credentials by which to legitimate its snooping, it finds itself fatally at a loss. It acknowledges no abstract norms or goals which could be a practicable alternative to those in force. Its exemption from the suggestive influence of the existing order lies precisely in the fact that, without favoring them, it accepts the bourgeois ideals, whether those which that order's exponents still proclaim, in however distorted a form, or those which are still discernible as the objective purpose of institutions, both technical and cultural, despite all the manipulation. It believes that the division of labor exists for the sake of human beings and that progress leads to freedom. That is why it is liable to come into conflict both with the division of labor and with progress. It gives voice to the contradiction between belief and reality, paying close attention to phenomena conditioned by the time. Unlike the press, it does not attach more importance to gigantic mass murder than to the liquidation of a few asylum inmates. It does not place the intrigues of the statesman compromised by fascism above the modest lynching, or the advertising frenzy of the film industry above the intimate funeral announcement. The taste for the grandiose is foreign to it. Thus it is at the same time remote from the existing order and deeply complicit with it. It lends its voice to its subject, against the latter's will; it is the voice of the contradiction which otherwise would not be heard, but would triumph silently.

THOUGHT

It is, of course, mistaken to believe that the truth of a theory is the same as its fruitfulness. There are some, however, who appear to assume the opposite. For them, theory has so little need to find application in thought that it should dispense with thinking altogether. They misinterpret every utterance as a final profession of belief, an injunction, or a taboo. They seek to submit to the idea as to a god or attack it as an idol. They lack freedom in relation to it. But it is in the nature of truth that one is involved in it as an active subject. People may hear propositions which in themselves are true; but they experience their truth only by thinking as they hear and by continuing to think.

This fetishism manifests itself in a drastic form today. One is called to account for one's thoughts, as if they applied directly to praxis.* For this reason, not only is the utterance which attacks power found intolerable but the one which gropes forward experimentally, playing with the possibility of error. Yet to be unfinished and to know it is the mark even of the thought which opposes power, and especially of the thought for which it would be worth dying. The proposition that the true is the whole* proves to be the same as its antithesis, that truth exists only as a part. The most wretched of the excuses which intellectuals have found for executioners— and in the last century they have not been idle in finding them—is that the thinking for which the victim was murdered was fallacious.

MAN AND BEAST

Throughout European history the idea of the human being has been expressed in contradistinction to the animal. The latter's lack of reason is the proof of human dignity. So insistently and unanimously has this antithesis been recited by all the earliest precursors of bourgeois thought, the ancient Jews, the Stoics, and the Early Fathers, and then through the Middle Ages to modern times, that few other ideas are so fundamental to Western anthropology. The antithesis is acknowledged even today. The behaviorists only appear to have forgotten it. That they apply to human beings the same formulae and results which they wring without restraint from defenseless animals in their abominable physiological laboratories, proclaims the difference in an especially subtle way. The conclusion they draw from the mutilated animal bodies applies, not to animals in freedom, but to human beings today.* By mistreating animals they announce that they, and only they in the whole of creation, function voluntarily in the same mechanical, blind, automatic way as the twitching movements of the bound victims made use of by the expert. The professor at the dissection table defines such movements scientifically as reflexes; the soothsayer at the altar would have proclaimed them a sign from his gods. Humans possess reason, which pitilessly follows its path; the animals from which they draw their bloody conclusions have only unreasoning terror, the impulse to take flight on a path which is cut off.

The lack of reason has no words. Its possession, which dominates manifest history, is eloquent. The whole earth bears witness to the glory of man. In war and peace, arena and slaughterhouse, from the slow death of the elephant overpowered by primitive human hordes with the aid of the first planning to the perfected exploitation of the animal world today, the unreasoning creature has always suffered at the hands of reason. This visible course of events conceals from the executioners the invisible one: existence without the light of reason, the actual life of animals. It would be the proper subject matter for psychology, for only the life of animals runs its course according to inner impulses; where psychology has to explain human beings, they are already regressive and destroyed. When the help of psychology is sought among human beings, the meager field of their immediate relationships is narrowed still further, and even within it they are made into things. Psychology used to explain others is impertinent, and to explain one's own motives sentimental. Animal psychology, meanwhile, has lost sight of its object; engrossed with the chicanery of its traps and labyrinths, it has forgotten that to speak of and acknowledge a psyche or soul (*Seele*) is appropriate precisely and only in the case of animals. Even Aristotle, who attributed a soul to them, if an inferior one, preferred to speak of the bodies, parts, movements, and procreation of animals rather than the life peculiar to them.

The world of animals is without concepts. There is no word to hold fast the identical in the flux of phenomena, the same genus in the succession of specimens, the same thing in changing situations. Although the possibility of recognition is not absent, identification is restricted to vital patterns. There is nothing in the flux* that could be defined as lasting, and yet everything remains one and the same, because there is no fixed knowledge of the past and no clear prospect into the future. The animal responds to its name and has no self, it is enclosed in itself yet exposed, one compulsion is followed by another, no idea extends beyond it. Its loss of solace is not balanced by a reduction in fear, its lack of awareness of happiness by the absence of mourning and pain. For happiness to become substantial, for life to be endowed with death, identifying remembrance is needed, assuaging knowledge, the religious or philosophical idea, in short, the concept. There are happy animals, but how short-lived is that happiness! The animal's experience of duration, uninterrupted by liberating thought, is dreary and depressive. To escape the gnawing emptiness of existence some resistance is needed, and its backbone is language. Even the strongest animal is infinitely feeble. Schopenhauer's doctrine according to which the pendulum of life oscillates between pain and boredom, between brief moments of sated impulse and endless craving, is true of the animal, which cannot interrupt the fatal cycle with cognition. In the animal's soul the individual feelings and needs of human beings are vestigially present, without the stability which only organizing reason confers. The best days flit past in a bustling medley like a dream, which the animal can hardly distinguish from waking in any case. It is without the clear division between play and seriousness, the happy awakening from nightmare to reality.

In popular fairy tales the metamorphosis of humans into animals is a recurring punishment. To be imprisoned in an animal body is regarded as damnation. To children and peoples, the idea of such transformations is immediately comprehensible and familiar. Believers in the transmigration of souls in the earliest cultures saw the animal form as punishment and torment. The mute wildness in the animal's gaze bears witness to the horror which is feared by humans in such metamorphoses. Every animal recalls to them an immense misfortune which took place in primeval times. Fairy tales express this dim human intuition. But whereas the prince in the fairy tale retained his reason so that, when the time came, he could tell of his woe and the fairy could release him, the animal's lack of reason holds it eternally captive in its form, unless man, who is one with it through his past, can find the redeeming formula and through it soften the stony heart of infinity at the end of time.

For the being endowed with reason, however, concern for the unreasoning animal is idle. Western civilization has left that to women. They have no autonomous share in the capabilities which gave rise to this civilization. The man must go out into hostile life, must act and strive.* The woman is not a subject. She does not produce but looks after the producers, a living monument to the long-vanished time of the self-sufficient household. The division of labor imposed on her by the man was unfavorable. She became an embodiment of biological function, an image of nature, in the suppression of which this civilization's claim to glory lay. To dominate nature boundlessly, to turn the cosmos into an endless hunting ground, has been the dream of millennia. It shaped the idea of man in a male society. It was the purpose of reason, on which man prided himself. Woman was smaller and weaker, between her and man there was a difference she could not overcome, a difference set by nature, the most shaming, degrading agency possible within the male society. When domination of nature is the true goal, biological inferiority remains the ultimate stigma, the weakness imprinted by nature, the mark which invites violence. The church, which in the course of history has hardly missed an opportunity to take a leading voice in popular institutions, whether they be slavery, crusades, or simply pogroms, sided with Plato, despite the *Ave Maria*, in the assessment of woman. The image of the Mother of Sorrows was a concession to matriarchal residues. Yet the church used the very image which was supposed to redeem woman from her inferiority to sanction it. "The influence of Divine Law in a Christian land," proclaimed de Maistre, that law's legitimate son, "need only be extinguished or weakened to a certain degree by tolerating the freedom of women which has arisen from it, and freedom, though noble and moving in itself, will degenerate soon enough into shamelessness. Women would become the fatal instruments of a general decline, which would swiftly undermine the vital organs of the state. Engulfed by corruption, the state would spread shame and terror in its fiery ruin."[21] The witch trials used by the allied feudal rackets to terrorize the populace when they found themselves threatened were at the same time a celebration and confirmation of the victory of male domination over primeval matriarchal and mimetic stages of development. The *autos-da-fé* were the Church's pagan bonfires, a triumph of nature in the form of self-preserving reason, to the glory of reason's domination over nature.

The bourgeoisie reaped the benefit of feminine virtue and modesty as reaction formations of the matriarchal rebellion. Woman gained admission to the world of mastery on behalf of the whole of exploited nature, but in a broken form. Subjugated, she mirrors her conqueror's victory in her spontaneous submission, reflecting defeat back to him as devotion, despair as the beautiful soul, the violated heart as the loving breast. At the price of radical exclusion from praxis and withdrawal into a charmed circle, nature receives homage from the lord of creation. Art, morality, and sublime love are masks of nature, in which nature reappears transformed and becomes expressive as its own antithesis. Through its masks it acquires the gift of speech; in its distortion it manifests its essence; beauty is the serpent which displays the wound where once the fang was implanted. Yet behind man's admiration for beauty lurks always the ringing laughter, the boundless scorn, the barbaric obscenity vented by potency on impotence, with which it numbs the secret fear that it is itself enslaved to impotence, to death, to nature. When the deformed jesters whose capers and foolscaps once enacted the mournful gaiety of broken nature had escaped the service of kings, the planned cultivation of beauty was entrusted to women. Modern puritanical woman zealously took up the task, identifying herself fully with the *fait accompli*, with nature not in its wildness but in its domestication. What was left of the fans, songs, and dances of Roman slave girls was definitively reduced in Birmingham to piano playing and other handicrafts, until the last residues of female wantonness had been entirely sublimated as emblems of patriarchal civilization. Under the pressure of universal* advertising, powder and lipstick, rejecting their origin among courtesans, became skin care, the bathing suit an attribute of hygiene. Nothing can escape. Even love, through the mere fact that it takes place within the completely organized system of domination,* has the system's trademark imprinted on it. In Germany those entrapped by the existing order now demonstrate their obedience to it by promiscuity, as earlier by modesty, affirming by indiscriminate performance of the sexual act their rigid subordination to the dominant reason.*

Jutting into the present* like a fossil of the bourgeois esteem for woman is the termagant, the shrew. For measureless ages her nagging has avenged, within her own house, the wretchedness which has befallen her sex. Outside it, too, in the absence of the genuflection she fails to receive, the malevolent crone barks at the absent-minded man who fails to rise to his feet in her presence, knocking off his hat. That the head itself must roll, come what may, she has always demanded in politics, whether in reminiscence of the maenadic past or through outbidding man and his order in her impotent rage. The bloodthirstiness of women in pogroms eclipses that of men. The oppressed woman as Fury has outlived her time, continuing to display the grimace of mutilated nature in an age when domination is molding the well-trained bodies of both sexes, in whose uniformity the grimace has been effaced. Against the background of such mass production, the scolding of the shrew, who at least retained her own distinguishing face, becomes a sign of humanity, her ugliness a trace of spirit. If in past centuries the young girl wore her subjection in her melancholy features and her devoted love, an alienated image of nature, an aesthetic cultural object, at least the harridan of today has finally discovered a new female profession. As a social hyena she actively pursues cultural goals. Her ambition runs after honors and publicity, but her understanding of male culture is not yet sufficiently sharpened to prevent her, amid the injuries done her, from committing *faux pas* and showing that she is not yet at home in the civilization of men. Isolated, she seeks refuge in conglomerates of science and magic, misbegotten offspring of the idealistic privy councilor and the Nordic clairvoyante. She feels herself drawn to mischief. The last female opposition to the spirit of male society is degenerating in a morass of trivial rackets, sects, and hobbies, is turning into the perverted aggression of social work and theosophical gossip, venting its petty rancor in good works and Christian Science. In this quagmire, solidarity with creaturely life expresses itself not so much in the animal protection league as in neo-Buddhism and the Pekinese, whose distorted visage, now as in early paintings, reminds us of the physiognomy of the court jester left behind by progress. Like the hunchback's ungainly leaps, the little dog's features still represent mutilated nature, while mass industry and mass culture have learned to prepare the bodies of breeding bulls and humans according to scientific methods. The standardized masses are now so little aware of their own transformation, in which they have desperately collaborated, that they no longer require its symbolic display. Among the lesser news items on the second and third pages of newspapers, the front pages of which are filled with the horrifying exploits of human beings, circus fires and the poisoning of large animals are sometimes reported. We are reminded of animals when their last specimens, of the same species as the medieval fool, perish in endless torment, a capital loss to their owner who was unable to provide the loyal creatures with fire protection in an age of concrete buildings. The tall giraffe and the wise elephant are oddities which can no longer provide amusement for wised-up schoolboys. In Africa, the last part of the earth which has vainly sought to protect their poor herds from civilization, they form traffic obstacles to bombers landing in the latest war. They are being eradicated entirely. On an earth made reasonable there is no longer a need for the aesthetic reflection. The demons are driven out by directly imprinting humans. Domination no longer needs numinous images; it produces them industrially, the more reliably to insinuate itself into human beings.

The distortion which is inherent in every work of art, as mutilation is inherent in the luster of feminine beauty, the maiming which puts on show the wound in which subjugated nature recognizes itself—that maiming is again being done by fascism, but no longer as mere appearance. It is inflicted directly on the damned. In this society there is no longer any sphere in which domination can profess its contradictions, as it does in art; there is no longer any means of duplication by which the distortion might be expressed. But in earlier times such expression was called not only beauty but thought, intellect, language itself. Today language calculates, designates, betrays, initiates death; it does not express. The culture industry* has, like science, its own precise, external means of measurement by which to judge itself: facts. Film stars are experts, their performances are records of natural behavior, classifying modes of reaction; the directors and scriptwriters produce models of adapted behavior. The precision work of the culture industry* precludes distortion as a mere fault, an accident, something defectively subjective and natural. The deviation is analyzed to discover the practical cause which would link it back to rationality. Only then is it forgiven. Along with the reflection of power by nature, the tragic, like the comic, has disappeared; the rulers become serious in proportion to the resistance to be overcome, and humorous in proportion to the despair they perceive. Intellectual enjoyment used to be confined to the presentation of suffering, but they play with horror itself.

Sublime love attached itself to strength appearing through weakness, in woman's beauty, but they attach themselves directly to power: the idol of today's society is the masculine face which exhibits a certain rakish lordliness. The woman is used for work, childbearing; or, if presentable, she enhances the status of her mate. No longer does she sweep the man away in rapture. Adoration reverts to self-love. The world and its purposes demand the whole of man. None can give away any part of himself; he must keep it all within. But, in the eyes of praxis, nature is all that is without and underneath, an object—as the girl, in vulgar parlance, has always been for the soldier. Feeling confines itself to power in relation to power. As woman did earlier, man now lays down his arms before man, but with dark, unswerving coldness. He becomes a woman, with eyes only for power. In the fascist collective,* with its teams and work camps, everyone from tender youth is a prisoner in solitary confinement, which breeds homosexuality. Even the beast must wear the lordly features. The distinctive human face, which humiliatingly recalls our origin in nature and our enslavement to it, irresistibly invites expert homicide. The caricature of the Jew has always relied on this, and even Goethe's aversion to apes marked out the limits of his humanity. When captains of industry and fascist leaders have animals around them, they are not domestic poodles but Great Danes and lion cubs. They are there to add spice to power through the terror they inspire. So blind is the murderous fascist colossus in face of nature that he conceives of animals only as means of humiliating humans. Nietzsche's unjust accusation of Schopenhauer and Voltaire, that they "knew how to disguise [their] hatred of certain men and things as pity toward animals,"[22] applies truly to the fascist butcher. The precondition of the fascists' pious love of animals, nature, and children is the lust of the hunter. The idle stroking of children's hair and animal pelts signifies: this hand can destroy. It tenderly fondles one victim before felling the other, and its choice has nothing to do with the victim's guilt. The caress intimates that all are the same before power, that they have no being in themselves. For domination's bloody purposes the creature is only material. Thus the *Führer* flaunts his concern for innocents, who are plucked out without merit as others are killed without desert. Nature is filth. Only the devious strength which survives is in the right. But that strength itself is only nature; the whole ingenious machinery of modern industrial society is no more than nature dismembering itself. There is no longer any medium through which this contradiction can find expression. It unfolds with the glum obstinacy of a world from which art, thought, and negativity have vanished. Human beings are so radically estranged from themselves and from nature that they know only how to use and harm each other. Each is merely a factor, the subject or object of some praxis, something to be reckoned with or discounted.

In this world liberated from appearance—in which human beings, having forfeited reflection, have become once more the cleverest animals, which subjugate the rest of the universe when they happen not to be tearing themselves apart—to show concern for animals is considered no longer merely sentimental but a betrayal of progress. In the best reactionary tradition Göring linked animal protection to racial hatred, the Lutheran-Germanic joys of the happy murderer with the genteel fair play of the aristocratic hunter. The fronts are clearly drawn; anyone who opposes Hearst* and Göring is on the side of Pavlov and vivisection; anyone who hesitates between the two is fair game for both. Such a person is told to follow reason. The choice is obligatory and inescapable. Anyone who wants to change the world should at all costs avoid finishing up in the morass of petty rackets, where political sectarians, utopians, and anarchists go to ruin along with the spiritualists. Intellectuals whose thought is unattached to any active historical power, and orientates itself by neither of the poles toward which industrial society is heading, lose their substance; their thought becomes baseless.* The real is the rational. Anyone who does not join in, the progressives also tell them, is of no help to anyone. Everything depends on society, and thought, no matter how precise, must align itself with the powerful social tendencies, without which it becomes mere whimsy. This consensus unites all the righteous realists, who declare their allegiance to human society as to a mass racket within nature. The thought which does not pursue the aims of any of their departments incurs their boundless wrath. It reminds them that something which exists only to be smashed still has a voice: nature, with which the lies of the nationalist folklore-lovers are full to overflowing. When its sound interrupts, even for a moment, their chanting chorus, the dread they seek to drown with their voices, and which lives on in their rationalized, broken hearts as in every animal, makes itself heard. The tendencies brought into daylight by the expression of such thoughts are omnipresent and blind. Nature in itself is neither good, as was believed by the old Romanticism, nor noble, as is asserted by the new. As a model and goal it signifies anti-intellectualism, lies, bestiality; only when apprehended as knowledge does it become the urge of the living toward peace, the consciousness which, from the beginning, has inspired the unerring resistance to *Führer* and collective. What threatens the prevailing praxis and its inescapable alternatives is not nature, with which that praxis coincides, but the remembrance of nature.

PROPAGANDA

Propaganda directed at changing the world—what an absurdity! Propaganda turns language into an instrument, a lever, a machine. Propaganda fixes the composition which human beings have taken on under social injustice, by stirring them. It counts on their ability to be counted on. All people know in their innermost awareness that through this medium they are turned into media, as in a factory. The rage they feel in following it is the old rage against the yoke, reinforced by the dim knowledge that the way out pointed by propaganda is the wrong one. Propaganda manipulates human beings; when it screams freedom it contradicts itself. Mendacity is inseparable from it. It is the community of lies in which the leader and the led come together, even when its content as such is correct. In it even truth becomes a mere means, to the end of gaining adherents; it falsifies truth simply by taking it into its mouth. That is why true resistance is without propaganda. Propaganda is antihuman. It presupposes that the principle that politics should spring from communal insight is no more than a form of words.

In a society which prudently sets limits to the threatening abundance, what is recommended to everyone by others deserves mistrust. The warning against commercial advertisements, that no company gives anything away, is applicable everywhere, and, after the merger of business and politics, especially to the latter. The degree of eulogy increases with the decrease in quality: the Volkswagen, unlike the Rolls-Royce, depends on advertising. The interests of industry and consumers do not harmonize even when the former seriously has something to offer. Even propaganda for freedom can be a source of confusion in that it necessarily effaces the difference between theory and the particular interests of its addressees. The workers' leaders murdered in Germany were cheated even of the truth of their own action, since fascism belied their solidarity by the selectivity of its revenge. When intellectuals are tortured to death in concentration camps, that does not necessarily make the workers outside worse off. Fascism was not the same for Ossietzky and for the proletariat. Propaganda cheated both.

What is suspect is not, of course, the depiction of reality as hell but the routine invitation to break out of it. If that invitation can be addressed to anyone today, it is neither to the so-called masses nor to the individual, who is powerless, but rather to an imaginary witness, to whom we bequeath it so that it is not entirely lost with us.

IN THE GENESIS OF STUPIDITY

The emblem of intelligence is the feeler of the snail, the creature "with the fumbling face," with which, if we can believe Mephistopheles,[23] it also smells. Meeting an obstacle, the feeler is immediately withdrawn into the protection of the body, it becomes one with the whole until it timidly ventures forth again as an autonomous agent. If the danger is still present, it disappears once more, and the intervals between the attempts grow longer. Mental life in its earliest stages is infinitely delicate. The snail's sense is dependent on a muscle, and muscles grow slack if their scope for movement is impaired. The body is crippled by physical injury, the mind by fear. In their origin both effects are inseparable.

The higher animals have themselves to thank for their greater freedom; their existence is evidence that feelers were once stretched out in new directions and not repulsed. Each of their species is a monument to countless others whose attempts to develop were blocked at the outset, which gave way to fright if only a single feeler stirred in the path of their evolution. The suppression of possibilities by the direct resistance of surrounding nature is extended inwardly by the wasting of organs through fright. Each time an animal looks out with curiosity a new form of the living dawns, a form which might emerge from the clearly formed species to which the individual creature belongs. But it is not only this specific form which holds it back in the security of the old state; the force which its look encounters is the resistance, millions of years old, which has imprisoned it at its present stage from the first, and which, constantly renewed, inhibits every step which goes beyond that stage. That first, tentative look is always easily repulsed; behind it stand goodwill, fragile hope, but no continuous energy. In the direction from which it has been definitely scared off the animal becomes shy and stupid.

Stupidity is a scar. It can relate to one faculty among many or to them all, practical and mental. Every partial stupidity in a human being marks a spot where the awakening play of muscles has been inhibited instead of fostered. With the inhibition, the vain repetition of unorganized, awkward attempts originally began. The child's endless questions are already a sign of a secret pain, a serious question to which it has found no answer and which it cannot frame in its proper form.[24] The repetition half resembles playful determination, as when a dog endlessly leaps against a door it has not learned how to open, finally giving up if the handle is too high, and half corresponds to hopeless compulsion, as when a lion paces endlessly up and down in its cage or a neurotic repeats the defense reaction which has already proved futile. If the child has wearied of its repetitions, or if the thwarting has been too brutal, its attention can turn in another direction; the child is richer in experience, as one says, but at the point where its impulse has been blocked a scar can easily be left behind, a slight callous where the surface is numb. Such scars lead to deformations. They can produce "characters," hard and capable; they can produce stupidity, in the form of deficiency symptoms, blindness, or impotence, if they merely stagnate, or in the form of malice, spite, and fanaticism, if they turn cancerous within. Goodwill is turned to ill will by the violence it suffers. And not only the forbidden question but the suppressed imitation, the forbidden weeping or the forbidden reckless game, can give rise to such scars. Like the genera within the series of fauna, the intellectual gradations within the human species, indeed, the blind spots within the same individual, mark the points where hope has come to a halt and in their ossification bear witness to what holds all living things in thrall.

Reference Matter

Editor's Afterword

The Position of "Dialectic of Enlightenment"
in the Development of Critical Theory

Horkheimer's and Adorno's *Dialectic of Enlightenment* is undoubtedly the most influential publication of the Critical Theory of the Frankfurt School, and one of its most compressed theoretical statements. The book was written during the Second World War, between 1939 and 1944, and first published in 1944 in a limited edition, as a hectographic typescript of the Institute for Social Research, on the occasion of Friedrich Pollock's fiftieth birthday. It was published as a printed edition by Querido of Amsterdam, the most important publisher of German writers in exile, in 1947.

"What we had set out to do," the authors wrote in the Preface, "was nothing less than to explain why humanity, instead of entering a truly human state, is sinking into a new kind of barbarism."[1] Yet the work goes far beyond a mere critique of contemporary events. Historically remote developments, indeed, the birth of Western history and of subjectivity itself from the struggle against natural forces, as represented in myths, are connected in a wide arch to the most threatening experiences of the present. It is true that the book scarcely forms a unity in the formal sense. It consists of five highly unconnected chapters, together with a number of shorter notes, the subjects of which at first sight appear somewhat heterogeneous. The various analyses relate to phenomena such as the way in which science has become detached from practical life, formalized morality, an entertainment culture which has reverted to manipulation, and a paranoid behavioral structure, as expressed in aggressive anti-Semitism, which marks the limits of enlightenment. The common element which the authors perceive in these phenomena is the tendency toward the self-destruction of enlightenment's own guiding criteria which had been inherent in enlightenment thought from the beginning. The historical analyses are intended to elucidate the present. For this reason, the two historical chapters, concerned with decisive thresholds of enlightenment in Homeric Greece and in Central Europe in the eighteenth century, are relegated to the status of "excurses," although they are indispensable to the argument of the book as a whole. In this way, against the background of a pre-history of subjectivity, the authors show why the National Socialist terror was not an aberration of modern history but was rooted deeply in the fundamental characteristics of Western civilization.

The self-destruction of Western reason is seen to be grounded in an historical and fateful dialectic of the domination of external nature, internal nature, and society. Enlightenment, which split these spheres apart, is traced back to its mythical roots. Enlightenment and myth are not seen, therefore, as irreconcilable opposites but as dialectically mediated qualities of both real and intellectual life. "Myth is already enlightenment, and: enlightenment reverts to mythology."[2] This paradox is the fundamental thesis of the book. Reason appears as inextricably entangled with domination. Since the beginnings of history, liberation from the compulsions of external nature has been achieved only by introducing a power relationship of second degree. Both the repression of the internal nature of human drives, and social domination, are already at work in myth. Finally, fascism and the modern culture industry are the forms taken by a return of repressed nature. In the service of an advancing rationalization of instrumental thought modeled on the domination of nature and serving its purposes, enlightened reason is progressively hollowed out until it reverts to the new mythology of a resurrected relationship to nature, to violence. This theme is summed up in the opening sentences of the book: "Enlightenment, understood in the widest sense as the advance of thought, has always aimed at liberating human beings from fear and installing them as masters. Yet the wholly enlightened earth is radiant with triumphant calamity."[3]

The book took a considerable time to reach a wide audience, not least because of the peculiarly dense, allusive, and demanding nature of the text. But it has now become one of the most intensively read and widely discussed writings of Critical Theory. This is not the place to offer yet another critical or systematic discussion of the theoretical problems it raises. Instead, three questions relating to editorial matters, which can in part be clarified by reference to materials in the posthumous papers, will be examined in detail here. *First*: What were the specific individual contributions of the authors to the text they jointly composed? *Second*: Which especially important theoretical implications and, in particular, internal revisions to Critical Theory, present but not fully worked out in the text, are significant for its interpretation? This will also involve clarifying where *Dialectic of Enlightenment* is to be located in the development, in particular, of Horkheimer's theoretical thinking. However useful it may be to divide Horkheimer's development into "historical" periods, such an approach risks hypostatizing those periods. An overprecise diagnosis of discontinuities in the author's thought obstructs perception of the transitions within it, and therefore of the *preconditions* of those discontinuities. This account should therefore be seen as a counterweight to an often overschematic reception of Horkheimer's thought, its identity, and its changes. The discussion will therefore take account of a number of shorter pieces written in the 1940s which are thematically related to *Dialectic of Enlightenment*. *Third*, and last, there is the question of how the textual variations between the printed edition of 1947 and hectographic edition of 1944 are to be evaluated. The reasons for the prolonged resistance of the authors, especially Horkheimer, to a reedition of the book will also be considered—reasons bound up with their own later evaluation of their work.

1. Authorship and the "Tension Between Two Intellectual Temperaments"

The authors of *Dialectic of Enlightenment* repeatedly stressed their joint responsibility for the entire work. In the Preface to the new edition of 1969 they write: "No one who was not involved in the writing could easily understand to what extent we both feel responsible for every sentence. We dictated long stretches together; the *Dialectic* derives its vital energy from the tension between the two intellectual temperaments which came together in writing it."[4] That the authors did not make this assertion for reasons of academic politics or because of other strategic and external considerations is demonstrated by the following letter from Adorno to Horkheimer of 2 June 1949: "Dear Max, I am enclosing copies of two critical comments sent to me by their author, Karl Thieme of Basel. I immediately corrected the nonsensical contention that I am the author of 'Elements of Anti-Semitism.' People seem unable to resist the temptation to keep us apart, although I wrote to Thieme in February that *Dialectic of Enlightenment* is 'the joint work of Horkheimer and myself, to the extent that every sentence belongs to us both.' Warm regards, Teddie."[5]

The collaboration between the two was not confined to this book. Records from the years 1931/32 and 1938 to 1946 bear witness to intensive theoretical discussions.[6] Numerous essays and memoranda from that period, and from the 1950s, and even as late as the 1960s, bear traces of their joint work, as is clear from handwritten corrections to the typescripts. When the two writers decided to return to Frankfurt after the end of the war and thought about publishing again in German journals, it is clear that they planned for a time to combine their works once and for all vis-à-vis the public. The correspondence between the two demonstrates that the initiative came primarily from Adorno. In 1949 he drafted the following declaration—which, however, remained unpublished: "As our entire scholarly work, both theoretical and empirical, has for years been so fused together that our contributions cannot be separated, it seems timely for us to declare publicly that all our philosophical, sociological, and psychological publications should be regarded as composed by us jointly and that we share responsibility for them. This also applies to work signed by us individually."[7]

Indisputable as it is that Horkheimer and Adorno successfully engaged over long periods in a collaboration of which *Dialectic of Enlightenment* is only the best-known and historically most influential product, it is extremely doubtful whether both theories really form a seamless unity, as asserted in this declaration. Viewed from a temporal distance, the declaration throws less light on the actual relationship between the two authors than on their ideal, which they had approached so closely through joint work during the 1940s that the differences could largely be overlooked. With characteristic exuberance, Adorno proclaimed the complete identity between their views at the start of a new phase of collaboration at the Institut für Sozialforschung, reestablished in Frankfurt, as if he wanted to make permanent that period of joint writing, securing it against all countervailing tendencies.

With the work on *Dialectic of Enlightenment* the thought of the two authors drew together more closely than before or immediately afterward. All the same, the book had very different functions in the individual developments of the two authors. Reference to the manuscripts for *Dialectic of Enlightenment* preserved in the posthumous papers of the authors, and to recorded comments on the question of the book's authorship, provides a basis for answering the more far-reaching question concerning theoretical agreements, differences, and developments. Regardless of that, however, the fact remains that the authorship of the book, which cannot necessarily be reduced to the act of writing the text, must ultimately be attributed to both together. Any motives of playing one author off against the other, that may have been involved in similar exercises during their lifetimes, automatically cease to apply from the present historical distance.

In determining the respective contributions of the two authors to their communal text, two kinds of sources are available: the preliminary drafts contained in the posthumous papers (A) and comments transmitted verbally (B).

(A) *Posthumous papers*

(1) "Preface": This is present among Horkheimer's posthumous papers in a number of typed sections which bear numerous handwritten corrections and additions by Horkheimer and a few corrections by Adorno.[8] No draft is to be found in Adorno's posthumous papers.[9]

(2) "The Concept of Enlightenment": In the 1944 version the chapter has the title "Dialectic of Enlightenment," and in the typescripts it is titled "Myth and Enlightenment." Handwritten notes and text passages relating to this chapter by Horkheimer and, in smaller quantities, by Adorno, are preserved in Horkheimer's posthumous papers; fragments of typewritten versions with handwritten corrections by both authors are present in similar proportions.[10] Adorno's posthumous papers contain nothing relating to this chapter.

(3) "Excursus I: Odysseus or Myth and Enlightenment": Horkheimer's posthumous papers have no material on this chapter, while Adorno's contain a typescript with numerous handwritten corrections and additions.

(4) "Excursus II: Juliette or Enlightenment and Morality": the typescript is in Horkheimer's posthumous papers and has the title "Enlighten-

ment and Rigorism."[11] Adorno's posthumous papers contain nothing on this chapter.

(5) "The Culture Industry: Enlightenment as Mass Deception": Horkheimer's posthumous papers contain two versions of this chapter with the title "The Schema of Mass Culture."[12] The earlier of the two versions is marked "Second Draft," is dated "October 1942," and bears the name Max Horkheimer (on the cover page of the notebook) and the initials M.H. in his own handwriting (on the title page). This typescript has eighty-nine pages, the first forty-five having numerous handwritten corrections and additions by Horkheimer. Only the part of the chapter revised up to that point was included in the editions of 1944 and 1947. This version corresponds to the second typescript of the chapter in Horkheimer's posthumous papers. In the printed version it closes with the note "To be continued," which was, however, omitted from the new edition of 1969. The surviving drafts for this chapter show in exemplary form the problems which arise when trying to draw conclusions about authorship from the form of the material. They also give us deeper insight into the way the two authors worked. To anticipate the result: despite indications pointing to Horkheimer, Adorno is probably the author of the first version (not extant) of the chapter. His posthumous papers also include the typescript known as the "Second Draft"; it is in triplicate, one copy being uncorrected, another showing a few handwritten corrections by Adorno—it has the handwritten initials T.W.A. on the title page—and the third having numerous handwritten corrections and additions by Adorno on the first forty-five pages. Some of these notes agree word for word with those of Horkheimer, while others diverge from them. Judging from the materials, therefore, the contributions of the two authors to the *secondary* revision were about equal. Only recorded verbal comments can throw light on the authorship of the *first* draft, and they refer to Adorno as the author. If the form of the materials is taken as the basis, the course of work on this chapter could be reconstructed as follows: after Adorno, on the basis of discussions and notes no longer accessible, had produced a "Second Draft" and hurriedly corrected it, the two authors discussed the typescript sentence by sentence, at the same time inserting the corrections on which they agreed. Independently of each other—beforehand or afterward—each of them made handwritten revisions to the typescript. This process of revision came to an end at page 45 of the typescript, for con-

tingent reasons. The printed version was produced as a compilation of the two revised versions of the first part. According to this interpretation, the abbreviations M.H. and T.W.A. clearly do not refer to the author but to the "owner" of the typescript at the time, the reviser. The insertion of "Max Horkheimer" as the author's name on the cover sheet was not made by Horkheimer himself and appears to be a later, mistaken addition by a secretary. This reconstruction is the decisive reason why the Editor decided not to include the second, unrevised part of the chapter in Horkheimer's posthumous writings.[13]

(6) "Elements of Anti-Semitism. Limits of Enlightenment": No typescript of this chapter ready for publication is to be found in Horkheimer's posthumous papers, which do, however, contain numerous typewritten fragments, mostly with handwritten corrections and additions by Horkheimer, together with text passages handwritten by Horkheimer.[14] One of these handwritten texts follows directly after three pages written by Gretel Adorno (probably under dictation). This bundle also includes a few handwritten notes by Adorno and a six-page typescript by Adorno with the title "Draft." It also contains reports of discussions between the two authors on anti-Semitism.[15] Thesis VII of this chapter, not added until the printed version of 1947, is also to be found in several versions as a typescript with handwritten corrections and additions by Horkheimer.[16] Attached to this is a three-page typescript by Adorno, "Remarks on Thesis VII," with the date "Sept. 4 / 46" handwritten by him.[17] Adorno's posthumous papers contain no further materials for this chapter.

(7) "Notes and Sketches": These are to be found in Horkheimer's posthumous papers, each one usually in several typescript versions, with handwritten corrections by Horkheimer.[18] The parts added as "Postscripts" to some of the notes are missing. The aphorisms are collected in several bundles. Of the typescripts present here only about half were included in the printed version of *Dialectic of Enlightenment*. The notes not included in it[19] are brought together in two bundles, one of which is marked with the abbreviations M.H. and Dr. H. The other, the contents of which coincide largely with those of the first, is bound as a typescript and bears the title "Notes As an Addition to the Festschrift for Friedrich Pollock" and is preceded by the remark: "The notes have not been revised. They were excluded from the Notes and Sketches of the Festschrift as being too provisional."[20] The "Notes and Sketches" are the oldest parts of *Dialectic of*

Enlightenment. Those which are dated were written in 1939, 1940, and 1942. Adorno's posthumous papers contain no manuscripts or typescripts relating to them.

(B) *Oral comments*

(1) "The authorship of the individual chapters," writes Jürgen Habermas, "is by no means indivisible. Gretel Adorno once confirmed my conjecture, which, in any case, is obvious to a careful reader, that the title essay and the Sade chapter were written predominantly by Horkheimer, while the chapters on Odysseus and the culture industry can be attributed primarily to Adorno. This conclusion is based not only on stylistic differences."[21]

(2) More precise and comprehensive is a report by Rolf Tiedemann,[22] based on a verbal communication by Adorno. It is consistent with the evidence from the materials of the posthumous papers. According to this remark the two authors dictated the chapter on the "Concept of Enlightenment" jointly. (The materials indicate a certain preponderance of drafts by Horkheimer.) The first excursus, "Odysseus or Myth and Enlightenment," according to this report, was written almost exclusively by Adorno, while the second, "Juliette or Enlightenment and Morality," can be attributed to the same degree to Horkheimer. The chapter "The Culture Industry: Enlightenment As Mass Deception" is based on a draft by Adorno, which, however, was so intensively revised by Horkheimer that the contributions of both should be regarded as practically equal. The reverse is the case with the chapter "Elements of Anti-Semitism: Limits of Enlightenment," which was originally written by Horkheimer and intensively revised by Adorno. In addition, the "Preface" of 1944 refers to a considerable contribution by Leo Löwenthal to the formulation of the first three theses of this chapter.[23] According to this report the "Notes and Sketches" were written by Horkheimer and contain no interventions by Adorno. Adorno wrote the "Postscripts," which were not revised by Horkheimer.

2. Genesis of the Work: Theoretical Implications

Whereas *Dialectic of Enlightenment* fits more or less seamlessly into Adorno's *oeuvre*, in Horkheimer's case it represents the most pronounced expression of a phase in his intellectual development which differs sharply from that of the 1930s. Whereas the essays for *Zeitschrift* were still borne up by the confidence that it was possible to translate the central ideas of the philosophical and political Enlightenment into materialist terms and to realize them practically, Critical Theory now seems to hope for little more than to preserve the memory of those ideas in the vortex of an overwhelming process of disintegration. The critique derives its incisiveness from being directed against a modern concept of reason which took its standard from the progress of productive forces and still formed the basis of the most advanced critique of the relations of production which had existed up to then. Enlightenment thus becomes enlightenment on the origins and consequences of enlightenment. The change in the development of Horkheimer's Critical Theory first shows itself in the essays "The Authoritarian State" and "The End of Reason"[24] and is emphatically present in *Dialectic of Enlightenment*.

Since the early 1930s Horkheimer had been developing the idea of a materialism to be implemented in an interdisciplinary way. The journal he published, *Zeitschrift für Sozialforschung*, illustrates how a critical theory of society guided by philosophy and underpinned historically and psychologically was to articulate and develop theoretically the practical interest in the abolition of individual suffering and social injustice. According to this conception, the only political groups which had the strength to bring about a revolutionary transformation of society were those which were able to make use of a comprehensive theory which employed the most advanced scholarly instruments.

The form of this theory, however, and especially its philosophical foundations, were by no means clearly outlined. Toward the end of the 1930s, therefore, Horkheimer planned an extensive work on dialectics in which he aimed to elaborate further the philosophical content of his articles published in *Zeitschrift für Sozialforschung*. In a letter of 10 November 1938 Adorno wrote to Benjamin regarding Horkheimer: "He is currently in an extremely overburdened state connected with his move to Scarsdale. In the next few years he wants to free himself from all his administrative work in order to devote his undivided energy to the book on the dialectic."[25] We know about the plan for this book from a memorandum written by Horkheimer about the same time on "The Idea, Activities and Program of the Institut für Sozialforschung," which, however, was not published at that time. The planned work is mentioned there under the title of a "dialectical logic": "This is not a formalistic epistemology but a materialist theory of categories. The scholarly and political discussion of social problems makes use of categories about which differences of opinion arise as soon as closer definition is requested. They include concepts such as causality, tendency, progress, law, necessity, freedom, class, culture, value, ideology, dialectic, etc. [. . .] The definition of philosophical concepts is always at the same time a description of human society in its historically given embodiment. In this respect the planned book conceives of logic in a similar way to Hegel in his great work, not as a collection of abstract modes of thought but as a definition of the most important substantial categories of progressive consciousness in the present time."[26]

But it was not until spring 1941, when he moved to California, that the book on dialectics took shape—though not, admittedly, as a "theory of categories." Nevertheless, even now Horkheimer connected his undertaking with the aim of producing a major philosophical work. In a letter to Pollock of 27 November 1942 he wrote about his efforts, his moments of success, his ambitions and his awareness of the limits of his work: "It is true, the subjects which I am dealing with are the most difficult ones that exist, but the pains you suffer by working on them are at the same time the greatest experience you can have in life. [. . .] There is no doubt that the studies, which I am undertaking now and which are really the fulfillment of what we have dreamt to be our *raison d'être* when we were very young, cannot be achieved in one or two years. [. . .] If Husserl needed ten years to write his *Logical Investigations* and another thirteen years to publish his *Introduction to Pure Phenomenology*, not to speak of more famous works on philosophy and related subjects, and if you take my poor forces, education, and routine into consideration, you will appreciate what I am in for. What I definitely know, however, and what makes me happy, is that I am really doing what I can. *Ultra posse nemini obligatio.* We are really on our way."[27]

Even after his move from New York to California in spring 1941, Horkheimer was unable to withdraw to the extent he wished from the administrative tasks mentioned by Adorno. His original plan for a materialist reformulation of Hegel's *Logic* was changed, suspended, or abandoned in favor of other considerations. However, far more responsible for his decision was the circumstance that Horkheimer's intellectual position and self-reflection were being accompanied by a number of significant political and theoretical experiences and by outward and inward changes in his life. These changes concerned not merely the planned book but—notwithstanding the continuity of his philosophical intention—Horkheimer's thinking as a whole.

If one looks exclusively at the difference between "Traditional and Critical Theory" and *Dialectic of Enlightenment*, one risks misinterpreting these changes as an abrupt break. A closer examination of his less well-known publications, of the records of the history of the Institute for Social Research which have now been collected, and of writings from Horkheimer's posthumous papers from that time reveals a number of intermediate steps and mediating links which make the transformation comprehensible.

In Horkheimer's view the twofold linkage of a philosophically orientated, critical theory of society with traditional research, on the one hand, and with political action, on the other, became weaker and weaker during the 1930s. Adorno had originally tried to draw a sharp dividing line between research in individual disciplines and philosophical interpretation.[28] Now, from the perspective of a sketch of a dialectical logic, or of a dialectic of enlightenment and myth from the point of view of the philosophy of history, this division cast crucial doubt on the philosophical self-consistency of the categories within individual disciplines.[29] Critical Theory could no longer draw on individual disciplines in the same way as previously. Finally, in the Preface to *Dialectic of Enlightenment*, the authors write on this point: "In the present collapse of bourgeois civilization not only the operations but the purpose of science have become dubious."[30] The status of Critical Theory as an immanent critique of traditional theory is thus also called increasingly into question.

The full scope of the particular considerations and doubts relating to the purpose of science becomes clear only from the posthumous papers and letters of the two authors. Important examples of these doubts are Horkheimer's public reflections on the philosophy of language from 1939 onward, which are now published in Vol. 12 of his *Gesammelte Schriften*. They continue from earlier critical discussions of the ideological aspect of language, especially with regard to the conception of language of Logical Positivism, to be found in a number of essays from the 1930s. Horkheimer now radicalizes this earlier standpoint, making it into an aporetic critique of the concept itself. The critique remains aporetic because, by interpreting language as the preponderant relationship of the subject to the object, it renders obsolete its own standard of a language which is not instrumentally stunted. Language, Horkheimer writes in one of these notes from 1946, contains, inextricably mixed, both the power to suppress the particular and the strength to liberate it from that suppression, to reconcile the particular with the universal. Both the negative and the positive sides of this critique appear in *Dialectic of Enlightenment*, but without mediation. The thesis of the universality of blindness implies the complementary thesis that the spell could be lifted at a stroke from humans and things if only the redeeming word were spoken. The critique of a reason which reverts to myth requires as its background not only an historical philosophy of reconciliation but also a utopia of true language. In the notes from the 1940s in his posthumous papers, Horkheimer even seems to be aiming at a sublation of the philosophy of history in a critical philosophy of language.[31]

In Critical Theory, reflections of this kind on the concept of language and on the concept itself never have the self-satisfied character of solutions to the special problems of individual disciplines or of specialist philosophy. Rather, they are persistently seen by Horkheimer and Adorno in their relationship to social theory, and indeed to historical-political experience. The positivist conception of language, in the view of the two authors, concerned merely the real function of language within monopolistic society, a function which it misinterpreted. Not least because language threatened to forfeit its capacity conceptually to transcend the existing order, the unity of theory and political praxis—no matter how mediated—appeared to them to be irremediably shattered by the beginning of the 1940s. The hope for a radical transformation of conditions, indeed, any confidence in the possibility of historical progress at all, seemed to be without substance. The failure of a proletarian revolution to occur in the developed capitalist societies, the subjugation of workers' organizations to a consolidated and expanding fascism, the manipulative power of monopolistic mass society in the West and of state socialism on the Stalinist model in the East—all these political experiences lent impetus to the transition from the Critical Theory of the 1930s to the critique of instrumental reason during the 1940s, a critique which became at the same time theoretically more radical and practically more conservative. In addition, there were internal changes at the Institute which went hand in hand with the theoretical transformations. Especially significant in this context were, first, the break between

Fromm and the other members of the Institute[32] and, second, Adorno's move from Oxford to New York, which began the phase of particularly intensive collaboration between him and Horkheimer.

In the early 1930s Fromm had played a leading part in the elaboration of a concept of analytic social psychology by the Institute. The function of psychoanalysis in this project was, above all, to identify the psychical forces opposing rational interests which aimed at social change, forces which "form, as it were, the cement without which society would not hold together and which contribute to the production of the great social ideologies in all cultural spheres."[33] Horkheimer drew on this sketch for the general conception of *Studien über Autorität und Familie*,[34] according to which the authoritarian attitude mediated through family or state institutions should be understood as the medium by which individuals are adapted to the structures of social domination. Fromm took further the critique, contained in these studies, of Freud's conception of himself as a natural scientist in his later publications concerning a critique of the psychoanalytic theory of libido. The assumption of a basic sexual drive was to be replaced by the wider conception of a drive toward social connection. At the same time Fromm sharpened the criticism he had expressed earlier of Freud's pessimistic anthropology, which he regarded as a hypostatization of bourgeois-patriarchal family structures.[35]

By contrast, Horkheimer's evaluation of psychoanalysis changed in the opposite direction, one might say, during the same period. Against Fromm, whom he accused of lapsing into a psychology of common sense, he adhered more emphatically than ever to the Freudian theory of drives. However, he now interpreted this theory in a different way, as a precise expression of the disempowerment of the subject, which he saw as bound up with the decay of liberalism. Against the theoretical categories and the practical, therapeutic maxims of psychoanalytic ego-psychology he emphasized the socially critical implications of Freud's biological, physicalist materialism. Freud's pessimism regarding the possibility of subjugating destructive forces, founded on the theory of drives, appeared to Horkheimer all the more convincing the less he himself was able to attach such hopes to the abolition of domination by concrete social movements.

How important such an interpretation of psychoanalysis—orthodox yet reading Freud, so to speak, against the grain—was for the conception of *Dialectic of Enlightenment* can be seen from records of talks between

Horkheimer and Adorno from 1939, which can be regarded as preliminary discussions on the work they were planning together.[36] It appears that at times the authors had considered planning their joint work entirely or partly as a critique of psychoanalysis. This is indicated negatively by a formulation concerning the revision of such a plan: "Instead of the orientation to analysis, I propose orienting the book toward currently outlawed concepts like that of the saboteur."[37] In these discussions psychoanalysis is seen, on the one hand, as a variety of positivist thinking ultimately tending toward a false reconciliation between the mutilated individual and the social agencies to which it owes its suffering. On the other hand, however, the psychoanalytic concepts spring from an Enlightenment tradition of asserting truth against illusions and taboos, on which the authors wished to draw. Critical Theory was to subject the scientific concepts of "bourgeois" thought to a change of function corresponding to Marx's procedure with regard to classical political economy. Those concepts contained standards by which their failure to be realized in existing society was to be measured. They were to be stripped of their illusory ahistorical appearance. In the case of psychoanalysis, this applied, for example, to the concept of the individual: "The Progressive moment of analysis consists in the contributions it has made to an understanding of the individual as an arena. It might be said that the analytic categories, however distorted, are conducive to the insight that the individual itself is 'a history of class struggles.'"[38]

However, in *Dialectic of Enlightenment* itself the dispute with psychoanalysis is carried on much more behind the scenes. It is present in central ideas of the book even though it may not be visible at first sight. The psychoanalytic category of the return of the repressed, for example, itself returns in the dialectic of the domination of nature, in the thesis that: "the subjugation of everything natural to the sovereign subject culminates in the domination of what is blindly objective and natural. This tendency levels out all the antitheses of bourgeois thought, especially that between moral rigor and absolute amorality."[39] The proximity of Horkheimer's and Adorno's argumentation to psychoanalytic theory and empirical practice is unmistakable, above all, in the chapters on the culture industry and anti-Semitism. The culture industry is the regression, operating with enlightenment means in restricted form, from the effort of cultural sublimation. In anti-Semitism this regression reveals its deadly seriousness. It is based on the triumph of the projective manipulation of the world over the differentiations and inhibitions of rational thought and behavior: "Impulses which are not acknowledged by the subject and yet are his are attributed to the object: the prospective victim."[40]

In their Preface the authors stress the close connection between the chapter on anti-Semitism and the studies in social psychology of the Institute for Social Research during the 1940s, which were published in the five volumes of *Studies in Prejudice*.[41] The chapter "Elements of Anti-Semitism" should therefore be read as the historical, philosophical, and theoretical background to the empirical studies on prejudice, which in their turn were an attempt to translate the theory into quantitative investigations. Moreover, Adorno refers expressly to this connection in an essay from 1968; "The chapter 'Elements of Anti-Semitism' in *Dialectic of Enlightenment*, which Horkheimer and I wrote jointly in the strictest sense, that is to say, we literally dictated it together, strongly influenced my contribution to the investigations carried out later with the Berkeley Public Opinion Study Group. *The Authoritarian Personality* was the literary outcome of those investigations. [. . .] 'Elements of Anti-Semitism' placed racial prejudice theoretically in the context of an objectively oriented, critical theory of society. Admittedly, in contrast to a certain economic orthodoxy, we did not take an aloof attitude toward psychology but gave it its due place in our sketch as a moment of enlightenment. Never, however, did we leave any doubt as to the precedence of objective factors over psychology. [. . .] We regarded social psychology as a subjective mediation of the objective social system: without its mechanisms subjects could not have been kept in their place."[42]

Despite Adorno's stress on the connection between empirical work and the general theory of anti-Semitism, the gulf between the two, measured by Horkheimer's original program for an interdisciplinary materialism, cannot be overlooked.[43] Unlike earlier attempts to mediate between philosophical, sociological, and psychological knowledge, Horkheimer and Adorno contended that the split between these conceptual spheres corresponded to an actual breach between individual and society and therefore would be merely short-circuited by a purely conceptual approach. This had the result, however, that their evaluation of anti-Semitism was not wholly consistent in both areas. For example, whereas the empirical investigations into the authoritarian character limit its destructive potential by conceding the possibility of a nonrepressive education within existing society, the "Elements" chapter emphatically relates it to "the nature of the dominant reason and of the world corresponding to its image."[44] An end to prejudice could therefore be expected only from a radical break with the logic of the civilizing process up to now. In the empirical studies, therefore, the counterpart to the authoritarian, intolerant, and prejudice-ridden personality is represented by a subject type which, within the framework of *Dialectic of Enlightenment*, appears to be almost inextricably entangled with the principles of self-preservation, of the domination of internal and external nature.

In the extracts cited above from the report on the studies of the 1940s, Adorno points to a second strand of theory which, compared to psychoanalysis, was still more important for *Dialectic of Enlightenment*: economics, meaning the critique of Marx and his successors. But however decisive the link to the critique of political economy may have been, no less characteristic was its relegation to the level of the merely implicit. This was done still more thoroughly than in the case of psychoanalysis. Whereas, in the discussions of 1939 already cited, the authors were still considering an historical-materialist reformulation of the psychoanalytic concept of the individual as a "history of class struggles," the explanatory principle underlying the Marxian concept of history is largely absent from Horkheimer's and Adorno's historical-philosophical sketch. Its place is taken by the more general antagonism between domination of nature and enslavement to it.

The authors attempt to show how reason, having regressed to instrumental rationality, has combined in the present era with the domination of nature and social control to form a quasimythical compulsion. In the modern varieties of totalitarianism, only the always-calamitous intertwinement of reason and power is manifested. The historical phenomenon of fascism no longer appears, as in the orthodox Marxist view, as the last political stage of monopoly capitalism but is related in manifold ways to overarching structures of bourgeois thought and action. National Socialism, which needed military expansion and terror to achieve internal stability yet was bound to miss its goal by using these means, is interpreted as an unstable barbaric interlude on the way to the historically and generically irrevocable goal of the "administered world."

This does not mean, however, that the Marxian approach comprising a dialectic of productive forces and relations of production has been simply replaced by a general analysis of technological rationality. Rather, an abundance of links to the Marxist critique of political economy still remain. To give an example from "Elements of Anti-Semitism" just quoted: the role of the Jews is interpreted there not least as a socioeconomic function of the distribution sphere and its loss of power in monopoly capitalism, and anti-Semitism as a projective obfuscating of the nonequivalent exchange of equivalents in the sale of labor power. Such an interpretation is based on the continuing attempts of the Institut during the late 1930s to redefine the concept of monopoly capitalism and, on that basis, the concept of fascism. A decisive influence on *Dialectic of Enlightenment* in this respect was Pollock's thesis that fascism and bureaucratic socialism were variants of a new order of capitalism which differed fundamentally both from earlier private capitalism and from modern monopoly capitalism, and which he called "state capitalism."[45] In a contribution which follows this Afterword, Willem van Reijen and Jan Bransen discuss in more detail this thesis and its importance for the discussions at the Institute for Social Research.

The pessimism regarding the possibility of socialist politics dominant in Horkheimer's thought since the early 1940s has its *economic* foundation in the theory of state capitalism, its *political* foundation in the connected theory of "rackets" as a "basic form of domination."[46] According to Pollock's thesis there is in state capitalism no structural conflict between political objectives and economic necessities. In the "command economy" the productive forces and the laws of the market are stripped of their autonomy and thus of their explosive potential. The planned economy has become inevitable; the only decisive political question is whether it will be democratic or totalitarian, that is, the question as to how access to the administrative control of the economy and thus to the new ruling class is regulated. This provides the starting point for Horkheimer's theory of rackets, according to which social power, in keeping with its own economic principle, is transformed from the form mediated by exchange, via the form conferred on it by economic monopolies, into direct domination by force. By rackets Horkheimer means the groups, cliques, councils, boards, or committees formed in the most diverse epochs whose social function is largely supplanted by the imperative to preserve and increase their own power. The theory of rackets, which grew out of the discussions on the applicability of Marxian theory to the present form of society, is first of all an attempt to escape the myth of a revolutionary subject without falling back into illusory cultural criticism behind the screen of a critique of political economy. Beyond that, it aims to construct a theory of power which reveals the historically limited model of the rule of liberalism regulated by market laws to be a special case of the monopolization of advantages on the basis of social performance.

For Horkheimer, the topical application of the racket theory was to be found in the transfer of traditional class antagonism to the field of international relations, on the one hand, and to institutionally determined antitheses within the classes themselves, on the other. In postliberal capitalism, according to this theory, new forms of conflict conceal the basic contradiction between capital and labor. With state capitalism mechanisms have come into being to mitigate the economic crises which earlier had the potential to disintegrate the system. In this way the economic "base" loses its role in supporting the social totality. National Socialism and bureaucratic socialism or, more generally, a new "integral statism," can no longer be described only in terms of economic basic categories. Political analysis takes on greater importance to the extent that liberalism appears as an historical episode, after the downfall of which society reverts to direct methods of domination no longer mediated via the market. The fundamental economic factors leading to crisis are tending to become controllable by measures of state intervention, which can range from compensatory welfare legislation to overt terror.

This new form of the "primacy of politics" does not leave untouched the concept of the political itself, in comparison to its function in general capitalism. Above all, it should not be confused with the positivist substitution of historical, political, or psychological laws for economic ones. In a fragment written by Horkheimer about 1942, he describes politics in postliberalism as an illusion which affects not only the dominated masses but the political agents themselves: "Politics, the rediscovery of which in the Renaissance was a theoretical advance, has become, in thinking under monopoly, even more an ideological category than the laws of the market under liberalism: with its aid the surface is hypostatized. The dominated masses attribute world events to politics. They hear the appeal and the decree, they are informed about the lives of the powerful, which consist of facts in no need of theory; the masses experience the direct consequences of political actions, of negotiations between rackets, they feel the effects of emergency aid, of rising prices, of the new job, of war, and perceive big politics as fate and nature just as they earlier perceived the economic depression. And the protagonists share this belief: They know that they hold key positions; just as the entrepreneur mistook his business ventures, calculations and speculations, that he undertook on the basis of the economic cycle, for freedom, the presidents of unions and governments misconstrue their decisions as the beginnings of causal chains. Government, however, must bow to the same necessities as buying and selling: to the requirements of the reproduction of society within the power relationships as they are. This is not so different in the two periods. The opacity of the market which gave rise to the self-deception about freedom merely expressed the fact that the relationships of entrepreneurs among themselves were not rational but were governed by individual self-assertion. Today the struggles take place within much stronger groups, amid movements of highly concentrated masses of capital. The governments are executive mechanisms which cannot rationally understand the actual state of the forces on which they depend, but merely feel their concrete effects."[47]

The state capitalist "primacy of politics" can be understood as a perversion of the socialist idea of the planned economy which was supposed to replace the anarchy of private appropriation by rational decisions in the generalizable interest of society as a whole. What is expressed in fascism, in especially brutal form, is merely what characterizes democratic state capitalism as well as bureaucratic socialism of the Soviet kind: the end of liberal, legal agencies of mediation under the power politics of competing ruling cliques. These groups take over the now necessary planning of the economic process, whether that process is still democratically legitimized or is already an almost openly planned and organized piracy.

The starting point of the racket theory is therefore an analysis of contemporary society as a conglomerate of organized groups under the leadership of bureaucratic or quasibureaucratic elites. The relationship of a clique to its clientele is structured on the principle of protection in exchange for obedience. Since the individual rackets no longer even pretend to pursue intellectual ideals or objectives relating to society as a whole, the traditional ideologies, which used to make particularist interests appear universal, also disappear. They are replaced by the unashamedly pragmatic objectives of manipulation and the preservation of power. The ability to impose these objectives decides the selection and careers of the leading personnel within a racket.

Beyond that, this approach aims to produce an historically generalizable theory of relations of class and domination: "Under the conditions of monopolism and total domination," Horkheimer writes in 1943, "the permanence of oppression, its parasitic nature, becomes manifest. Every ruling class has always been monopolistic to the extent that it excluded the overwhelming majority of human beings. The structure corresponded to that of competing rackets. Even the socially useful functions which the ruling classes used to perform have been transformed into weapons against the oppressed population and against competing groups within their own class. The racket pattern, which used to be typical of the behavior of rulers toward the ruled, is now representative of all human relationships, even those within the working class. The difference between the racket within capital and the racket within labor lies in the fact that in the capitalist racket the whole class profits, whereas the racket of labor functions as a monopoly only for its leaders and for the worker-aristocracy. The laboring masses are the objects of both forms; they merely have to pay for the whole system. The similarity between the most highly respected historical formations, such as the medieval hierarchies, to the modern rackets is obvious. The concept of the racket applies to both large and small enterprises; they all struggle for the largest possible share of added value. In this respect the highest capitalist corporations resemble the small interest groups which operate among the lowliest strata of the population, both within and outside the legal boundaries. [. . .] A true sociology of the racket as the living element of the ruling class in history could serve both a political and a scientific purpose. It could help to clarify the goal of political praxis: a society with a pattern different to that of the racket, a racket-less society. It could contribute to defining the idea of democracy which still leads a shadowy life in the heads of human beings. [. . .] Expressed in scientific terms, a more appropriate philosophy of history could evolve from the sociology of the racket. [. . .] The modern concept contributes to describing social relationships of the past. 'The human anatomy is the key to the anatomy of the ape.' "[48]

The political and economic basis for a theory of rackets and of state capitalism was developed within the Institute primarily by Horkheimer and Pollock; dissenting voices were not lacking among their colleagues, particularly those of Neumann and Kirchheimer. Although Horkheimer adhered fundamentally to the thesis, the criticism may have retarded early publication of his reflections on racket theory. Adorno's contribution,[49] too, remained unpublished. These beginnings of the theory were not elaborated in detail later.

They were, however, the decisive factor in the transition from the earlier form of Critical Theory, represented by the essays in *Zeitschrift für Sozialforschung* during the 1930s, to an historical and generic critique of instrumental reason, of which *Dialectic of Enlightenment* is the most important document. But the specific economic and political arguments do not appear, or appear only in rudimentary form, in this book. Nevertheless, they provide the background of social theory against which the scientific, moral, cultural, and psychological phenomena of the self-destruction of enlightenment were interpreted. Since the authors limit the application of the Marxian categories essentially to liberalism—which, especially with regard to the, at least partial, achievement of bourgeois freedom, is presented as a transient episode in a history of power always dominated by the law of the racket—it is understandable why those categories are pushed into the background in *Dialectic of Enlightenment*. Racket theory, of course, has as its occasion and subject the fate of the once oppositional workers' organizations.[50] It shows how far the class struggle had been transformed under monopoly capitalism into a system of transactions between monopolistic units and thus into a medium of adaptation.

3. Textual Variants. Theoretical Revisions and Misgivings Regarding the Dissemination of the Theory

The reason for the decision initially not to commit *Dialectic of Enlightenment* to print was certainly not only the slender financial means and uncertain academic, political, and geographical future of the Institute in the mid-1940s. This is indicated by the facts that the hectographic edition was limited to about 500 copies and distributed only to specific recipients; that an American edition was not seriously considered; and, finally, that the text for the printed edition published three years later was subjected to thorough revision. None of this is surprising in the case of authors who were always concerned to ensure that their own theoretical utterances or those of others never became entirely detached from their systematic, historical, and social contexts. All the more revealing from the historical standpoint, therefore, are the revisions to the content and terminology of the text undertaken not only in that first period but also more than two decades later. In this edition, these changes, when they go beyond mere orthographic corrections and minor changes of wording, are indicated in the form of footnotes. These were produced on the basis of comparisons between the different editions (1944, 1947, and 1969) made by Willem van Reijen and Jan Bransen. In their commentary, which follows this Afterword, they relate the textual changes (between 1944 and 1947) to the evolution of the economic and political theory underlying them.

Clearly, there are a number of different motives for the later interventions in the text. That becomes clear if the textual variants are classified. The following groups of revised formulations can be distinguished.

(1) Formulations which tie the text directly to its time of origin. These include editorial explanations ("When, two years ago, we began this work . . ."[51]), qualifications reflecting contemporary history ("fascist present"[52]), or overly specialized historical on geographical examples ("The German and Russian pavilions at the Paris World Exposition seemed of the same essence,"[53] "the monumental buildings of monopoly, the skyscrapers of Wrigley and Rockefeller"[54]).

(2) Obscure or elaborate formulations which required stylistic simplification or unraveling, but without replacing theoretically or politically loaded terms (for example, "the official spokesmen [. . .] are repudiating the thought to which they owe their place in the sun" becomes "the official spokesmen [. . .] are liquidating the theory to which they owe their place in the sun"[55]).

Terminological changes based on theoretical considerations, such as the replacement of the expression "mass culture" originally used by "the culture industry," can be included in this group.[56]

(3) Formulations in which monopoly capitalism, totalitarianism, and fascism were equated too indiscriminately. In these cases what had been said in general terms about "class society," "monopolism," or the "totalitarian order" is made more concrete and is restricted to "fascism" or "German fascism."[57] There is clearly also an intention to soften excessively crass judgments on Western democracy or liberalism.[58] Two formulations referring especially critically and inclusively to Jewish functionaries and Christian churches can also be included in this group.[59]

(4) Formulations in which certain theoretically, historically, or polit-ically loaded terms from Marxian or Marxist theory were used. This group not only preponderates quantitatively—it includes more than half the amended passages—but is also far more interesting historically than the others. The politico-economic terms are replaced as a rule by neutral eco-nomic, sociological, or moral-practical expressions—for example, "prole-tarians" by "workers,"[60] "capitalist" by "entrepreneur,"[61] "throughout class history" by "until today,"[62] "exploitation" by "suffering."[63] More than half of these offending formulations include a single concept, that of "monop-oly" (and, again, the great majority of these cases is found in the chapter on "The Culture Industry").

One important motive for such reformulations was undoubtedly the concern to avoid making political enemies, which might possibly have had threatening consequences for the Institute or individual members of it. As early as the 1930s Horkheimer had had serious doubts about the lasting sustainability of a liberal right of asylum in face of opposition from inter-est groups involved in domestic or foreign politics. The terminological changes, therefore, do not reflect a single break but rather a continuum in Horkheimer's thinking. Even the terminology from this period relating to the proletariat and the revolution was characteristically modified in the publications of the *Zeitschrift*.[64] And even as late as the 1950s and 1960s in postwar Germany he constantly anticipated the possibly fatal conse-quences of ill-considered utterances; indeed, he even feared the return of a situation in which people would be able to communicate only, as it were, in whispers.[65]

Such "translations" of Marxist concepts in keeping with the tradition of philosophical and political enlightenment were all the more natural since Critical Theory, starting with its name, represented a reaction to the repudiation of Marxian theory by the authoritarian forms of socialism. The use of language, and reference to the "classics," especially under inte-gral statism of the Soviet kind, had, in the authors' view, lost any truly crit-ical power and, indeed, had itself become a means of repression. For this reason Critical Theory not only was able to draw on the established disci-plines and concepts of scholarly tradition but also considered the "ten-dencies opposed to official science"[66] to have become obsolete. For, as they write, alluding to Soviet Marxism, "They suffer the fate which has always been reserved for triumphant thought. If it voluntarily leaves behind its critical element to become a mere means in the service of an existing order, it involuntarily tends to transform the positive cause it has espoused into something negative and destructive."[67] This interpretation is fundamental to *Dialectic of Enlightenment* but was not carried out in the book itself. In his "Remarks on Thesis VII [of "Elements of Anti-Semitism"]," Adorno noted critically in 1946 that in *Dialectic of Enlightenment* the authoritarian "ticket thinking" present in Bolshevism was neglected: "The thesis applies there in its classical form. [. . .] This whole process of the extermination of humanity in the name of socialism was untouched in the *Fragments*.[68] It is, however, essential to an understanding of the situation as a whole and can no longer be ignored."[69] As early as "The Authoritarian State" Horkheimer had criticized bureaucratic socialism as the most advanced form of authoritarian rule, and there was no lack, subsequently, of unmistakable statements regarding Soviet Marxism by both authors. But they never produced a comprehensive critique of that system and therefore were constantly in fear of being confused with it.

Independently of such questions concerning the prejudiced reception the book might receive, however, there was also a more narrowly theoretical motive. The change in their evaluation of Marxian theory and its applicability to state capitalism and integral statism, on the one hand, and of economic and political reality, of the political tendencies and the chances of changing them, on the other, needed to be reflected in the terminology. The elimination of fascist rule in Central Europe as a result of the war required a redefinition of certain terms which earlier had implicitly equated totalitarianism, fascism, and monopoly capitalism; and the regular focus of the diagnosis of the present on "monopoly" in the earlier version of the text suggested an indiscriminately economistic or subjectivist approach which stood in flat contradiction to the acuity of their analysis elsewhere: economic monopoly could neither causally explain the dialectic of enlightenment in its full breadth nor identify the historical subject of the fateful history of the species. And, not least important, it was necessary to address the thesis that the monopoly capitalism which had existed up to then was in the process of undergoing a qualitative change to become "state capitalism." In this respect the racket theory held an ambiguous position. On the one hand, the identification of fascist rule as an unmediated form of power and *at the same time* the legitimate heir of bourgeois monopoly capitalism[70] prepared the way for a generalized racket theory of domination which went beyond the limited model of the criminal gang. On the other, however, such a theory was in danger—as Horkheimer himself was aware[71]—of merely replacing an oversimplified economic concept ("monopoly") by an oversimplified political one ("rackets"). Probably for this reason, the textual changes affected both terms: "monopoly" is replaced by "the influential clique"[72] and "rackets" by "the completely organized system of domination."[73]

Despite this critical distance, at the time of the book's first publication in printed form the authors continued to regard themselves as Marxists. In the report of a discussion in 1946 about the planned continuation of their joint work after the completion of the printed version, Horkheimer writes: "We see this moment of unity [in the analysis of politics and philosophy] in holding fast to the radical impulses of Marxism and, in fact, of the entire Enlightenment—for the rescue of the Enlightenment is our concern—but without identifying ourselves with any empirically existing party or group. Our position is, in a sense, a materialism which dispenses with the prejudice of regarding any moment of existing material reality as directly positive. The paradox, the dialectical secret of a true politics, consists in choosing a critical standpoint which does not hypostatize itself as the positive standpoint. [. . .] [W]e are [. . .] Stoics because there is no party."[74]

Adorno objected to this stoic conception of oneself on the grounds that it was inappropriate to an advanced technology which could now eliminate all material poverty. His counterproposal for their continuing work was, however, no closer to the reality of politics. For he went back to the original conception of a materialist theory of categories dating from 1938. Political and economic questions should not be taken as the starting point for philosophical analyses, as Horkheimer envisaged; rather, "one should begin by analyzing logical and epistemological categories. The task would be to subject categories like concept, judgment, subject, substantiality, essence, and suchlike to the kind of examination that was already begun in the *Fragments*. This should include not only purely logical but also historical and social discussions. The historical and social substance of the categories and their present status should be determined from their immanent meanings, and such an analysis would lead on to a judgment on the correct and false moments of the categories concerned."[75]

The two authors failed to agree, however, on the question of the

proper relationship between political and philosophical analysis. Horkheimer, from the outset, placed greater emphasis on the political. To which
Adorno responded: "What you fear is a heavy chunk of professorial philosophy. My fear is that the leap from logic to reality will be made in a
dogmatic or analogistic way."[76] Perhaps this dissent should be seen as one
of the—undoubtedly numerous—reasons why the planned continuation
of *Dialectic of Enlightenment* did not materialize. Horkheimer put the
emphasis on the question of how his intention to "rescue the Enlightenment"[77] was to be reconciled with the radical nature of a self-referential
critique of reason: "I should like to see one main theme, e.g.: What can
theory do in the present situation? What is its place? Or: How can the
abstractness of the concept be overcome by the concept itself?"[78] Adorno,
for his part, came down much more squarely on the negative side of this
aporia: "[. . .] reason is its own sickness."[79]

In this way *Dialectic of Enlightenment* also remained a fragment in
the sense that its planned continuation did not come about. It formed the
indispensable starting point and reference point for Horkheimer's thought
during the two decades after his return from emigration.[80] But this reference point remained latent, and of uncertain usefulness. On the one hand,
the epochs of fascism and postwar democracy in Western countries,
despite their deep-seated differences, were, for Horkheimer, connected by
a continuum: the preponderance of bureaucratic structures over the free
subject, which they buried beneath them. On the other, he saw in Western
democracies very serious possibilities of opposing this tendency, which he
regarded as irreversible in the history of the species; to preserve the scope
for freedom which, despite everything, still existed, was for him a practical postulate. To express this contradiction, the resolution of which he did
not believe possible, he coined, and applied to himself, the notion of a
complementarity of theoretical pessimism and practical optimism.[81]

This dichotomy is also present in a similar form in the relationship
of Critical Theory to science. The rejection of established and departmen-
talized science announced in the Preface to *Dialectic of Enlightenment* is
anything but consistently carried through in the book itself, in which the
authors continue frequently to base their argument, whether affirmatively
or critically, on the findings of individual disciplines. Irrespective of the
philosophical reflection which rejects both sense data and judgments as
mediated immediacies, they concede even here that "practically fruitful

scientific enterprises call for an unimpaired capacity for definition, for shutting down thought at a point designated by social need, for demarcating a field which is then investigated in the minutest detail without passing outside it."[82] From this point of view, the empirical research projects which the Institute had planned from the early 1940s and carried out until the end of that decade belie the radical nature of their rejection of science. And after their return to Frankfurt both the reestablishment of the Institut and Horkheimer's and Adorno's intensive academic work and involvement in educational politics during the 1950s and 1960s bear witness to their continuing and vigorous confidence in the enlightening potential of science. Nevertheless, all these concessions to the "business" of science are subject to a general reservation: science, Horkheimer writes in one of his notebooks in the early 1950s, is inherently subject to "standards adapted to the purpose of domination,"[83] and the true philosophy which aims to resist the negative course of the world must beware of secretly wishing to submit to scientific standards.

The question whether a new edition of *Dialectic of Enlightenment* should be published did not arise until the early 1960s—up to then copies of the first edition had still been available. At that time the initial decision on such matters was in the responsibility of Pollock. In January 1961 he compiled, for the first time, a list of "problematic" passages and expressions in the text and noted: "Reacquaintance with *Dialectic of Enlightenment* leads distressingly to two conclusions: How many significant ideas are contained in it, and in an adequate and convincing form; and how little or, rather, how much less than fifteen years ago, one can say without incurring the fury of the mob. [. . .] My question marks and crosses predominantly indicate misgivings about the too-unguarded use of language. Only in a few places did I think it necessary to express doubts, as an 'expert,' on the correctness of the content. All in all, I come to the dismal conclusion that the content of *Dialectic* is not suitable for mass circulation. However, individual chapters, somewhat amended here and there, should be republished in the planned collection."[84] It is reported that Adorno did not share such misgivings to the same extent as Horkheimer and that he tried, vainly at first, to persuade the latter to agree to a largely unamended new edition. The particular reasons for Horkheimer's hesitation have not been recorded; but they were, no doubt, political concerns which probably are approximately reflected in Pollock's formulations. That Adorno, too, shared such misgivings, at least in part, is shown by a draft he produced for a letter, written in summer 1962, in which he and Horkheimer jointly replied to Marcuse, who had emphatically supported the idea of a new edition. In this draft he writes: "The situation is simply that, on the one hand, there are certain hazardous formulations, especially concerning organized religion, that we are afraid about, should the book achieve the circulation which is now to be expected; on the other hand, we wish to keep the text intact and not to water it down because of any concerns and considerations. [. . .] One gradually grows too old to be able to pay overmuch attention to matters of security. The 'pro' for republication is therefore beginning to tilt the scales against the 'contra.'"[85] However, in the final text of the letter redrafted by Horkheimer, this is replaced by the general formulation: "The well-known reasons which had deterred us from agreeing to the second edition become less weighty with each year that we get older."[86]

By now an Italian translation had been ready for printing for some time—the authors had agreed to its production, by Renato Solmi, as early as 1955;[87] it finally came out in 1966. In this text, and in line with the preceding misgivings, a considerable number of changes were made, which Pollock justified in a draft for a preface, written for Horkheimer and Adorno, and certainly after agreeing to the content with them. Because this draft clearly characterizes the authors' political self-understanding at this time, as well as their view of the context of the book's production, it will be quoted in full here:

The German text of *Dialectic of Enlightenment* is a fragment. About the end of the war it was intended to form the introduction to the theory of history and society which we had conceived during the National Socialist period of rule. The attempt to use Hitler's regime to accelerate the regression to the bourgeois-individualistic world, because the power struggles in the new period of world history, in both war and peace, require an absence of economic and administrative friction which is difficult to achieve under the conditions of democracy, had failed. The rapacious nationalism of the East had not been eliminated by its crazy half-brother in the West; rather, war had unleashed developments in Asia, Africa, and South America from which nationalism finally benefits. Life in Europe is threatened by a new migration of peoples which overshadows the earlier one in violence and terror. If physical resistance finally gives way, at least something of its capacity for experience, for reflection and critical consciousness shall live on, just as the critique of power lived on at the end of Antiquity.

That was the mood in which the fragment was written—and we do not disclaim it today. However, instead of developing the theory further we moved back to Germany to try to assist by teaching, despite the dark horizon. Meanwhile the calamity which seems to hang over Europe has been symbolically concretized in the divided Germany. In the Eastern regions people live like slaves, while in the West they subordinate everything else to the will to protect themselves from such slavery. Culture threatens to become a mere means. That is why we believe the book to be still topical today. But the terror inflicted by the National Socialist murderers in the 1940s lives on in the more up-to-date and historically more powerful form which the tyrants of the Eastern mass empires disseminate today.

This has affected the content of the book with no intervention from us. The terminology used in our critique of totalitarian terror has hardened through its use by terror's representatives in the East to a litany which contradicts what it once meant. No word is immune to its own history. We sincerely thank the translator, Dr Renato Solmi, for the dedication to which his work bears witness. As far as we can judge, he has masterfully fulfilled our request to convey the book's meaning.

Our analysis of cultural phenomena from the 1930s and 1940s, which we in no way intend to moderate, is supplemented by our hope that the overthrow of the totalitarian Nazi rule has awakened forces which, despite everything, will resist the temptation which will not fail to emerge one day in every country. Through its theme, our book points out the regressive tendencies which arise from economic, social, and cultural progress itself. We know of no linguistic sphere which contains a more sensitive organ for this task than the Italian.[88]

Solmi responded by advising urgently against most of the textual changes and asked Horkheimer, as the latter writes to Adorno, "almost on bended knee," "to omit the substantive discussion [in the Preface], because it would unleash political controversy."[89] Horkheimer, however, attributed these misgivings mainly to concerns about the political tendency of the publishing house. The authors therefore insisted on the textual changes, but dispensed with the substantive preface on the grounds that "it does no good to encourage the reader to start searching for changes."[90] In the event, no Italian reviewer noticed the changes to begin with; they were discovered only about ten years later and subjected, in some cases, to political debate.[91] In Germany, however, twenty-nine amended passages were painstakingly listed as early as 1967, in an article in a Frankfurt students' newspaper, refuting the assurances in the prefaces that no essential changes had been made. Annoyance at what was taken to be an abandonment of Marxism was unavoidable: "What is left of Critical Theory's claim to be critical if its sting is removed in the way indicated by the Italian edition?"[92]

This experience with the Italian edition is unlikely, on the one hand, to have exactly encouraged the authors to bring out a new German edition but probably did, on the other hand, contribute to the fact that, when the new edition finally appeared in 1969, it was largely spared further interventions in the content. A year earlier, in his "Letter to S. Fischer Verlag," Horkheimer had unequivocally distanced himself from the hopes regarding the future that he had expressed in his early writings but without abandoning the *intention* which underlay those essays: "My hesitation [regarding republication] springs from the difficulty of reexpressing the old ideas, which were not independent of that time, without harming what seems to me true today: the need to renounce the belief in the imminent realization of the ideas of Western civilization and yet to advocate those ideas—without Providence, indeed, against the progress attributed to them."[93] In fact, Horkheimer had already renounced the belief in the imminent "realization of the ideas of Western civilization," as he here paraphrases the proletarian revolution in terms of cultural philosophy, in *Dialectic of Enlightenment*. Nevertheless, this statement also throws light on his evaluation of his critique of society and reason in the 1940s. For common to both phases of Horkheimer's Critical Theory is the impulse to withstand the contradiction of "expressing the frightening tendencies of the present while not giving up the idea of something different."[94]

But it was not only external pressures or the pirated editions of the text already in circulation which are likely to have induced Horkheimer finally to agree to the new, authorized publication. Another decisive factor may have been that in the course of the 1960s Horkheimer's thinking once more drew closer to the theoretical standpoint of *Dialectic of Enlightenment*. In this period, as we can read in *Notizen 1950–1969*, his thinking was marked by a deep-seated skepticism with regard to reason, which took up some features of those earlier ideas and radicalized them further. Adorno, on his return to Frankfurt, had been able to connect *directly* with this text and the other work from those years in his new writing. It was not until the end of the 1950s, however—the year of his retirement, 1959, could be mentioned as the decisive moment—that Horkheimer returned to a position extremely close in some respects to that of Adorno.[95] However, he expressed this position only in the *Notizen*, which were unpublished in his lifetime. In these notes, negative metaphysics and negative religion are joined in a precarious unity. The "true yearning for something different" springs from the fundamental experience of ineradicable suffering in the social context and of a metaphysical, global negation of meaning. Philosophy seems possible only in the vanishing private sphere. It has thus become obsolete in face of historical progress. Such reflections, however, must set themselves philosophical demands if they are not to remain trapped in empty skepticism. Horkheimer's late philosophy is marked by this contradiction, already prefigured in *Dialectic of Enlightenment*: to recognize that the path to the realization of reason in history is blocked and yet, despite all the criticism, to assume the purpose and possibility of enlightenment.

The Disappearance of Class History in "Dialectic of Enlightenment"

A Commentary on the Textual Variants (1947 and 1944)
by Willem van Reijen and Jan Bransen

Since the early 1940s scholars at the Institute for Social Research had devoted themselves with special intensity to analyzing the causes and consequences of fascist rule, with the aim of carrying out extensive research projects. In the course of this work two opposed views emerged. On one side, Horkheimer, Adorno, Pollock, and Löwenthal developed the thesis that National Socialism, as compared to traditional capitalism, represented a new order. While they regarded fascist state capitalism as the most recent outcome of capitalist logic, they believed that this outcome manifested a new quality: the dominance of politics over economics. In his essay entitled "Is National Socialism a New Order?"[1] Pollock, on whose specialist knowledge of economics the other advocates of this view relied, answered this question in the affirmative. On the other side, Neumann, Kirchheimer, and Gurland supported the thesis that the National Socialist economic order was a continuous development of capitalism, so that one could not speak of a new order. This controversy over the primacy of politics or economics in postliberal capitalism, as authors such as Dubiel and Söllner or Brick and Postone show,[2] impinged deeply on the theoretical self-understanding of the members of the Institute for Social Research.

Pollock's study of the development of capitalism had been a permanent part of the Institute's work since the early 1930s. In his early essays[3] he followed Marx in locating the contradictions threatening the capitalist system in the growing tension between productive forces and the relations of production. He argued that the quality of the new economic crisis demonstrated that liberal capitalism, with its attempts to regulate crises through the market, must fail. It was therefore time for a transition to a new economic order which, although based on the old one and therefore to be seen as a development of it, exhibited the novel quality of a planned economy. The latter, according to Pollock, was possible in two forms: as a capitalist planned economy on the basis of private ownership of the means of production, or as a Socialist planned economy on the basis of socialized ownership of the means of production. Pollock contradicted the Marxian theory of the collapse of capitalism and went still further in prophesying its permanence: "What is coming to an end is not capitalism but only its liberal phase."[4]

In the early 1940s Pollock refined and sharpened his analysis.[5] He now applied the term "state capitalism" both to the National Socialist economy and to the economy of the Soviet Union. Both were totalitarian forms of the economic order. Typical of both these forms of state capitalism was the "fusion of leading bureaucracies from the worlds of business, state, and party"[6] to form a new ruling class. By contrast, in the democratic form of state capitalism to be found in the USA, for example, the state apparatus was, to be sure, controlled by the people but had in common with the totalitarian varieties the fact that state activity rendered the key function of the market inoperative. While there were still profits, prices, and wages, these no longer predominantly determined economic actions. And the influence on decisions of the private ownership of the means of production had disappeared. The individual capitalist, separated from the centralized decision-making agencies and "overruled" by the state administration, had become a mere recipient of annuities.[7] There were no longer any autonomous economic problems, only administrative problems. For this reason impulses for social change no longer emanated from the economic sphere. It had become static. All initiatives issued from politics—unless problems of political legitimation arose, for example, in connection with unemployment or the failure of the standard of living to rise. Pollock therefore replaced the tension between the relations of production and the productive forces, regarded as fundamental by Marx, by the tension between the relations of production and distribution. The switch from the primacy of economics to that of politics takes place within the distribution sphere: it is the switch from unconscious to conscious distribution and control. In both cases Pollock assumed a primacy of the mode of distribution.[8]

The concept of "state capitalism" did not remain uncontested within the Institute. Neumann, in particular, took a critical view.[9] His position makes clear the theory of the paramount role of economics which is also implicit in *Dialectic of Enlightenment*. For Neumann continued to advance the thesis of continuity in the development from liberal capitalism to National Socialism. Neumann considered Pollock's concept to be a *contradictio in adjecto*. Either, he argued, National Socialist society is capitalist—in which case market, competition, and profit continue to function as before; or the state determines economic processes—in which case society is not capitalist in the Marxian sense. Unlike Pollock, Neumann put the emphasis on the fact that the contradictions in developed capitalism had not been resolved but intensified. As empirical evidence he cited various measures of totalitarian rule and economic regulation which did not curtail the importance of competition and profit.

But Neumann's work, too, contains a number of ideas by which he sought to account for the qualitative changes in the relationship of monopoly capitalism to totalitarian rule. He did not dispute the functional increase of politics compared to economics which he, too, perceived as continuing in the postfascist states and in which he saw a "developmental product of capitalism."[10] Finally, he attempted to incorporate Pollock's analyses, in reinterpreted form, in his own approach: "Control over the state apparatus is [. . .] the pivot on which everything turns. This is the only possible meaning of the primacy of politics over economics."[11] In arguing this, however, he did not mean to call into question the fundamentally capitalist mode of operation of "totalitarian monopoly capitalism," to use his expression, which has remained a standard term until today.

Naturally, Horkheimer's own work was not uninfluenced by this controversy. In 1937 he still unquestioningly accepted the Marxian thesis of the contradiction between the productive forces and the relations of production; what had changed under fascism was, above all, that the techniques of power and manipulation had been perfected. The culture taken over by fascism, Horkheimer argued, no longer held resources for criticism and opposition. In 1942, in the essay "The Authoritarian State," however, he based himself on Pollock's theory of state capitalism. National Socialism and bureaucratic Socialism of the Soviet kind were distinguished, at most, by the composition of the ruling cliques, but in both cases politics had gained dominance over economics. As "integral statism" the Soviet system appeared as the most logical form of the authoritarian state.

If the two versions of *Dialectic of Enlightenment* are compared—the mimeographic publication of the Institute of Social Research of 1944 and the first printed copy of 1947—it is clear how deeply the debate over the primacy of economics over politics had affected the self-understanding of its two authors. To be sure, Horkheimer and Adorno assert in their Preface to the book edition, which follows the original Preface, that "The book contains no essential changes to the text completed during the War."[12] But few things are more open to dispute than the question as to what is essential; the textual changes made for the book edition of 1947 can be called, at least, significant. This will be shown by a few representative passages:

Throughout the book the authors replaced terms such as "monopoly," "capital," and "profit," which had become charged with specific meanings through the debate over state capitalism, with *less charged expressions.* "Monopoly" becomes "the economic apparatus";[13] or the term is replaced by "the agencies of mass production,"[14] "the system of modern industry,"[15] "the culture industry,"[16] "those in control,"[17] or, more neutrally, "the system."[18] However, the term "monopoly" is not infrequently replaced by "trusts" and "combines."[19] The "monopoly rulers" are transformed into "managing directors."[20] "Capital" becomes "the economy,"[21] its "power" the "power of the economically strongest,"[22] or "capitalism" disappears completely.[23]

From the postwar perspective in which the printed version was produced, fascist phenomena are *more precisely qualified,* whereas earlier they had been referred to generally as economic phenomena: the "collective of the totalitarian monopoly" becomes the "fascist collective,"[24] "monopoly" becomes "fascism."[25] There is an increasing *distance from Marxian terminology.* The "relations of production" become "economic forms,"[26] "class domination" becomes "domination,"[27] "exploitation" becomes the more neutral "enslavement,"[28] "control" becomes "utilization,"[29] "those in control" become "leaders."[30] "Class history" disappears completely.[31] "Monopoly" becomes "industry"[32] or no longer appears at all.[33]

The almost complete elimination of the term "monopoly" from all important passages, and the transformation of "capital" into "economy" and similar terms in most places, are not sufficiently explained by political misgivings and considerations alone. Rather—and this is more important for a theoretical and systematic understanding of *Dialectic of Enlightenment*—they show that in the mid-1940s Horkheimer and Adorno, in keeping with Pollock's analyses, had distanced themselves definitively from a form of Marxism which assumed the primacy of economics. Instead, the importance of control through politics and the culture industry moves clearly into the foreground.

It would nevertheless be mistaken to conclude that Horkheimer and Adorno had thereby turned their backs on Marxian theory altogether. The references to fascism, which emerged more emphatically in the book version than in the first publication, should be understood not only as anxious reminders that the dangers issuing from fascism still persisted but also as evidence of the authors' view that capitalism and fascism were still intertwined as social principles and that capitalism continued to have the tendency to prevent the realization of the "realm of freedom." Horkheimer and Adorno decisively rejected a mechanistic interpretation of Marx of the kind adopted by theoreticians of the Second International and by the Soviet orthodoxy, but they did not deny the fundamental importance of the economic order for the totality of social orders in the modern period. For this reason the Marxian approach continued to be fundamental to Critical Theory.

Notes

[Bracketed numbers are the page numbers on which asterisk notes appear; other numbers refer to the numbered notes. "It. tr." = from the Italian translation.]

DEDICATION

[vii] "Pollock" / 1944: Pollock for his fiftieth birthday on 22 May 1944; 1947: "Pollock for his fiftieth birthday."

PREFACES

[xiii] "Preface to the Italian Edition": Translated from the Italian by Philipp Rippel with reference to the German draft by M.H. and T.W.A.

[xiv] "When" / 1944/47: "When, two years ago."

[xiv] "a . . . of" / 1944: "renewed."

[xiv] "with an increasing" / 1944: "readily with the."

[xiv] "The tireless . . . humanity" / 1944: "The end of enlightenment by its own hand, hypocritically celebrated by crude advocates of the totalitarian order in their propaganda speeches and naively executed by the smart attorneys of the victims in their respective branches of the culture industry."

[xv] "friendship" / 1944: "friendship, in the Action Française."—"Action Française": extreme right-wing movement in France between 1898 and 1944.

[xv] "place in . . . sun": allusion to an imperialist slogan coined in Wilhelmine Germany.

[xv] "liquidating . . . completely." / 1944: "repudiating the thought to which they owe their place in the sun before it has had time to prostitute itself completely in the service of those now basking there."

[xvi] "the regression" / 1944: "its reversal."

[xvi] "headlong" / 1944: "in such a way."

[xvi] "rational" / 1944: "a rational."

[xvii] "In the . . . increase" / 1944: "The powerless and pliability of the masses increase."

[xvii] "Today, however," / 1944: "In the name of enlightenment."

[xvii] "increased sufferings" / 1944: "increased exploitation."

[xvii] "melting down . . . crucible" / 1944: "application of the national melting pot to all cultural entities."

[xviii] "Volkswagen" / 1944: "chewing gum."

[xviii] "curtain" / 1944: "veil."

[xix] "demonstrates" / 1944: "defines."

[xix] "fragmentary" / 1944: "fragmentary. Large parts, written long before, need only final editing. In them the positive aspects of mass culture will also be dealt with."—The second part of the chapter, not finally edited at that time, has now been published with the title "Das Schema der Massenkultur" as an appendix to *Dialektik der Aufklärung* in Adorno, *Gesammelte Schriften*, Vol. III, Frankfurt am Main 1981, pp. 299ff.

[xix] "empirical . . . Research" / 1944: "the research project of the Institute of Social Research."

[xix] "anthropology" / 1944: "anthropology.

In selecting the fragments from the work of the previous two years we opted for those with clear internal coherence and unity of language. We excluded all English works produced in the same period, regardless of their thematic connection to the fragments. We would mention the lecture series "Society and Reason"; the essays "Sociology of Class Relations" and "The Revival of Dogmatism"; the extensive analysis of anti-Semitic propaganda, "The Psychological Technique of Martin Luther Thomas' Radio Addresses," and our other studies in contributions to the project on anti-Semitism. Collaboration in this study carried out in New York, Los Angeles, and Berkeley took at least half our time.—Of the German preliminary studies to the whole work, which include the fragments themselves, we left out the pieces on logic, among others. The already formulated parts of the planned section concerned with a critique of sociology are also omitted.

If the good fortune of being able to work on such questions without the unpleasant pressure of immediate purposes should continue, we hope to complete the whole work in the not too distant future. We are encouraged to believe this by the confidence, undeflected by the vicissitudes of the time, of the person to whom the part completed so far is now dedicated."

"Society and Reason": under this general title Horkheimer gave five lectures at Columbia University, New York, in February and March 1944. They were later used as the basis of *Eclipse of Reason* (New York 1947), German title *Zur Kritik der instrumentellen Vernunft*, Frankfurt am Main 1967.

"Sociology of Class Relations": essay by Horkheimer from 1943 now published with the title "Zur Soziologie der Klassenverhältnisse" in *Gesammelte Schriften*, Vol. XII, Frankfurt am Main 1985, pp. 75ff.

"The Revival of Dogmatism. Remarks on Neo-Positivism and Neo-Thomism": Horkheimer's manuscript with his title later formed the basis of Chapter 2 of *Eclipse of Reason*.

THE CONCEPT OF ENLIGHTENMENT

[1] "The concept" / 1944: "The dialectic."

[1] "disenchantment of the world": "allusion to a formulation of Max Weber's; cf. Weber, "Wissenschaft als Beruf" (1919) in *Gesammelte Aufsätze zur Wissenschaftslehre*, Tübingen 1968, p. 594.

1. Voltaire, *Lettres philosophiques,* ed. F. A. Taylor, London 1992, p. 36.

2. "In Praise of Knowledge," in *Francis Bacon*, ed. Arthur Johnston, London 1965, p. 15.

[2] "enslavement" / 1944: "exploitation."

[2] "economic system" / 1944: "capitalism."

[2] "exploitation . . . others" / 1944: "control of foreign work."

3. Cf. Bacon, *Novum Organum, The Works of Francis Bacon*, ed. Basil Montagu, London 1825, Vol. XIV, p. 31.

4. Bacon, "Valerius Terminus: Of the Interpretation of Nature." *Miscellaneous Tracts upon Human Knowledge, Works*, Vol. I, p. 281.

[3] "spirit-seer": allusion to Kant's dispute with Swedenborg: "Dreams of a spirit-seer elucidated by dreams of metaphysics" in Kant, *Theoretical Philosophy*, trans. David Walford, Cambridge/New York 1992.

5. Cf. *Hegel's Phenomenology of Spirit*, trans. A. V. Miller, Oxford 1977, pp. 331f.

6. Xenophanes, Montaigne, Hume, Feuerbach, and Salomon Reinach are at one here. Cf. Reinach, *Orpheus,* trans. F. Simmons, London and New York 1909, pp. 6ff.

7. Bacon, *De augmentis scientiarum, Works*, Vol. VIII, p. 152.

8. J. de Maistre, "Les Soirées de Saint-Pétersbourg." 5ième entretien, *Oeuvres complètes*, Lyon 1891, Vol. IV, p. 256.

9. Bacon, *Advancement of Learning, Works*, Vol. II, p. 126.

10. *Genesis* I, 26

11. Archilochus, fr. 87, quoted by Deussen, *Allgemeine Geschichte der Philosophie*, Vol. II, Pt. 1, Leipzig 1911, p. 18.

12. Solon, fr. 13.25 et seq., quoted by Deussen, *op. cit.*, p. 20.

13. Cf. Robert H. Lowie, *An Introduction to Cultural Anthropology*, New York 1940, pp. 344f.

14. Cf. Freud, *Totem and Taboo*, in *The Complete Psychological Works of Sigmund Freud*, trans. James Strachey, London 1991, pp. 85ff.

15. *Ibid.*, p. 89.

[7] "industrial technology" / 1944: "the technology of monopoly."

[8] "insufficient righteousness": allusion to the positivists' charge that metaphysical philosophers lacked sufficient correctness, honesty, and uprightness, a charge generally leveled by "enlightened" thought against the preceding philosophical systems. (It. tr.)

[9] "doubtless" / 1944: (missing).

16. *Hegel's Phenomenology of Spirit, op. cit.*, p. 342 (where *Trupp* is translated more neutrally as "group").

17. Cf. W. Kirfel, "Geschichte Indiens," in *Propyläenweltgeschichte*, Vol. III, pp. 261ff, and G. Glotz, "Histoire Grècque," Vol. 1, in *Histoire Ancienne*, Paris 1938, pp. 137ff.

[9] "subjugated people" / 1944: "objects of exploitation."

18. G. Glotz, *op. cit.,* p. 140.

19. Cf. Kurt Eckermann, *Jahrbuch der Religionsgeschichte und Mythologie*, Halle 1845, Vol. I, p. 241, and O. Kern, *Die Religion der Griechen*, Vol. I, Berlin 1926, pp. 181f.

[10] "link" / 1944: "link" (n. 20 here).

20. Hubert and Mauss describe the nature of "sympathy" or mimesis as follows: "L'un est le tout, tout est dans l'un, la nature triomphe de la nature." H. Hubert and M. Mauss, "Théorie générale de la Magie," in *L'Année Sociologique* 1902–3, p. 100.

21. Cf. Westermarck, *Ursprung der Moralbegriffe*, Leipzig 1913, Vol. I, p. 402.

[13] "total art" / an allusion to Richard Wagner's concept of the total art work (*Gesmtkunstwerk*) (It. tr.).

22. Cf. Plato, *The Republic*, Book 10.

23. Schelling, *Erster Entwurf eines Systems der Naturphilosophie*. S. 5, *Werke*, Abt. 1, Vol. II, p. 623.

24. *Ibid.*, p. 626.

[15] "twentieth century": allusion to Alfred Rosenberg's *Der Mythos des zwanzigsten Jahrhunderts* (1930).

[16] "the consolidated . . . privileged" / 1944: "class domination."

25. Cf. E. Durkheim, "De quelques formes primitives de classification," *L'Année Sociologique*, Vol. IV, 1903, pp. 66ff.

26. Cf. *The New Science of Giambattista Vico*, trans. 3rd ed. Thomas Goddard Bergin and Max Harold Fisch, New York 1961.

[17] "industrial trusts" / 1944: "social upheaval caused by monopoly."

27. Hubert and Mauss, *op. cit.*, p. 118.

28. Cf. Tönnies, "Philosophische Terminologie," in *Psychologisch-Soziologische Ansicht*, Leipzig 1908, p. 31.

29. Hegel, *Phenomenology*, *op. cit.*, p. 51.

[18] "value" / 1944: "word."

30. Edmund Husserl, *The Crisis of European Sciences and Transcendental Phenomenology, an Introduction to Phenomenological Philosophy*, trans. David Carr, Evanston, 1970.

31. Cf. Schopenhauer, *Parerga and Paralipomena*, trans. E. F. J. Payne, Oxford 1974, Vol. II, §356, p. 610.

[20] "spirit-seer": Cf. note [6], p. 255.

[21] "industrialism . . . things." / 1944: "industry makes souls into things. The rule of the monopolists, as of individual capitalists earlier, is not expressed directly in the commands of the rulers."

[21] "The countless . . . culture" / 1944: "Monopoly."

[22] "value" / 1944: "exchange value."

32. Spinoza, *Ethics*, trans. A. Boyle, London/New York 1948, Part IV, Propos. XXII, Coroll.

[23] "merely an aid . . . apparatus" / 1944: "an apparatus in the perpetuating monopoly."

[23] "unitary knowledge": The "unity of knowledge" postulated by the Vienna Circle, especially Neurath and Carnap.

[24] "pleasure": allusion to the National Socialist promotion of physical culture for racial, genetic ends, which went hand in hand with the lifting of certain taboos in the private sexual sphere ("Strength Through Joy," "Lebensborn e.V," etc. Cf. Friedrich Pollock, "Is National Socialism a New Order?" in *Studies in Philosophy and Social Science*, Vol. IX, 1941, pp. 448f.

[24] "The German . . . self-contempt" / 1944: "Pleasure, which the neopagans and administrators of war fever wanted to set free, has, on its way to totalitarian emancipation, internalized meanness as self-contempt."

33. Homer, *Odyssey*, trans. E. V. Rieu (amended), Harmondsworth 1965, p. 194.

34. *Ibid.*

35. *Hegel's Phenomenology of Spirit*, *op cit.*, p. 116.

[29] "society" / 1944: "class society."

[29] "rulers" [*Lenker*] / 1944: "those in control" [*Verfügende*].

[29] "of . . . injustice" / 1944: "of exploitation."

[30] "of the cliques . . . embodied" / 1944: "of monopoly, the last incarnation of economic necessity."

[30] "Intuitions," "dynamic worldview," "mission," and "fate" were common terms in "educated" National Socialist jargon.

[30] "company chairmen" / 1944: "monopoly controllers."

[30] "of those still" / 1944: "the hands needed to operate the increasing fixed capital."

[30] "Poverty" / 1944: "Increasing misery."

[30 "the economy" / 1944: "capital."

[30] "rackets": Systems for extorting protection money; in a wider sense, groups securing the system of power. Also see Editor's Afterword, pp. 233ff.

[31] "the reason of the reasonable" / 1944: "this."

[31] "industrialists . . . This" / 1944: "those in power . . . This twofold."

[31] "that thinking": Refers to the Marxian concept of the period of history preceding the socialist society.

[31] "truth": The authors are paraphrasing the scholastic formulation: "verum index sui et falsi" (It. tr.).

[32] "eternal": Cf. Marx, *Capital. A Critique of Political Economy*, trans. David Fernbach. Harmondsworth 1991, Vol. III.

[33] "unfettered technology" / 1944: "the unfettered technical forces of production."

36. "The supreme question which confronts our generation today—the question to which all other problems are merely corollaries—is whether technology can be brought under control . . . Nobody can be sure of the formula by which this end can be achieved . . . We must draw on all the resources to which access can be had . . ." (*The Rockefeller Foundation. A Review for 1943*. New York 1944, pp. 33ff).

[33] Cf. note 2, p. 255.

EXCURSUS I

1. Nietzsche, *Nachlass, Werke*, Vol. XIV, Leipzig 1904, p. 206.

2. *Ibid.*, Vol. XV, p. 235.

[37] "Borchardt": An earlier draft of the manuscript (Theodor W. Adorno Archiv) contains a reference to Borchardt's afterword to his translation of the poems of Pindar *Pindarische Gedichte*, Munich 1929/30 (private impression), pp. 99, 103, and 93; cf. "Einleitung in das Verständnis der Pindarischen Poesie," in *Gesammelte Werke*, Prosa II, Stuttgart 1959, pp. 161ff.

3. *Ibid.*, Vol. IX, p. 289.

[37] "rational" / 1944/47: "more rational."

4. Hölderlin, "Patmos," *Poems and Fragments*, trans. Michael Hamburger, Cambridge and New York 1980, p. 463.

5. Direct evidence in support of this argument is found early in Book XX. Odysseus notes the maids' nightly visits to the beds of the Suitors. "Odysseus'

gorge rose within him. Yet he was quite uncertain what to do and he debated long. Should he dash after them and put them all to death; or should he let them spend this one last night in the arms of their profligate lovers? The thought made him snarl with repressed fury, like a bitch that snarls and shows fight as she takes her stand above her helpless puppies when a stranger comes by. So did Odysseus groan to himself in sheer revolt at these licentious ways. But in the end he brought his fist down on his heart and called it to order. 'Patience, my heart!' he said. 'You had a far more loathsome thing than this to put up with when the savage Cyclops devoured those gallant men. And yet you managed to hold out, till cunning got you clear of the cave where you had thought your end had come.' But though he was able by such self-rebuke to quell all mutiny in his heart and steel it to endure, Odysseus nevertheless could not help tossing to and fro on his bed . . ." (*The Odyssey, op. cit.*, p. 304). The subject is not yet articulated to form a firm inner identity. Affects, courage, the "heart" still rise up independently. "At the beginning of this episode, his heart, *kradie* or *etor* (the two words are synonyms for "heart," 17.22), snarls and growls within him, and Odysseus beats his breast, that is, his heart, and addresses it. His heart beats violently; this part of his body is stirring against his will. That he speaks to it is not, therefore, a mere formal device, as when hand or foot is addressed in Euripides to set them in motion; his heart acts autonomously" (Wilamowitz-Moellendorff, *Die Heimkehr des Odysseus*, Berlin 1927, p. 189). The affect is equated with an animal which the human being is subduing: The metaphor of the bitch forms part of the same stratum of experience as the metamorphosis of Odysseus's companions into swine. The subject, still split and forced to do violence to nature both within himself and outside, "punishes" his heart, compelling it to be patient and denying it direct satisfaction in the present for the sake of a more distant future. Beating one's breast later became a gesture of triumph: What the victor really expresses is that his victory is over his own nature. The achievement is accomplished by self-preserving reason. ". . . the speaker thought first of his wildly beating heart; his *metis* [cunning], which is thus seen a separate inner force, was able to master it, and saved Odysseus. Later philosophers would have contrasted it as *nus* [mind] or *logistikon* [reasoning] to the unreasoning parts of the body" (Wilamowitz, *op. cit.*, p. 190). But the "self"—*autos*—is not mentioned until line 24, after the impulse has been successfully mastered by reason. If the choice and sequence of the words are taken as evidence, the identity-forming self is regarded by Homer as resulting from a mastery of nature within the human being. This new self trembles inwardly, as a thing, the body, when the heart within it is punished. At any rate, Wilamowitz's juxtaposing of separately analyzed moments of the psyche, which often speak to each other, seems to confirm the loose cohesion of the subject, whose substance consists only in the coordination of these moments.

6. In contrast to Nietzsche's materialistic interpretation, Klages understood sacrifice and exchange entirely in terms of magic: "The general necessity to offer sacrifices affects everyone, because everyone, as has been seen, receives his or her share of life, and all the goods of life they can obtain—the original *suum cuique*—only through the constant exchange of gifts. This, however, is not exchange in the ordinary sense of exchanging goods (although at the very beginning that, too, was consecrated by the idea of sacrifice) but of exchanging fluids or essences by abandoning one's own soul to the supporting and nurturing life of the world" (Ludwig Klages, *Der Geist als Widersacher der Seele*, Leipzig 1932, Vol. III, Part 2, p. 1409). However, the twofold character of sacrifice—the magic self-abandonment of the individual to the collective (in whatever form) and the self-preservation achieved through the technology of this magic—implies an objective contradiction which necessitates further development of the rational element in sacrifice. Still under the influence of magic, rationality, as the behavior of the performer of the sacrifice, becomes cunning. Klages himself, the zealous apologist of myth and sacrifice, came up against this contradiction and found himself obliged, even within the ideal image of Pelagianism, to distinguish between genuine and false communication with nature. However, he was unable to derive from mythical thinking itself any opposing principle to set against the illusion of the magical mastery of nature, because that very illusion constitutes the essence of myth. "It is no longer merely pagan belief but pagan superstition which compels the king of the gods, on ascending his throne, to swear that henceforth he will cause the sun to shine and the field to be covered in fruits" (Klages, *op. cit.*, p. 1408).

7. In keeping with this, human sacrifices in the literal sense do not occur in Homer. The epic's civilizing tendency is manifested in the selection of the incidents narrated. "With one exception . . . both Iliad and Odyssey are completely expurgated of the abomination of Human Sacrifice" (Gilbert Murray, *The Rise of the Greek Epic*, Oxford 1911, p. 150).

[40] "The representative character . . . deity." / 1944: "The idea of magic representation implied in sacrifice, which he affirms, cannot be separated from the victim's status as the elect. But this status results from the priests' transposition of the victim to the heaven of the gods. An element of this projection, which elevates the perishable person as the bearer of the divine substance, has always been detectable in the ego, which owes its origin to projection. It bears the features of the idolized victim: not without reason was Odysseus continually regarded as a secularized deity."

8. Probably not at the earliest stages. "The custom of human sacrifice . . . is far more widespread among barbarous and half-civilized peoples than among true savages, and it is hardly found at all at the lowest levels of culture. It has been observed that in some peoples this custom has become increasingly predominant

in the course of time"—on the Society Islands, in Polynesia, in India, among the Aztecs. "With regard to Africa Winwood Read states that 'the mightier the nation the more prominent the custom of sacrifice'" (Eduard Westermarck, *Ursprung und Entwicklung der Moralbegriffe*, Leipzig 1913, Vol. I, p. 363).

9. Among cannibal peoples like those of West Africa, "neither women nor adolescents . . . were allowed to taste the delicacy" (Westermarck, *op cit.*, Leipzig 1909, Vol. II, p. 459).

10. Wilamowitz places *nus* in "sharp opposition" to *logos* (*Glaube der Hellenen*, Berlin 1931, Vol. I, pp. 41f). For him myth is "a story one tells oneself," a fairy tale, an untruth, but also, without distinction from that, the ultimate, undemonstrable truth, as in Plato. While Wilamowitz is aware of the illusory character of myths, he equates them with poetry. In other words, he looks for myths only in significative language, which has already come into objective contradiction with its intention, and seeks to resolve it as poetry: "Myth is in the first place spoken discourse; the words are indifferent to the content" (*ibid.*). By hypostatizing this late concept of myth, which presupposes reason as its explicit counterpart, he arrives—in an implicit polemic against Bachofen, whom he dismisses as merely fashionable without mentioning him by name—at a clear distinction between mythology and religion (*op. cit.*, p. 5), whereby myth appears not as the older but the younger state: "I attempt . . . to trace the evolution, the transformations and the transition from faith to myth" (*op. cit.*, p. 1). The Hellenistic scholar's rigid departmental arrogance blocks his perception of the dialectic of myth, religion, and enlightenment: "I do not know the languages from which the currently modish words 'taboo,' 'totem,' '*mana*,' and '*orenda*' are taken but consider it legitimate to confine myself to the Greeks, and to think about Greek matters in Greek terms" (*op. cit.*, p. 10). How his unexplained contention that "the germ of the Platonic deity" was present "in the earliest Hellenic culture" is therefore to be reconciled with the historical view, put forward by Kirchhoff and taken over by Wilamowitz, that the earliest core of the Odyssey is contained in the mythical encounters of the *nostos*, remains unclear, just as the central concept of myth itself lacks adequate philosophical articulation in Wilamowitz. Nevertheless, his opposition to the irrationalism which idolizes myth and his insistence on the untruth of myths reveal unmistakable insight. His repugnance for primitive thinking and prehistory shows up all the more clearly the tension which has always existed between the deceptive word and truth. The arbitrariness of fabrication which Wilamowitz criticizes in later myths must already have been contained in the earliest ones, by virtue of the *pseudos* [substitute] of sacrifice. This *pseudos* is related to precisely the Platonic deity which Wilamowitz dates back to archaic Hellenism.

11. The conception of Christianity as a pagan sacrificial religion is fundamental to Werner Hegemann's *Geretteter Christus* (Potsdam 1928).

[43] "society's predicament" / 1944: "the predicament of the whole of class history."

12. For example, when he refrains from killing Polyphemus at once (IX, 302); when he has to endure the mistreatment of Antinous in order not to give himself away (XVII, 460ff). Also compare the episode of the winds (X, 50ff) and Teiresias's prophecy in the first visit to the Underworld (XI, 105ff), which makes his homecoming dependent on mastery of his heart. To be sure, Odysseus's renunciation is more a postponement than a final state; he usually performs the deeds of vengeance all the more thoroughly for having delayed them; his endurance is patience. His behavior still displays relatively openly, as a natural objective, something which was later concealed in total, imperative renunciation, thereby taking on the irresistible violence which subjugated everything natural. Through being transposed inside the subject and emancipated from its mythical content, this subjugation becomes "objective," confronting the special purposes of humans as an independent entity and becoming the universal rational law. In Odysseus's patience—quite clearly after the death of the Suitors—vengeance is already turning into judicial procedure: the ultimate fulfillment of the mythical impulse becomes the objective instrument of domination. Law is vengeance which is capable of renunciation. But since this judicial patience is generated by something outside itself, the longing for the homeland, it takes on human traits, almost a quality of trust, which point beyond vengeance postponed. In fully developed bourgeois society, however, both are annulled: with the idea of vengeance longing, too, is tabooed—thereby, of course, enthroning vengeance, mediated as the self's revenge on itself.

13. Max Weber, *Wirtschaftsgeschichte*, Munich and Leipzig 1924, p. 3.

14. Victor Bérard has strongly emphasized the Semitic element in the *Odyssey*, though not without some apocryphal interpretation. Cf. the chapter "Les Phéniciens et l'Odyssée" in *La Résurrection d'Homère*, Paris 1930, pp. 111ff.

[48] "capitalist economy" / 1944: "exploitation."

[48] "make use . . . worker" / 1944: "have anyone to exploit."

[48] "entrepreneur" / 1944: "capitalist."

[48] "moral . . . profit" / 1944: "moral justification for the plunder raked in by the privileged."

[49] *nostos*: Greek: "journey," "homecoming."

15. *Odyssey*, Book IX, *op. cit.*, p. 141.

16. *Ibid.*, p. 349.

17. *Ibid.*, p. 141.

18. Jacob Burckhardt, *History of Greek Culture*, trans. Palmer Hilty, London 1963, p. 180.

19. *Odyssey*, *op. cit.*, p. 141.

20. In Indian mythology Lotus is the earth goddess. (Cf. Heinrich Zimmer, *Maja*, Stuttgart and Berlin 1936, pp. 105f.) If there is a connection between this and the mythical tradition on which the old Homeric *nostos* is based, the encounter with the Lotus-eaters might be characterized as a stage in the struggle with the chthonic powers.

21. *Odyssey, op. cit.*, p. 142.

22. According to Wilamowitz the Cyclopes are "really animals" (*Glaube der Hellenen*, Vol. I, p. 14).

23. *Odyssey, op. cit.*, p. 148.

24. *Ibid.*, p. 142.

25. *Ibid.*

26. *Ibid.*, p. 150.

27. *Ibid.*, p. 151 (adapted).

28. *Ibid.*, p. 146.

29. *Ibid.*, p. 146.

30. *Ibid.*, p. 149.

31. "The mindless creature's frequent stupidities might be seen as a kind of stillborn humor" (Klages, *op. cit.*, p. 1469).

32. *Odyssey, op. cit.*, p. 148.

33. *Ibid.*, p. 163.

34. Cf. *ibid.*, p. 159. Cf. F. C. Bauer, *Symbolik und Mythologie*, Stuttgart 1824, Vol. I, p. 47.

35. Cf. Baudelaire, "Le vin du solitaire," *Les Fleurs du Mal.*

36. Cf. J. A. K. Thomson, *Studies in the Odyssey*, Oxford 1914, p. 153.

37. *Odyssey, op. cit.*, p. 161.

38. Murray refers to the "sexual expurgations" to which the poems of Homer were subjected while being edited (cf. *op. cit.*, pp. 141ff).

39. "Pigs are in general the sacrificial animals of Demeter" (Wilamowitz-Moellendorff, *Der Glaube der Hellenen*, Vol. II, p. 53).

40. Cf. Freud, *Complete Psychological Works*, trans. James Strachey, Vol. XXI, London 1978, p. 99, fn. 1.

41. In a note Wilamowitz points to a surprising connection between the notions of snuffling and of *noos*, autonomous reason: "Schwyzer has very convincingly linked *noos* to snorting and snuffling" (Wilamowitz-Moellendorff, *Die Heimkehr des Odysseus, op. cit.*, p. 191). Wilamowitz doubts, however, whether the etymological relationship contributes to elucidating the meaning.

42. *Odyssey, op. cit.*, p. 161.

43. The consciousness of her irresistibility was later expressed in the cult of Aphrodite Peithon, "whose magic brooks no refusal" (Wilamowitz-Moellendorff, *Der Glaube der Hellenen, op. cit.*, Vol. II, p. 152).

[56] "Aeaea": Circe's island; old name for Colchis.

44. *Odyssey*, p. 164.

45. *Ibid.*

46. *Ibid.*, p. 166.

47. *Ibid.*

48. Cf. Bauer, *op. cit.*, pp. 47, 49.

49. *Odyssey*, p. 343.

50. Goethe, *Wilhelm Meister's Years of Apprenticeship*, trans. H. M. Waidson, London 1977, p. 62.

51. *Odyssey*, p. 346.

[59] "Underworld": Greek: sacrifice offered for the dead; Greek title of Book XI of the *Odyssey*.

52. Cf. Thomson, *op. cit.*, p. 28.

53. "My eyes filled with tears when I saw her there, and I was stirred to compassion. Yet, deeply moved though I was, I would not allow her to approach the blood out of turn, before I had had speech with Teiresias" (*Odyssey*, p. 173).

54. "I see the soul of my dead mother over there. She sits in silence by the blood and cannot bring herself to look her own son in the face or say a single word to him. Tell me, my prince, is there no way to make her know that I am he" (*ibid.*, p. 175)?

55. "I cannot avoid believing that the whole of Book XI, with the exception of a few passages . . . is a fragment of the old *nostos* and therefore of the oldest part of the poem" (Kirchhoff, *Die homerische Odyssee*, Berlin 1879, p. 226).

56. *Odyssey*, p. 174.

57. He was originally the "husband of the earth" (cf. Wilamowitz, *Glaube der Hellenen*, Vol. I, pp. 112ff) and only became the sea god at a late stage. Teiresias's prophecy may be an allusion to his twofold nature. It is conceivable that his propitiation by means of an earthly sacrifice far from any sea implies a symbolic restoration of his chthonic power. This restoration might reflect the superseding of the sea voyage in search of booty by agriculture: The cults of Poseidon and Demeter merged (cf. Thomson, *op. cit.*, p. 96, fn).

58. Translated from Grimm, *Kinder- und Hausmärchen*, Leipzig n.d., p. 208. Closely related motifs are passed down from antiquity, especially regarding Demeter. "Demeter came to Eleusis in search of her daughter after she had been abducted and was given lodging by Dysaules and his wife Baubo; but in her great sorrow she refused to touch food or drink. Thereupon her hostess Baubo made her laugh by suddenly lifting up her dress and exposing her body" (Freud, *Complete Psychological Works*, Vol. XIV, London 1962, p. 338; cf. Salomon Reinach, *Cultes, Mythes et Religions*, Paris 1912, Vol. IV, pp. 115ff).

[60] "up to now" / 1944: "throughout class history."

59. Hölderlin, "Autumn," *Poems and Fragments, op. cit.*, p. 595.

60. *Odyssey*, p. 340.

61. Wilamowitz considers that the execution was "carried out with satisfaction by the poet" (*Die Heimkehr des Odysseus, op. cit.*, p. 67). But when the authoritarian scholar enthuses over the simile of the snares, which "conveys the dangling of the maids' corpses in an apt and modern way" (*ibid.*, also cf. *ibid.*, p. 76), the satisfaction appears to be largely his own. Wilamowitz's writings are among the most striking documents of the German intermingling of barbarism and culture, which is fundamental to modern Philhellenism.

62. Gilbert Murray draws attention to the consoling intention of this line. According to his theory, scenes of torture have been expunged from Homer by civilizing censorship. The deaths of Melanthios and the maids have been retained (*op. cit.*, p. 146).

EXCURSUS II

1. Kant, "An answer to the question: What is Enlightenment?" *Practical Philosophy*, trans. Mary J. Gregor, Cambridge 1996, p. 17.

2. *Immanuel Kant's Critique of Pure Reason*, trans. Norman Kemp Smith, London 1973, p. 533.

3. *Ibid.*

4. *Ibid.*, p. 542.

5. *Ibid.*, p. 534.

6. *Ibid.*

7. *Ibid.*, p. 148.

8. *Kant's Critique of Judgment*, trans. J. H. Bernard, London and New York 1892, p. 24.

9. *Ibid.*, p. 25.

10. *Metaphysische Anfänge der Tugendlehre, Kants Werke. Akademie-Textausgabe*, Berlin 1968–, Vol. VI, p. 449.

11. Spinoza, *Ethics*, trans. A. Boyle, London/New York 1948, Pt. III, Pref., p. 84.

[67] "fascism" / 1944: "monopoly."

[68] [German text:] *Leistungsfähigkeit* / 1944: "efficiency."

12. *Critique of Pure Reason*, 2nd ed., *op cit.*, p. 154.

[68] "is revealing . . . form." / 1944: "monopoly is outgrowing itself in a fascistically rationalized form."

13. Translated from de Sade, *Histoire de Juliette*, Holland 1797, Vol. V, pp. 319f.

14. *Ibid.*, pp. 322f.

15. *Ibid.*, p. 324.

[71] "economic system" / 1944: "capitalism."

[71] "as . . . individuals": An allusion to Marx's formulation in *Capital* (Marx, Engels, *Collected Works*, Vol. 35, London 1996, p. 89).

[71] "industrial reason" / 1944: "monopoly and its reason."

[72] "system" / 1944/47: "system, the reason of capital."

16. E.g. *Critique of Practical Reason*, Kant, *Practical Philosophy*, trans. Mary J. Gregor, Cambridge 1996, p. 165.

17. *Nouveaux Essais sur l'Entendement Humain*, ed. Erdmann, Berlin 1840, Book 1, Ch. II, § 9, p. 215.

18. Cf. Heinrich Mann's introduction to the Insel Verlag edition.

19. *Metaphysische Anfänge der Tugendlehre, op. cit.,* p. 408.

20. *Juliette, op. cit.,* vol. IV, p. 58.

21. *Ibid.,* pp. 60f.

22. Spinoza, *Ethics,* Pt. IV, Prop. LIV, *op. cit.,* p. 178.

23. Spinoza, *ibid.*

24. *Metaphysische Anfänge der Tugendlehre, op. cit.,* p. 408.

25. *Ibid.,* p. 409.

26. *Juliette, op. cit.,* Vol. II, p. 114.

[76] "bourgeois" / 1944: "bourgeois in democracy."

27. *Ibid.,* Vol. III, p. 282.

28. Nietzsche, *Umwertung aller Werte. Werke,* Kröner, Vol. VIII, p. 213.

29. *Juliette, op. cit.,* Vol. IV, p. 204.

30. E. Dühren pointed out this affinity in *Neue Forschungen,* Berlin 1904, pp. 453ff.

31. Nietzsche, *op. cit.,* Vol. VIII, p. 218.

32. *Juliette, op. cit.,* Vol. I, pp. 315f.

33. Nietzsche, *The Birth of Tragedy and The Genealogy of Morals,* trans. Francis Golffing, New York 1956, pp. 174f.

34. *Juliette, op. cit.,* Vol. I, p. 300.

35. *Histoire de Justine,* Holland 1797, Vol. IV, p. 4 (also quoted by Dühren, *op. cit.,* p. 452).

36. *Genealogy of Morals, op. cit.,* p. 178.

37. *Justine, op. cit.,* Vol. IV, p. 7.

38. *Nachlass, op. cit.,* Vol. XI, p. 214.

39. *Genealogy of Morals, op. cit.,* p. 258.

40. *Juliette,* Vol. I, p. 208ff.

41. *Ibid.,* pp. 211f.

42. *Beyond Good and Evil,* trans. R. J. Hollingdale, London (Penguin Classics) 1990, p. 97.

43. *Nachlass, op. cit.,* Vol. XII, p. 108.

44. *Juliette, op. cit.,* Vol. I, p. 313.

45. *Ethics*, Pt. IV, Appendix, XVI, *op. cit.*, p. 194.

46. *Ibid.*, Pt. IV, Prop. L, Note, p. 176.

47. *Ibid.*, Prop. L, p. 175.

48. *Juliette, op. cit.*, Vol. II, p. 125.

49. *Ibid.*

50. *Nietzsche contra Wagner, op. cit.*, Vol. VIII, p. 204.

51. *Juliette, op. cit.*, Vol. I, p. 313.

52. *Ibid.*, Vol. II, p. 216.

53. *Beobachtungen über das Gefühl des Schönen und Erhabenen, op. cit.*, Vol. II, pp. 215f.

54. *Ibid.*

55. *Nachlass, op. cit.*, Vol. XI, pp. 227f.

56. Nietzsche, *Thus Spoke Zarathustra*, trans. R. J. Hollingdale, Harmondsworth 1984, p. 189.

[81] "fascist masters" / 1944: "masters."

57. *Genealogy of Morals, op. cit.*, p. 249.

[81] "Annie Henry": In 1940 she shot a man by whom she and a companion had been taken for a walk, after having threatened him with a pistol and humiliated him for hours; cf. *Los Angeles Examiner*, 29.11.1942.

58. *Juliette, op. cit.*, Vol. III, pp. 78f.

59. *Ibid.*, Vol. IV, pp. 126f.

60. R. Caillois, "Théorie de la fête," *Nouvelle Revue Française*, Jan. 1940, p. 49.

61. Cf. *ibid.*

62. Cf. *ibid.*, pp. 58f.

[83] "Benzedrine": A strong stimulant administered by the Nazi commanders to their troops (It. tr.).

63. *Nachlass, op. cit.*, Vol. XII, p. 364.

[84] "appeased . . . industry" / 1944: "hypostatized as an accomplished reconciliation. Under monopoly."

[84] "system . . . industry" / 1944: "monopoly."

[84] "white trash"; derogatory expression for white workers.

64. *Juliette, op. cit.*, Vol. II, pp. 81f.

65. *Ibid.*, Vol. III, pp. 172f.

66. *Ibid.*, pp. 176f.

67. Private edition by Helpey, p. 267.

68. *Juliette, op. cit.*, Vol. III, pp. 176f.

69. *Ibid.*, pp. 178f.

70. *Ibid.*, pp. 188–99.

71. *Juliette, op. cit.*, Vol. IV, p. 261.

72. *Ibid.*, Vol. II, p. 273.

73. *Ibid.*, Vol. IV, p. 379.

74. *Aline et Valcour*, Brussels 1883, Vol. I, p. 58.

75. *Ibid.*, p. 57.

76. Victor Hugo, *The Laughing Man*, Book VIII, Ch. 7.

77. *Juliette, op. cit.*, Vol. IV, p. 199.

78. Cf. *Les 120 Journées de Sodome*, Paris 1935, Vol. II, p. 308.

79. *Der Fall Wagner, op. cit.*, Vol. VIII, p. 10.

80. R. Briffault, *The Mothers*, New York 1927, Vol. I, p. 119.

[89] "German fascism" / 1944: "the class society."

81. *Nachlass, op. cit.*, Vol. XI, p. 216.

82. *Ibid.*, vol. XIV, p. 273.

83. Kant, *Practical Philosophy*, trans. Mary J. Gregor, Cambridge 1996, p. 82.

84. Nietzsche, *Joyful Wisdom*, trans. Thomas Common, New York 1973, p. 279.

85. *Ibid.*

86. Cf. Nietzsche, *Nachlass, op. cit.*, Vol. XI, p. 216.

87. Cf. Le Play, *Les ouvriers européens*, Paris 1879, Vol. I, esp. pp. 133ff.

88. *Juliette, op. cit.*, Vol. IV, pp. 303ff.

89. *Les 120 Journées de Sodome, op. cit.*, Vol. I, p. 72.

90. Cf. *Juliette, op. cit.*, Vol. II, p. 235, n.

91. *La Philosophie dans le Boudoir, op. cit.*, p. 185.

92. Cf. Democritus, Diels Fragment 278, Berlin 1912, Vol. II, pp. 117f.

93. *La Philosophie dans le Boudoir, op. cit.*, p. 242.

94. S. Reinach, "La prohibition de l'inceste et le sentiment de la pudeur," in *Cultes, Mythes et Religions,* Paris 1905, Vol. I, p. 157.

95. *La Philosophie dans le Boudoir, op. cit.*, p. 238.

96. *Ibid.*, pp. 238–49.

97. *Ibid.*

98. *Juliette, op. cit.*, Vol. IV, pp. 240–44.

99. *La Philosophie dans le Boudoir, op. cit.*, p. 263.

100. *Aline et Valcour, op. cit.*, Vol. II, pp. 181ff.

101. *Juliette, op. cit.*, Vol. II, pp. 181ff.

[92] "prehistory": Cf. note [31], p. 258 ("that thinking").

102. Nietzsche, *Joyful Wisdom*, trans. Thomas Common, New York 1973, p. 209.

THE CULTURE INDUSTRY

[94] "The" / 1944: "The German and Russian pavilions at the Paris World Exposition (of 1937, Ed.) seemed of the same essence, and the."

[94] "the total power of capital" / 1944: "monopoly."

[95] "those whose . . . strongest" / 1944: "capital."

[95] "economy today" / 1944: "profit economy."

[96] "Soap operas": alludes to the fact that such programs were originally broadcast at times when housewives were at home doing their washing (It. tr.).

[96] "selection" / 1944: "selection. The operations of the large studios, including the quality of the highly paid human material populating them, is a product of the monopoly system into which it is integrated."

[96] "subjected . . . purges" / 1944: "expropriated even before fascism."

[98] "at film" / 1944: "at the film monopoly."

[98] "agencies . . . business" / 1944: "monopolistic agencies."

[100] "industrial society" / 1944: "the machinery."

[100] "gigantic economic machinery" / 1944: "gigantic machinery of monopoly."

[101] "tolerated" / 1944: "tolerated, used by monopoly."

1. Nietzsche, *Unzeitgemässe Betrachtungen. Werke*, Leipzig 1917, Vol. I, p. 187.

[102] "Zanuck": Film producer, cofounder of 20th Century Pictures.

[104] "present society" / 1944: "monopoly society."

[105] "Pathé": French film magnates.

[105] "Hugenberg": Founders of German publishing combines.

2. A. de Tocqueville, *De la Démocratie en Amérique*, Paris 1864, Vol. II, p. 151.

[106] "Hays Office": Voluntary censorship agency (It. tr.), set up in 1934 in Hollywood.

[106] "Mickey Rooney": See note [126], p. 271.

[107] "ready-to-wear trade or" / 1944: "Jewish clothing trade or the Episcopal."

[107] "some omnipresent agency" / 1944: "a Rockefeller Institute, only slightly more omnipresent than the one in Radio City,"—"Radio City": the name given since the early 1930s to a part of the Rockefeller Center in New York containing several theatres, radio studios, and the Radio City Music Hall.

[107] "Casino de Paris": Music hall in Paris, famous for its luxurious furnishings.

[107] "society" / 1944: "class society."

[108] "Lombardo": Orchestra leader especially known for his annual musical broadcasts on New Year's Eve.

[109] "novelty songs": Hit songs with comic elements.

[110] "cruelty" / 1944: "lust for murder."

[110] "of the" / 1944: "of the kiss, but not of the."

[111] ". . . overwhelming": The idea expressed here dates from a time when television was not in widespread use (It. tr.).

[111] "possibilities" / 1944: "productive forces."

[111] "culture industry" / 1944: "mass culture."

[111] "Hays Office": See note [106], p. 269.

[112] "Laughter . . . ended": On this twofold function of laughter cf. pp. 60f (It. tr.).

[112] "*res . . . gaudium*": Seneca, Letter 23; letters to Lucilius (*Letters from a Stoic*, trans. Robin Campbell, Harmondsworth 1969).

[113] "constitutes its essence": Cf. Adorno, "Über Jazz" (1937), in *Gesammelte Schriften*, Vol. 17, Frankfurt am Main 1982, p. 98.

[113] "the system" / 1944: "prevailing in monopolistic society."

[114] "funnies": Amusement pages in newspapers with jokes and comic strips.

[114] "Ludwig": Primarily a writer of popular biographies.

[114] "Mrs. Miniver": Leading role in a radio family serial; also filmed.

[114] "Lone Ranger": Title figure in a radio western serial, the type of the lone cowboy fighting for the good; also filmed.

[114] "Lombardo": See note [108], p. 269.

3. Frank Wedekind, *Gesammelte Werke*, Munich 1921, Vol. IX, p. 426.

[115] "women's serials": Light novels in women's magazines.

[115] "Adler": Neo-Thomist popular philosopher who defended film with arguments from scholastic philosophy (It. tr.)—Cf. Horkheimer, "Neue Kunst und Massenkultur," in *Gesammelte Schriften*, Vol. 4.

[116] "the culture industry" / 1944: "the monopoly system."

[117] "planning" / 1944: "monopoly planning."

[117] "life has been transformed" / 1944: "monopoly has transformed life."

[117] "those in control" / 1944: "monopoly."

[118] "Industry" / 1944: "Monopoly."

[118] "proof": A play on the various philosophical-theological (ontological, cosmological, etc.) proofs of the existence of God.

[120] "giant corporation" / 1944: "monopoly."

[120] "the thinking subject" / 1944: "liberalism."

[120] *Hans Sonnenstößers Höllenfahrt. Ein heiteres Traumspiel.* Radio play by Paul Apel (1931), revised version by Gustaf Gründgens (1937).

[120] "*Life with Father*": Popular American radio family serial after a stage play by Clarence Day.

[120] "the latest society" / 1944: "monopoly society."

[120] "Formal freedom . . . answer officially" / 1944: "Bourgeois democracy guarantees formal freedom for everyone. No one is officially responsible to the government."

[120] "Dagwood": Character in the comic strip *Blondie*.

[121] "established" / 1944: "established by monopoly."

[121] "leaders of industry" / 1944: "monopolists."

[121] "provision" / 1944: "provision by the monopoly."

[121] "winter aid": *Winterhilfswerk*: National Socialist organization to support the unemployed and other needy persons under the direction of the Ministry of Propaganda.

[122] "even now" / 1944: "even under monopoly."

[123] "women's serial": See note [115], p. 270.

[123] "the pressure of the system" / 1944: "monopoly."

[124] "the system" / 1944: "monopoly."

4. Nietzsche, *Götzendämmerung, Werke, op. cit.*, Vol. VIII, p. 136.

[124] "those in command" / 1944: "monopoly."

[125] "bourgeois" / 1944: "German bourgeois."

[126] "Mature . . . Rooney": Well-known film actors, embodiments of the hero and the antihero.

[126] "cultural conglomerate" / 1944: "cultural conglomerate and monopoly."

[126] "Something . . . everyone" / 1944: "Monopoly serves up something for everyone."

[127] "The . . . purpose": Cf. Kant, *Critique of Judgment, op. cit.*, p. 68.

[128] "inner . . . commodities" / 1944: "composition of cultural commodities in terms of use value and exchange value."

[128] "What . . . replaced" / 1944: "Use value is being replaced in the reception of cultural assets."

[128] "The consumer . . . escape." / 1944: (missing).

[128] "Mrs. Miniver": See note [114], p. 270.

[128] "deception" / 1944: "swindle."

[129] "the commercial radio system" / 1944: "broadcasting."

[129] "the sovereign whole" / 1944: "monopoly as the sovereign whole."

[129] "combines" / 1944: "monopolies."

[129] "invented by the sociology of religion": Allusion to Max Weber's concept of charismatic authority; cf. *Economy and Society*, Vol. I, ed. Guenther Roth and Claus Wittich, Berkeley 1978, pp. 241ff.

[130] "Even . . . use value" / 1944: "Use value."

[130] "screenos": Bingo games played by the audience between pictures.

[130] "radio": Television was still in its infancy when the authors were writing (It. tr.).

[131] "the Warner brothers": Owners of large film studios.

[131] "hopes" / 1944: "waits."

[131] "labor time . . . in advertising" / 1944: "social labor time, but saved it. Today, when the free market is at an end, monopoly is entrenching itself in advertising."

[131] "the combines" / 1944: "monopoly."

[131] "wielders of influence . . . economic councils" / 1944: "class remains among its peers, as a preliminary form of the resolutions of economic councils of industrialists."

[132] "It benefits . . . names." / 1944: "Its termination by an individual firm represents only a loss of prestige, in fact an offence against the class discipline which monopoly imposes on its members. In wartime, commodities which can no longer be supplied continue to be advertised merely in order to keep the institution, and naturally also the war economy, in operation."

[132] "the big companies" / 1944: "monopoly, the skyscrapers of Wrigley and Rockefeller."

[133] "blackshirt": A term for fascists, after the black shirts of their uniforms, especially in Italy but also in other countries.

[134] "people" / 1944: "people, which still determines life in monopoly society."

[135] "*Schriftleiter*": The term *Schriftleiter* [lit. director of writing] was preferred by the National Socialists to the "foreign" word *Redakteur* (It. tr.).

[135] "such language" / 1944: "the language of monopoly."

[136] "false." / 1944/47: "false." After paragraph break: "(to be continued)."

ELEMENTS OF ANTI-SEMITISM

[137] "Now that . . . reasons," / 1944: "In the age when political domination is obsolete."

[137] "workers" / 1944: "proletarians."

[137] "appropriation" / 1944: "exploitation."

[138] "discharged." / 1944: "discharged. That would be the classless society."

[138] "existing society" / 1944: "the class society."

[138] "the existing order" / 1944: "capitalism."

[139] "that order" / 1944: "class society."

[139] "The respectable . . . disreputable ones" / 1944: "Monopoly, the respectable rackets, condone it, and the fascists, the disreputable ones."

[140] "vagrants" / 1944: "Negroes, Mexican wrestling clubs."

[142] "take possession of" / 1944: "appropriate."

[142] "parasites of old": Allusion to the Nazis' anticapitalist propaganda distinction between "productive" [*schaffend*] and "parasitic" [*raffend*; lit. "grasping"] capital, i.e., between industrial and bank capital; cf. Franz Neumann, *Behemoth* (1942), Frankfurt/Main 1977, p. 376.

[142] "of the economic system in general" / 1944: "of all capital."

[142] "what is withheld" / 1944: "what capital withholds."

[143] "society" / 1944: "class."

[144] "knights of industry . . . creators" / 1944: "capitalist bloodsucker who has to justify himself as a creator."

[144] "salvation." / 1944/47: "salvation, now that the churches have been reduced entirely to the function of social control."

[145] "German Christians": The Protestant movement "Deutsche Christen" sought a union between Church and National Socialism.

[148] "recognition in a concept": Kant, *Critique of Pure Reason, op. cit.*, pp. 79ff [B 103].

1. Cf. Freud, "The Uncanny," *The Complete Psychological Works, op. cit.*, Vol. XVII, pp. 219ff.

[152] "Coughlin": Charles Edward Coughlin, Catholic priest, demagogic anti-Semitic radio preacher.

2. *Kant's Critique of Pure Reason, op. cit.*, p. 183 [B 180f].

[160] "any . . . country" / 1944: "even lynching."

3. Freud, *Totem and Taboo, op. cit.*, Vol. XIII, p. 73.

[163] "culture industry" / 1944: "economic and cultural monopoly."

[164] "big industry" / 1944: "monopoly."

[164] "workers" / 1944: "proletarians."

[165] "until now" / 1944: "in liberalism."

[165] ". . . turning-point of history": Allusion to Marx's "Zur Judenfrage," in *Aus den Deutsch-Französischen Jahrbüchern* 1843/44.

[165] "VII": The whole of section VII ("But . . . of enlightenment.") was not contained in the 1944 edition.

[165] "the Ahlwardts and the Knüppelkunzes": Hermann Ahlwardt: author of anti-Semitic pamphlets, Reichstag deputy at the end of the nineteenth century; for years his appearances were accompanied by uproar and scandal.

Hermann Kunze: teacher at the Cadet School, Chairman of the Deutsch-Soziale Partei, anti-Semitic demagogue; his nickname [*Knüppel*; stick, cudgel] resulted from the frequent brawls at his meetings.

[166] "ticket": single list of a party's candidates in the American electoral system.

[166] "Jew-free": From the National Socialist term *judenrein*.

[167] ". . . without mediation": Allusion to Kant's proposition: "Thoughts without content are empty, intuitions without concepts are blind," *Critique of Pure Reason, op. cit.*, p. 93 [A 51].

NOTES AND SKETCHES

[173] "Chamberlain . . . Bad Godesberg": Chamberlain met Hitler three times in September 1938; the second meeting took place in Bad Godesberg.

[175] "In this country": In America [It. tr.].

[175] "Spoke . . . loneliness": Translated from *Die chinesische Flöte*, Nachdichtungen von Hans Bethge, Insel-Bücherei, p. 17 [It. tr.].

1. Paul Deussen, *Sechzig Upanishad's des Veda*. Leipzig 1905, p. 524.

2. Matthew 2, 17–19. [I think it should be ch. 11—tr.]

3. Above all Brhad-aranyaka Upanishad 3, 5, 1 and 4, 4, 22. Deussen, *op. cit.*, pp. 436f and 479f.

4. *Op. cit.*, p. 436.

5. Mark, 1, 6.

6. Translated from *Vorlesungen über die Geschichte der Philosophie*, Vol. 2, *Werke*, Vol. XIV, pp. 159f.

7. *Ibid.*, p. 168.

8. Cf. Deussen, *op. cit.*, p. 373.

9. Cf. Eduard Meyer, *Ursprung und Anfänge des Christentums*, Stuttgart/Berlin 1921, Vol. I, p. 90.

10. Diogenes Laertius, IV, 15.

11. Cf. *Politeia*, 372; *Politikos*, 267ff and Eduard Zeller, *Die Philosophie der Griechen*, Leipzig 1922, Part 2, Section 1, pp. 325f note.

12. Cf. Deussen, *Das System des Vedanta*, Leipzig 1906, 2nd ed., pp. 63ff.

13. Hermann Oldenberg, *Buddha*, Stuttgart/Berlin 1914, pp. 174f.

14. *Ibid.*, p. 386.

15. *Ibid.*, pp. 393f.

16. Cf. *ibid.*, pp. 184ff and pp. 424ff.

[180] "*Soirées de Petersbourg*": Joseph de Maistre, *Les Soirées de Saint Petersbourg* (1821).

[180] "circles of Hell": Allusion to Dante's *Divine Comedy*, Inferno III, 4ff (It. tr.).

[180] "Animal psychology": In the 1944 edition this entry comes directly after "Against knowingness."

[185] "Economic . . . forms" / 1944: "Relations of production, forms of class domination, culture."

[185] "troglodyte": Paleolithic cave dweller.

[186] "dictum": Cf. Marx, *Die deutsche Ideologie*, in *Marx-Engels Werke*, Vol. 3, Berlin 1969, pp. 34f.

[186] "The poor figure . . . them": Cf. Marx, Engels, *Die Heilige Familie*, in *Marx-Engels Werke*, Vol. 2, Berlin 1958, p. 85; also Marx, "Zur Kritik der Hegelschen Rechtsphilosophie," in *Marx-Engels Werke*, Vol. 1, Berlin 1957, pp. 385f.

[187] "Blum government": Popular front government 1936–37, introduced extensive social reforms.

[187] "From a theory of the criminal": Cf. the full text, "Theorie des Verbrechers," in *Gesammelte Schriften*, Vol. 12, Frankfurt/Main 1985, pp. 266ff.

[187] "rising . . . labor power" / 1944: "a regular need for labor power, increased production."

17. Leibniz, *The Monadology and Other Philosophical Writings*, trans. Robert Latta, Oxford 1925, § 7, pp. 219f.

18. Cf. *ibid.*, § 51.

19. Cf. R. Caillois, *Le Mythe et l'Homme*, Paris 1938, pp. 125ff.

[190] "fascism" / 1944: "monopoly."

[190] "state" / 1944: "order."

[191] "executioner: each operation . . . forgetting." / 1944: "executioner. But that is not to say enough. Is not death the radical loss of the 'residual capacity of the nerve substance'? Life would not be a dream but a narcosis. We would behave toward other people, not to mention all other creatures, as, in Flourens's view, the patient behaves towards the interval when he or she was under the influence of the drug: deludedly. The narcosis acts like the *principium individuationis*. The positivists, however, could learn from this how far they have advanced with their science: their note taking would be limited in principle to the postnarcotic period. It would be the utterance of a life which had forgotten itself under the influence of narcotics, or rather of death, from which one can remember nothing. They would, in their thing-language, have "mortificated" it. Reality would be left to metaphysics and to antiquated French physiologists. Admittedly, a test of the objective justification of such speculations would call for a discriminating analysis of Schopenhauer's notion, which still contributes too much to Flourens's positivism."

[195] "The 'tragic' world-view of the fascists": An allusion to the vulgarized reception of Nietzsche by some National Socialist authors in the early 1930s.

[197] "Chaplin's film": *The Great Dictator* (1940).

20. Translated from *Die Nachsokratiker*, ed. Wilhelm Nestle, Jena 1923, Vol. I. 72a, p. 195.

[198] "big business" / 1944: "monopoly."

[203] "praxis." / 1944: "praxis. In Europe there is now hardly a country in which one would not be shot for a slip of the tongue."

[203] "The proposition . . . the whole": Hegel's *Phenomenology of Spirit*, op. cit., p. 11.

[204] "today" / 1944: "under monopoly."

[205] "flux" / 1944: "transience."

[206] "The man . . . strive": Allusion to Schiller's poem, "Das Lied von der Glocke."

21. Cf. *Éclaircissement sur les Sacrifices. Oeuvres*, Lyon 1892, Vol. V, pp. 322f.

[207] "universal" / 1944: "monopolistic."

[207] "completely . . . domination" / 1944: "system of big rackets."

[207] "In Germany . . . reason": Cf. note [24], p. 257 ("pleasure").

[207] "present" / 1944: "fascist present, in which she no longer needs meta-

phorically to put on mannish trousers because she is already in desexualized slacks, machining bombs."

[209] "culture industry" / 1944: "mass culture."

[210] "fascist collective" / 1944: "collective of the totalitarian monopoly."

22. *Joyful Wisdom, op. cit.*, p. 136.

[211] "Hearst": William Randolph Hearst, founder of the USA's largest press conglomerate.

[211] "baseless" / 1944: "baseless; on this Heidegger and Lukács agree."

23. Goethe, *Faust*, Part I, 4068.

24. Cf. Karl Landauer, "Intelligenz und Dummheit," in *Das Psychoanalytische Volksbuch*, Bern 1939, p. 172.

EDITOR'S AFTERWORD

1. P. xiv of this edition.

2. P. xviii of this edition.

3. P. 1 of this edition.

4. P. xi of this edition.

5. Max-Horkheimer Archiv der Stadt- und Universitätsbibliothek Frankfurt am Main (abbreviated henceforth to MHA): VI 1D.210.

6. Published in Horkheimer, *Gesammelte Schriften*, Vol. 12, Frankfurt am Main 1985.

7. MHA: VI 1D.66—The declaration was to be issued in connection with the publication of essays by both authors in the periodical *Der Monat*. As contributions by Horkheimer, "Vernunft und Selbsterhaltung" [Engl.: "The End of Reason," see n. 24, Afterword], "Autorität und Familie in der Gegenwart" [Engl.: "Authoritarianism and the Family Today," in *The Family: Its Function and Destiny*, ed. R. N. Anshen, New York 1949, pp. 359–374], or a section from *Eclipse of Reason* (Oxford 1947) were considered (cf. MHA: VI 1 D.158, 161A). However, Horkheimer then withdrew his permission. The joint declaration, too, was not published. The reasons for this emerge only partly from the correspondence between Horkheimer and Adorno. They have to do, above all, with misgivings about a further political declaration which was to be combined with this first one. However, there is no reason to assume that the two authors were unwilling to endorse the content and formulation of the first declaration.

8. MHA: XI 6.86.

9. My thanks go to Rolf Tiedemann for information on the content of Adorno's posthumous papers here and elsewhere.

10. MHA: XI 6.2.

11. MHA: XI 6.3.

12. MHA: XI 6.4.

13. It is to be found under the title "Das Schema der Massenkultur" as an appendix to *Dialektik der Aufklärung* in Theodor W. Adorno, *Gesammelte Schriften*, Vol. 3, Frankfurt am Main 1981, pp. 299ff.

14. MHA: X 17.1–17.

15. Published in Horkheimer, *Gesammelte Schriften*, Vol. 12, pp. 587ff.

16. MHA: XI 6.64.

17. MHA: XI 6.65.

18. MHA: XI 6.5–110; XI 6a.1–3: XI 7a.3–5.

19. Now published in Horkheimer, *Gesammelte Schriften*, Vol. 12. The designation *Fragments*, which *Dialectic of Enlightenment* bears as its subtitle (and as its main title in the original version of 1944), therefore has not only the metaphorical meaning of a kind of thinking opposed to the compulsion of a system but also the literal meaning that the printed version does not include everything initially written for it. Adorno also wanted to include *The Philosophy of Modern Music* as an excursus for *Dialectic of Enlightenment*; cf. Adorno, *Gesammelte Schriften* Vol. 12, Frankfurt am Main 1975, p. 11.

20. MHA: XI 6.43–62.

21. Jürgen Habermas, "Bemerkungen zur Entwicklung des Horkheimerschen Werkes," in *Max Horkheimer heute: Werk und Wirkung*, ed. Alfred Schmidt and Norbert Altwicker, Frankfurt am Main 1986, p. 171.

22. Verbal communication to the Editor on 22.10.1985.

23. Cf. p. xix of this edition.

24. "The Authoritarian State," tr. The People's Translation Service, Berkeley, in *The Essential Frankfurt School Reader*, ed. Andrew Arato and Eike Gebhardt, pp. 95–117, New York 1982; German: "Autoritärer Staat," in *Gesammelte Schriften*, Vol. 5, Frankfurt am Main 1987, pp. 293ff; "The End of Reason," *The Essential Frankfurt School Reader*, op. cit., pp. 26–48; German: "Vernunft und Selbsterhaltung," in *Gesammelte Schriften*, Vol. 5, Frankfurt am Main 1987, pp. 320ff.

25. Theodor W. Adorno, *Über Walter Benjamin*, Frankfurt am Main 1970, p. 143. The straightforward identification by the editor of that volume, Rolf Tiedemann, of the "book on the dialectic" mentioned in the letter with the later book *Dialectic of Enlightenment*, seems to me questionable, especially in the light of the memorandum about to be cited.

26. "Idee, Aktivität und Programm des Instituts für Sozialforschung," in Horkheimer, *Gesammelte Schriften*, Vol. 12, Frankfurt am Main 1985, pp. 156f.

27. MHA: VI 33.62–63.

28. Cf. Adorno, "Die Aktualität der Philosophie" (1931), in *Gesammelte Schriften*, Vol. 1, Frankfurt am Main 1973.

29. Cf. Horkheimer, Adorno, "Diskussion über die Differenz zwischen Posi-

tivismus und materialistischer Dialektik," in Horkheimer, *Gesammelte Schriften*, Vol. 12, pp. 467ff.

30. P. xiv of this edition.

31. Cf. Horkheimer "Vertrauen auf Geschichte," in *Gesammelte Schriften*, Vol. 12, *op. cit.* Also compare the more detailed interpretation in Gunzelin Schmid Noerr, "Wahrheit, Macht und die Sprache der Philosophie. Zu Horkheimers sprachphilosophischen Reflexionen in seinen nachgelassenen Schriften zwischen 1939 und 1946," in *Max Horkheimer heute: Werk und Wirkung, op. cit.*

32. Cf. Martin Jay, *Dialektische Phantasie*, Frankfurt am Main 1973, pp. 125ff, and Wolfgang Bonß, "Psychoanalyse als Wissenschaft und Kritik. Zur Freud-rezeption der Frankfurter Schule," in *Sozialforschung als Kritik*, ed. Wolfgang Bonß and Axel, Honneth, Frankfurt am Main 1982, esp. pp. 391ff.

33. Erich Fromm, "Über Methode und Aufgabe einer analytischen Sozial-psychologie," in *Zeitschrift für Sozialforschung*, Vol. I, 1932, p. 50.

34. Paris 1936.

35. Cf. Horkheimer, "Ernst Simmel und die Freudsche Philosophie," *Gesammelte Schriften*, Vol. 5, Frankfurt am Main 1987, pp. 396ff.

36. Horkheimer, Adorno, "Diskussionen über die Differenz zwischen Positiv-ismus und materialistischer Dialektik," in Horkheimer, *Gesammelte Schriften*, Vol. 12, esp. pp. 433–451; "Diskussionen über Sprache und Erkenntnis, Naturbe-herrschung am Menschen, politische Aspekte des Marxismus," *ibid.*, pp. 510–512.

37. Horkheimer, Adorno, "Diskussionen über die Differenz zwischen Positiv-ismus und materialistischer Dialektik," *op. cit.*, p. 443.

38. *Ibid.*

39. P. xviii of this edition.

40. P. 154 of this edition.

41. New York 1949–50; one of these volumes is *The Authoritarian Personality* (New York 1950), written by Adorno, Else Frenkel-Brunswick, Daniel J. Levinson, and R. Nevitt Sanford, mentioned by Adorno and in the following quotation.

42. Adorno, "Wissenschaftliche Erfahrungen in Amerika," in *Gesammelte Schriften*, Vol. 10.2, Frankfurt am Main 1977, pp. 721–723.

43. Martin Jay discusses this in more detail in "The Frankfurt School in Exile," in *Perspectives in American History*, Vol. VI, pp. 348–355.

44. P. xix of this edition.

45. Cf. especially Pollock, "State Capitalism," in *Studies of Philosophy and So-cial Science* IX, 1941, and "Is National Socialism a New Order?" *ibid.* Horkheimer himself explains this concept in his essay "The Authoritarian State" [see n. 24, Afterword].

46. "Aufzeichnungen und Entwürfe zur *Dialektik der Aufklärung* 1939–1942," in *Gesammelte Schriften*, Vol. 12, *op. cit.*, p. 287.

47. "Zur Ideologie der Politik heute (Fragment)," in *Gesammelte Schriften*, Vol. 12, *op. cit.*, pp. 317f.

48. "Zur Soziologie der Klassenverhältnisse," in *Gesammelte Schriften*, Vol. 12, *op. cit.*, pp. 101–104. That Horkheimer's theory of rackets, which, in the end, was developed to only a rudimentary level, aimed to go far beyond a sociological analysis in the narrower sense becomes clear from an analogy with his reflections on linguistic philosophy mentioned earlier. In an essay of 1946 he described the function of the concept on the basis of the racket model, protection in exchange for oppression: "In the concept fulfillment is inseparable from suffering. Its fixity only faithfully reflects the society which serves life by oppressing it, which develops human beings by mutilating them and knows of homeland only as the protection which suppresses the protected." ("Vertrauen auf Geschichte," in *Gesammelte Schriften*, Vol. 12, *op cit.*, p. 124).

49. "Reflexionen zur Klassentheorie" (1942), in Adorno, *Gesammelte Schriften*, Vol. 8, Frankfurt am Main 1972.

50. Cf. Horkheimer, "Zur Soziologie der Klassenverhältnisse," *op. cit.*, pp. 75ff.

51. P. xiv of this edition.

52. P. 207 of this edition.

53. P. 94 of this edition.

54. P. 132 of this edition.

55. P. xv of this edition.

56. E.g., p. 209 of this edition.

57. E.g., p. 67 and p. 89 of this edition.

58. E.g., p. 76 and p. 120 of this edition.

59. P. 107 and p. 144 of this edition.

60. P. 137 of this edition.

61. P. 48 of this edition.

62. P. 60 of this edition.

63. P. xvii of this edition.

64. For example, in a note written probably in the early 1930s and at any rate not later than 1935, Horkheimer writes of the "independence of the revolutionary fighter" (MHA: XI 16.4a, p. 5). The note was incorporated in "Bemerkungen zur philosophischen Anthropologie," published in 1935, where, however, he writes of the "independence of the person who pursues this goal [of a free humanity]" (*Zeitschrift für Sozialforschung*, Vol. IV, 1935, p. 16).

65. According to a verbal communication to the Editor from Rudolph Hirsch in November 1983.

66. P. xv of this edition.

67. P. xv of this edition.

68. The original main title of the book was *Philosophical Fragments*.

69. MHA: XI 6.65.

70. Cf. "Reason and Self-Preservation," *op. cit.*

71. Cf. "Zur Ideologie der Politik heute (Fragment)," in *Gesammelte Schriften*, Vol. 12, *op. cit.*, pp. 316ff. This text reads like a critique of a positivistically abbreviated reading of Pollock's theory of state capitalism.

72. E.g., p. 131 of this edition.

73. P. 207 of this edition.

74. Horkheimer, Adorno, "Rettung der Aufklärung. Diskussion über eine geplante Schrift zur Dialektik" (1946), in Horkheimer, *Gesammelte Schriften*, Vol. 12, *op. cit.*, pp. 597–599.

75. *Ibid.*, p. 600.

76. *Ibid.*, p. 604.

77. *Ibid.*, pp. 594, 598.

78. *Ibid.*, p. 601.

79. *Ibid.*, p. 602.

80. Cf. The Editor's Afterword to Vols. 7 and 8 of Horkheimer's *Gesammelte Schriften*, in Vol. 8, esp. pp. 461–465.

81. Cf. e.g., "Kritische Theorie gestern und heute" (1969/72), in *Gesammelte Schriften*, Vol. 8, Frankfurt am Main 1985, p. 353; "Pessimismus heute" (1971), in *Gesammelte Schriften*, Vol. 7, Frankfurt am Main 1985, p. 232; "Das Schlimme erwarten und doch das Gute versuchen. Gespräch mit Gerhard Rein" (1972/76), *ibid.*, p. 467.

82. P. 161 of this edition.

83. *Notizen 1950 bis 1969*, Frankfurt am Main 1974, p. 12.

84. MHA: VI 40.245 c.

85. MHA: VI 4.146.

86. MHA: V 118.3.

87. Cf. Solmi's letter to Horkheimer of 5.7.1961 (MHA: V 61.21).

88. MHA: V 61.13–14.

89. Letter of 26.2.1962 (MHA: VI 4.181).

90. Letter from Horkheimer to Solmi of 15.8.1962 (MHA: V 61.1). In the Italian edition Solmi's name finally no longer appeared but was replaced by the pseudonym Lionello Vinci—clearly a sign of distancing.

91. My thanks go to Furio Cerutti of Florence for this information.

92. Nico Pasero, Rudolph Bauer, "Aufklärung auf Italienisch," in *Diskus. Frankfurter Studentenzeitung*, Vol. 17, July 1967, p. 4.

93. In *Kritische Theorie*, Vol. II, Frankfurt am Main 1968, p. XI.

94. *Ibid.*, p. IX.

95. Cf. Alfred Schmidt, "Die geistige Physiognomie Max Horkheimers," Introduction to Horkheimer, *Notizen 1950–1969*, Frankfurt am Main 1974, pp. XLIX, L, LXVIII.

THE DISAPPEARANCE OF CLASS HISTORY

1. In *Studies in Philosophy and Social Science*, Vol. IX, 1941, pp. 264ff.
2. Helmut Dubiel, Alfons Söllner, "Die Nationalsozialismusforschung des Instituts für Sozialforschung—ihre wissenschaftsgeschichtliche Stellung und ihre gegenwärtige Bedeutung," in *Wirtschaft, Recht und Staat im Nationalsozialismus . . .*, *op. cit.*, pp. 7ff; Barbara Brick, Moishe Postone, "Kritischer Pessimismus und die Grenzen des traditionellen Marxismus," in *Sozialforschung als Kritik*, ed. Wolfgang Bonß and Axel Honneth, Frankfurt am Main 1982, pp. 179ff. In what follows we base ourselves substantially on these texts, without discussing them in detail. Regarding the context described in these works cf. also: Martin Jay, *Dialektische Phantasie*, Frankfurt am Main 1981, Ch. V, and Alfons Söllner, *Geschichte und Herrschaft*, Frankfurt am Main 1979, Ch. 3.3.6.
3. "Die gegenwärtige Lage des Kapitalismus und die Aussichten einer planwirtschaftlichen Neuordnung," in *Zeitschrift für Sozialforschung*, Vol. I, pp. 8ff; "Bemerkungen zur Wirtschaftskrise," *ibid.*, Vol. II, pp. 321ff.
4. Quoted from Brick, Postone, *op. cit.*, p. 184.
5. Cf. "State Capitalism: Its Possibilities and Limitations," in *Studies in Philosophy and Social Science*, Vol. IX, 1941, pp. 200ff.
6. Quoted from Brick, Postone, *op. cit.*, p. 185.
7. Cf. *ibid.*
8. Cf. *ibid.*, pp. 189f.
9. Franz L. Neumann, *Behemoth*, New York 1942.
10. Quoted from Dubiel, Söllner, *op. cit.*, p. 18.
11. *Ibid.*
12. P. xix of this edition.
13. P. 23 of this edition.
14. P. 21 of this edition.
15. P. 84 of this edition.
16. P. 116 of this edition.
17. P. 117 of this edition.
18. P. 124 of this edition.
19. P. 17 of this edition.
20. P. 30 of this edition.
21. P. 30 of this edition.
22. P. 95 of this edition.
23. P. 138 of this edition.

24. P. 210 of this edition.
25. P. 190 of this edition.
26. P. 185 of this edition.
27. *Ibid.*
28. P. 2 of this edition.
29. *Ibid.*
30. P. 29 of this edition.
31. Pp. 43 and 60 of this edition.
32. P. 118 of this edition.
33. Pp. 100, 101, 104, and 118 of this edition.

Cultural Memory | in the Present